THE
BATTLEFIELD
WALKER'S
HANDBOOK

By the same author

All for a Shilling a day
Captain Carey's Blunder
At Them With the Bayonet!
Colonial Small Wars 1837–1902
Conflict in Hampshire
The Bowmen of England
The Weapons and Equipment of the Victorian Soldier
Victoria's Enemies – 19th Century Colonial Wars
Victorian Military Campaigns in Africa
Victorian Military Campaigns in India
Khartoum; the Gordon Relief Expedition 1884/5
Tel-el-Kebir; the War with Egypt 1882
Omdurman: Kitchener's Dongola Campaign 1896/8
Campaigning with the Duke of Wellington; the Peninsular War 1808/1814
Khaki and Red: N.W. Frontier India 19th Century
Redcoats for the Raj; 'Tales from a Victorian Barrackroom' – an historical novel

Twenty-seven hardback books on Wargaming: Fighting tabletop Battles with Model Soldiers

Nine books on Physiotherapy Treatments: Sports, Industrial, Ballet etc Injury – Prevention and Treatment

DONALD FEATHERSTONE

THE
BATTLEFIELD
WALKER'S
HANDBOOK

Airlife
England

Copyright © Donald Featherstone 1998

First published in the UK in 1998
by Airlife Publishing Ltd

British Library Cataloguing-in-Publication Data
A catalogue record for this book
is available from the British Library

ISBN 1 85310 881 2

Typeset by Phoenix Typesetting, Ilkley, West Yorkshire
Printed in England by MPG Books Ltd., Bodmin, Cornwall

Airlife Publishing Ltd
101 Longden Road, Shrewsbury, SY3 9EB, England.

Preface

Some of the worst days of my life were spent on battlefields in North Africa and Italy, made bearable only by discipline and the presence of probably less fearful comrades. However, that has been more than balanced since, while walking possibly 250 fields of fifty-two wars, in twenty-two countries, in three continents – all in the good company of assorted bands of amicable and knowledgeable Britons, Americans, Belgians, French, Portuguese, Spaniards and South Africans. Walking battlefields is an exercise in comradeship, a most salubrious and far less frightening means of perpetuating the fellowship cherished in the Forces.

Every battlefield described or referred to in this book has been walked by the author, and writing about them has been a nostalgic business arousing a sadly impossible yearning to turn back the clock and do it all over again.

The addictive aspects of battlefield walking are strongly recommended!

Donald Featherstone

Dedication

To Lee Angel, Bill Betenson, David Chandler, Ken Chapman, Richard Ellis, John Flight, John Gaylor, Bob Malone, Chris Scott and Roger Snell with whom, over more than twenty-five years, I have walked dozens of battlefields in three continents.

AND

My comrades on American battlefields, whose friendship and open hearts have added another dimension to my life – Dick Bryant, Leo Cronin, Jim Getz, Sam Gill, Greg Nicholl, Dave Paddock, Jim Butters and members of HATSOFF, along with others too numerous to name.

Contents

Foreword

Dr David Chandler MA(Oxon) FRHist S, FRGS, formerly Head of the Department of War Studies at the Royal Military Academy Sandhurst and President of the British Commission for Military History, is an internationally renowned authority on Marlborough and Napoleon. He has conducted countless battlefield tours throughout the world, and is an author of innumerable books on military history.

Haunted Acres

by

David Chandler

Visiting battlefields has become a holiday attraction
for many tourists besides old soldiers

Professional soldiers have always displayed considerable interest in the sites of battlefields, whether ancient or modern, hoping to improve their military education by attempts to relate historical events to the actual ground. Sometimes their application to this pastime has had special significance. Napoleon, for example, developed an obsession with Marengo – a battle he so nearly lost – and revisited the ground on 11 May 1805, covering 50 miles during the day and exhausting five horses in the process. The result of this energetic tour was an order to the much-tried officers of the historical section of the *Depôt de la Guerre* in Paris demanding a major revision of the official account of the events of 14 June 1800. The motivation, alas, did not spring from a wish to correct a point or two of detail, but rather from a determination to place his generalship in a more favourable light. It was not only pulpits that the recently crowned Emperor desired to 'tune', but also the pages of history.

A century later, General Sir Edmund Allenby was noted by Wavell (then an officer on his staff) as always carrying his Old Testament with him on ground reconnaissances during the Palestinian Campaign of 1917–18. 'The Bull' spent no little time trying to relate the martial achievements of Gideon and other ancient Israelite generals to the actual ground. It was suitable that the decisive victory over the Turks was eventually won in September 1918 at Megiddo – the supposed site of the legendary battle of Armageddon (the supreme conflict between the nations), and, probably more historically, the place where Thutmose III crushed the rebel King of Kadesh and his allies in 1479 BC. Allenby was not alone this century in his interest in the practical application of military history. General George Patton spent considerable time visiting ancient battle sites in Algeria and Tunisia in 1943, and even came to believe that he was the reincarnation of a Roman tribune. Lieutenant-General Sir Brian Horrocks had no such mystical illusions, but late in 1944 he felt slightly cheated when the German Ardennes Offensive was halted some little way short of the battleground he had prepared with his British Corps for the showdown – around no less a place than Waterloo; an artillery observation post had been established upon the famous Lion Mound, but on this occasion history did not repeat itself.

If the interest of many soldiers in former battlefields is understandable, that of a growing number of civilians of all age groups and callings – and indeed of both sexes – needs a little more explanation. The practice of battlefield visiting has naturally long been resorted to by many military historians in search of evidence to support their impressions or in corroboration of their researches among archives, memoirs and war diaries. A notable English example was F Loraine Petre, who explored many of Napoleon's battlefields, with the invaluable assistance of an Edwardian bicycle, during the first decade of this century. His notable quintet of campaign studies, covering the military events of 1806, 1807, 1809, 1813 and 1814 in Napoleon's Europe, did much to establish the writing of military history as a respectable academic activity, one that had somewhat lapsed since the great history of the Peninsular War in six volumes published by General Sir William Napier between 1828 and 1840, and that on *The Invasion of the Crimea* by Kinglake, of which eight volumes appeared between 1865 and 1886. No less important a generation later than Petre was the contribution of Lieutenant-Colonel Alfred Burne, whose studies of the battlefields of England, and of the Crécy and Agincourt campaigns, are classics of military history researched not only in the library but also in the field.

Today the appeal of battlefield touring is becoming increasingly broad-based. In July 1965, the correspondent Clare Hollingworth wrote in *The Guardian* that 'the excitement of a battle hangs over the site for hundreds of years long after grass, towns, or dust have covered horrors' and went on to claim that 'from Granada in Southern Spain through France and Italy, the most amusing trips I can recall have been to battlefields'. Here indeed is a lady whom H G Wells, in years long before the Sexual Discrimination Act, would have included among the chosen to whom he dedicated his book on war-gaming, *Little Wars*, namely 'boys of every age from twelve to 150

. . . girls of the better sort, and a few rare and gifted women'. One hopes that Miss Hollingworth's enthusiasm, which sprang from a love of history engendered at school, managed to survive the rigours of reporting the later years of the Vietnamese War. She is not, however, by any means unique. On a Peninsular War tour, which the author of this article conducted to Spain for Captain Gordon Battlefield Tours in April 1976, no less than five members were women; two, it is true, were wives accompanying their husbands to the scenes of Wellington's achievements, but of the remaining three, one was a novelist from Wales in search of local colour, a second was from Oxford fulfilling what she described as a lifetime ambition, and the third, the doyenne of the whole party, was a senior lady of amazing energy and great charm who revealed that she was the last descendant of Lieutenant-General Sir John Lambert, KCB, who commanded one of the Guards' Brigades at Waterloo, and also through him connected to Captain Harry Smith, her Great-Great-Uncle, the dashing soldier of the 95th who rescued the beautiful Juanita from the drink-maddened soldiery after the storm of Badajoz in April 1812 – a lady who later achieved further fame by having the town of Ladysmith in South Africa named after her.

It must be admitted, these instances notwithstanding, that battlefield touring attracts more men than women. The interest would seem to stem from several sources, attracting very different types of people although one and all share a deep and abiding regard for military history. The growing pastime of war-gaming accounts for many in the younger age bracket of those who accompany, for example, the Military Historical Society's annual tour. Interest in *kriegsspiel* is by no means restricted to those of tender years, but the older generation often join their preference for this type of instructive holiday with an interest in the collection of militaria and a certain amount of nostalgia for former wars and campaigns in which they feel they were privileged to serve. The recent MHS tour to Verdun, Cambrai and the Somme, for instance, included in the party two veterans of the Tank Corps, one of whom had served in 'D Battalion' under Brigadier-General Hugh Elles' command on that cold November day in 1917 which saw the first use of tanks on a large scale in war. The recollections of such survivors of great events, however restricted to their own field of experience, serves to illuminate the human angle of twentieth-century battles in a way that no amount of reading or documentary research can hope to equal. Two-thirds of the party had military experience of one sort or another, most of it dating from the Second World War or from the days of National Service. But the common experience of having been in the army is rarely the main motive for joining a tour. Collectors with a Peninsular Medal often feel an urge to retread the paths and visit the battlefields fought over by the original recipient. Others with regimental associations and interests find satisfaction in following the fortunes of their military predecessors in earlier campaigns. And lastly the teachers, scholars and writers of military history naturally find these excursions of both value and interest – although in many cases the pleasure obtained is somewhat marred by an inability to resolve particular problems in the time available. On the other hand, there are also golden moments when some obscure aspect of a battle is suddenly understandable with the ground literally before one's eyes, or when a windfall occurs: the presentation of an 1810 cannon-ball to every member of the party by a Portuguese official at Almeida in 1974 was one such; another was the discovery of First World War mementos on the actual ground – by no means a rare occurrence at Cambrai or the Somme, where the chalk is continually extruding these and even grimmer relics of battles of sixty years ago.

A visit to a battlefield can also be a very moving experience. Whether it is a rough memorial on a Spanish battlefield or a well-kept War Graves Commission Cemetery in France or Flanders, the impression of the loss and waste of human life is inescapable and horrifying. The macabre splendour of the Ossuaire at Verdun, the repository of the mortal remains of 130,000 unidentified French dead, is matched by the many white stones in the myriad British War Cemeteries marked simply 'Known unto God'. For relations and descendants, or former comrades of the fallen, a visit to such a battlefield is often an act of both homage and remembrance. And this can be equally affecting for the visitor with no personal ties.

Of course, a battlefield tour needs careful preparation if the best possible use is to be made of time. It is important not to try to see too much, or mental indigestion can set in, and it is a good idea to intersperse the days of travel and battlefield-visiting with occasional distractions. A visit to a famous art gallery, museum or country mansion often serves as a valuable contrast. Similarly, it is also a good idea to visit the occasional site of an engagement of a different century not associated with the particular period or campaign being studied, as this can add an element of depth and an awareness of the successive generations of soldiers of one's own and other countries who have served, one after another, in the same general area.

Two pre-requisites are vital for a successful tour: a carefully considered programme of preparatory reading before the visit, and the obtaining of good modern maps. The reading material selected should be based on sound general accounts – Sir Charles Oman's famous history is virtually compulsory reading for the would-be visitor to the Peninsula. Rifleman Harris's recollections of the campaigns and battles he served in under Moore and Wellesley are as illuminating as Robert Graves's recorded experiences in Flanders of a century later. Cavalié Mercer's account of the Waterloo campaign and battle – as seen by an officer commanding a troop of Royal Horse Artillery – also makes compelling and illuminating reading. Whenever possible it is desirable to read some account 'from the other side of the hill' – the recollections of Colonel Baron Marbot of Napoleon's Hussars or Sergeant Coignet of the Imperial Guard can add a great deal to one's comprehension of both armies and events. Neither should good historical fiction, nor poetry, be neglected. C S Forester's *The Gun, or Death to the French* illuminates the roles of Spanish guerrillas and individual soldiers with great perception. His book, *The General*, throws equal light on the problems of senior command in London and at the front during the First World War. Miss Georgette Heyer's novels *An Infamous Army* and *The Spanish Bride* also have much to recommend them. Where poetry is concerned, the poems of Rupert Brooke or Siegfried Sassoon have obvious relevance, but a visitor to the Pass of Roncesvalles in the Pyrenees may also find a reading of *Le Chanson de Roland* a moving experience, while a copy of J G Lockhart's translation of *Ancient Spanish Ballads* is a suitable companion for a visit to Granada, as is D Roberts's *The Military Adventures of Johnny Newcome* for a tour of Vitoria. A cassette of *Songs of the Redcoats* – discreetly employed on a coach or car radio – can also add to the atmosphere, or serve as a welcome distraction, during the inescapable road journeys.

Where maps are concerned, a combination of the old with the new is desirable. Photocopies of such useful documents as Lieutenant Unger's sketches of Talavera, Albuera and Busaco – or of some Oman's or Sir Charles Fortescue's maps – will prove of great value. The best scale of modern map for pre-twentieth-century battlefields is 1/25,000; for the study of battles of the present century, a scale of 1/100,000 or even 1/250,000 is often more practicable. Of course, it is also necessary to take along a compass and to develop some facility at map-reading. It is also advisable to make enquiries in advance about the current state of the original battle site. Nothing is more disappointing than to arrive at a location after a tedious journey to find that a railway marshalling yard has been placed on top of the area. Reafforestation programmes have played havoc with such battlefields as Culloden in Scotland and Busaco in Portugal, and the suburbs of Brno in Czechoslovakia are creeping inexorably towards the battlefield of Austerlitz, while the Lesser Teson at Ciudad Rodrigo on the Spanish frontier has recently received a large housing estate. On the other hand, many sites are unspoilt and virtually unchanged – pre-eminent among those that spring to mind being Waterloo, Blenheim, Ramillies, Verdun, Cambrai, Salamanca and Talavera. Often the trees and forests have shrunk away, but the basic topography remains unaltered, and the size of many villages and small towns in Spain and Belgium has not changed too much over the years. Careful study of maps in advance will reveal the best viewpoints to head for, and a logical sequence should be worked out so as to trace the development of an action through its various stages. There is also much to be said for following a complete campaign from beginning to end, and in April 1977 the author of this article took a party to retrace the steps of Sir John Moore's army from Lisbon to Corunna over eight days by way of Castelo Branco, Salamanca, the

Escorial, Benavente and Sahagun, examining each place of action in turn, and in the process coming to appreciate the distances involved for men marching on their feet or on horseback during the last months of 1808 and the first of 1809. One should always allow enough time for such an enterprise – for an unseemly rush spoils the impact of the events being studied, and also robs the visitor of time to enjoy the scenery and to savour the wines and cuisine of the regions they are passing through.

Battlefield tours, therefore, have much to offer as an unusual form of holiday with a definite purpose in mind. The amount of physical endeavour involved can be adjusted to suit the individual's wishes: some prefer to spend several hours walking the battlefields; others are content with scaling one or two local eminences to obtain an overview. Everybody, however, must be prepared – when a tour of Spain or Portugal is envisaged – for long car or coach journeys over roads of varying quality. A pair of stout shoes, binoculars, perhaps a shooting stick, besides one's notes and one or two carefully chosen volumes, are other desirable pieces of personal equipment – together with a camera. In the experience of the author, gained over at least a dozen tours in the past ten years whether for Sandhurst or specialist societies and travel groups, these enterprises are well worth the amount of work and preparation involved. Besides the attraction of reliving in the mind and on the ground some dramatic moments of military history, a fine spirit of camaraderie invariably affects the party after the first day of slightly hesitant introductions and weighings-up, and even those who have only come along for the ride become infected with the fascination of bringing to life old names half remembered from school or university days. And that, after all, is exactly what the study of history is all about. It can be made into a living as well as an academic experience, and in the process a great deal of enjoyment as well as valuable experience is obtainable.

This article was originally printed in *History Today*, November 1976.

Introduction:
The Art of Battlefield Walking

The author is proud to be a member of that steadily decreasing band of men who, many years ago, young and uniformed in drab khaki, were shipped off on prolonged tours of foreign countries – with all expenses paid. They had no choice as to where they went, troopships and facilities were primitive to the extreme, hotel accommodation was non-existent, and there was no guarantee of ever returning home. One common factor marked the perambulations of so many young and gauche soldiers let loose among the towns and villages of Belgium, France, Germany, Italy, North Africa and the Far East – a total disdain for art and history amid an insatiable quest for wine, women and song. In those far-off days not many people travelled abroad, today there are few who are not familiar with the more exotic corners of the world, thus when resuming civilian status, the author's interest in military history aroused an inevitable urge to travel abroad, to personally chosen places, free of such irksome factors as being shot at, shouted at, or compelled to be indoors by 23.59 hours.

Subsequently, since the mid-1960s, each successive year has produced its eagerly anticipated period of foreign travel, seeking and exploring those fields of war which, along with museums and kindred sites, paint a vivid picture of world history. Far more than just pre-planned rambles through Europe, Africa or America, they are memorable occasions warmed by the presence of a galaxy of like-minded comrades who always seem ready to undertake an expedition to some military site in four continents of the world. To date, the score is 234 battlefields visited, of thirty-two wars, spread over seven centuries, in nine countries, each and every one of them carefully researched, explored, photographed and logged.

Besides finding and 'walking' these areas of conflict, the varied projects entailed travelling many thousands of miles by land, sea and air. Each year's expeditions have been memorable, some more memorable than others, as in 1979 in South Africa for the centenary of the Zulu War, two spaced trips to Portugal and Spain for the Peninsular War, plus an autumn tour of fields in France and Belgium. These battlefield walking expeditions have long assumed the aspects of a mid-summer ritual, beginning when compatible comrades drive onto the cross-channel ferry (when the tunnel was but a dream) or do battle with the multi-hazards of Gatwick and Heathrow.

However, these annual pilgrimages begin much earlier in the year, when winter's dark evenings are spent in the stimulating study of maps, brochures, regimental and military history books, all arousing almost unbearable senses of anticipation. Beyond purely military aspects, details are noted of other places of interest – castles, châteaux, museums, ruins, galleries and noted beauty-spots – there are very few countries so barren as to deserve nothing more than singleminded dashes from one battlefield to another. Eventually the itinerary takes shape, divided into daily sections detailing mileages, map-locations, keyed references to notes and books, with every battlefield well researched and in its own labelled folder containing relevant maps, diagrams, notes, quotes, etc., much being photocopied to avoid overloading the car. During the journey the folders become hand-baggage, studied diligently on ferry or in aircraft, when our increasing anticipation breathes life into the venture.

Possible over-night stops are also researched as gastronomy plays a big part in the success of these tours, and recommended or known-to-be-good restaurants are sought for what is invariably one of the day's highlights. Custom decrees each evening meal to be a social event when weary limbs are rested and assuaged by the balm of good food and wine, while the day's explorations are assessed and those for the morrow discussed. Searching for appealing restaurants is a saga in itself, a long-running tale of modest repasts in Relais-Routier establishments, or gargantuan platters in American diners, plus some off-beat dishes like monkey-gland steaks in Ladysmith and Pretoria during the South African trip. Not unexpectedly, it has been found that the best food is usually served in those establishments noticeably full of 'locals'.

When the group camped, the tent was frequently erected on some of Europe's most famous battlefields, and often in the dark after a good dinner when mallets hit fingers more often than tent-pegs. We were proud to be 'Campers Sauvages' – Wild Campers – pitching our temporary home on a suitable site by dead of night and away before eight o'clock in the morning – luxury campsites with toilets, showers, shops and other civilised amenities were scorned. Then to the nearest town or village for croissants and coffee, usually taken at a table outside a bar, from where the novel foreign street-scene is observed. Next, the daily browse around the *épicerie*, selecting a picnic lunch from a mouthwatering assortment of cheeses, pâtés, sausages, meats, crusty breads, melons, peaches, nectarines and the like, all washed down with local wine.

Without in any way diminishing our respect for those who immortalised the area, such fare becomes a banquet when eaten on an historic battlefield – memories abound of feasting at Waterloo, Omaha Beach, Arnhem, St Nazaire, Dieppe, Cambrai, Mons, Spion Kop, Rorke's Drift,

Isandhlwana, most of the Peninsular War fields in Portugal and Spain, Agincourt, Crécy, Poitiers, and – of late – Bull Run, Antietam and Gettysburg, and Saratoga or Yorktown.

When the era of camping ended, the search for a campsite was replaced by seeking an hotel when, in many cases, the sole choice lay in the village's only such establishment. Clear memories of these one-night stays in foreign hotels range from the sublime to the ridiculous, if only because the predominance of double-beds in continental hotels on hot summer nights renders a pair of fully grown men uncomfortable bed-fellows! In such emergencies, humour comes to the rescue – as it did at a hotel in Eupen-en-Malmédy, where a vast bedroom housed TWO double-beds with a single massive headboard. After a notably good dinner, the high ceiling echoed to the hilarity of four bed-mates in a row, leaning back against the huge rear upright panel of the bed(s).

Such 'lows' if it can be termed such, are balanced by such nights as that spent in a luxurious hotel at Viseu in Portugal, with a lobby graced by an ornamental lake and palm trees. After swimming in the pool, a dinner of roast goat – a dish of the province – with wine, cognac and all the trimmings, plus ornate bedrooms, and substantial breakfasts – all for £15 per head!

Gracious living is well worth the extra cost of the unique state-run Pousadas and Paradors in Portugal and Spain, both countries offering a network of them. Some are ancient castles, such as that at Obidos where the battlefield of Rolica could be located from the bedroom window, or the Moorish castle in the unchanged and historic town of Ciudad Rodrigo, subject to renowned sieges during the Peninsular War.

Long experience has taught us battlefield walkers to do our homework, contemplating and studying each individual site before proceeding to it; once on the spot, in order of priority, those places are sought out where significant events are known to have occurred. Every effort is made to shut twentieth-century attitudes and beliefs from the mind, in the effort to become one with our marching forebears, sharing their apprehensions, deeds and sacrifices. Occasionally this causes conflict with accepted and publicised accounts which, all too often in the manner of recorded history, tend to be perpetuations of initial errors or misjudgements. Seeing it for oneself, on the ground, backed by experience in reading military history and – for some of us – the personal experience of soldiering and being under fire, besides confirming that the emotion of fear is timeless, arouses a controversial or different assumption, which is well argued out!

But rest assured, none of us ever walks a battlefield, least of all one fought over by our own countrymen, without an awareness of that inestimable factor common to all fields of war – that they are hallowed by the courage of self-sacrifice of the soldiers who fought upon them.

Linger with this final thought, when comfortably cruising along endless dusty roads under a blazing sun, remember that those soldiers of historic wars marched every mile, carrying heavy musket and ammunition, a pack containing all their meagre possessions, with feet sore and muscles aching.

Part One
Battlefield Walking

1 *Why Battlefields?*

Not unreasonably, it might be asked 'Why should one want to visit a battlefield, knowing it to be a place where men fought and died? Is this not a glorification of War itself?' There can be no simple or straightforward answer, apart from the awareness that warfare is a pursuit thrust upon Man by powers beyond his control, encouraged by the disturbing awareness that throughout the ages Man has found fighting and violence to be evocative, stirring the imagination and quickening the blood. Long before film-makers realised this, William Shakespeare wrote, with discernment:

> In peace there's nothing so becomes a man
>> As modest stillness and humility:
> But when the blast of war blows in our ears,
>> Then imitate the action of the tiger;
> Stiffen the sinews, summon up the blood,
>> Disguise fair nature with hard favour'd rage;
> Then lend the eye a terrible aspect;
>> Now set the teeth and stretch the nostrils wide;
> Hold hard the breath, and bend every spirit
>> To his full height . . .
> (*Henry V*, Act III Scene I, William Shakespeare)

And so on.

It has to be acknowledged that, from the beginnings of time, war has brought out the best and the worst qualities in Man – courage and fear, dignity and abjectness, nobility and brutality, selflessness and selfishness – the entire spectrum of human emotion can be seen on the field of battle. Even the most passive of persons, imbued with an innate respect for bravery and brave men, and with an awareness of what occurred over the very ground upon which they are standing, should be awed by knowing that it has been hallowed by courage, forthrightly recognised by British Field-Marshal Bill Slim, who once said:

> I do not believe there is any person who, in his heart of hearts, would not rather be called brave than have any other virtue attributed to him. Courage is the basic virtue in Man and Beast, without it there are no other virtues. (*Courage*, FM W Slim (1957))

Arguably more blatantly than in any other aspect of life, stark courage is required in battle, where every ounce of it has to be dredged-up to bolster skill and strength. This must have been recognised on ancient fields where every soldier knew he faced life or death hand-to-hand combat; later generations knew it when facing the bounding roundshot, cavalry charges and the bayonet; their descendants faced high-explosives and slicing shrapnel along with the scything machine-guns, before the arrival of the screaming dive-bomber or the clattering tank, all inexorably leading to the mind-boggling horrors of nuclear weapons. These facts can be recognised on many old battlefields, where the clamour and tumult of battle has long ceased but has generated an aura causing them to be explored with an uneasy mixture of awe and admiration, even a degree of self-identification sending a noticeable tremor up the spine. Such an emotion may not affect him who has never soldiered, and is unaware of the warrior's age-old touchstone, that optimistic conviction that whatever may befall nearby comrades he will remain unharmed – without such blind hope only the truly brave or the stupid man will stand firm.

Battlefield walking tends to encourage such unfashionable traits as chauvinism and patriotism, so that when exploring the Hundred Years War field of Agincourt in France, one recalls Shakespeare again who wrote of our warlike forebears:

> . . . like so many Alexanders, have in these parts
> From morn 'til even fought,
>   And sheathed their swords for lack of argument
> (*Henry V*, Act III Scene I, William Shakespeare)

However, such thoughts never occur when on those immortal fields of the American Civil War or the Franco-Prussian War of 1870 – here we soberly consider their equal sacrifice, withholding not a fraction of our respect for the enemy either – be he Boer, Frenchman, German or Zulu.

Unconvinced? Then, how about personal pride in one's national inheritance? It is hard to understand today and tomorrow without considering yesterday and, for the Briton, much of what our nation has been for the past 600 years is built on foundations laid at Crécy, Poitiers and Agincourt, from 1346 to 1415. Picture a young nation in an exciting and colourful era, feeling its feet and a little unsteady, being uplifted by the incomparable English archer who so efficiently wielded his crude yew longbow as to transform all concepts and traditions of warfare. These proud yeomen were the forerunners of the common British soldier, the man-in-the-ranks who carved-out a great empire and was victorious in most of his battles, earning reluctant praise from his enemies at his rare defeats.

They fought with Marlborough at Blenheim and in the Low Countries; through inefficient commanders, lost America at Saratoga and Yorktown; scaled the Heights of Abraham at Quebec with Wolfe;

triumphed with Wellington in the Peninsula and at Waterloo; beat the Russians in the Crimea and rebellious sepoys in the Indian Mutiny; won innumerable colonial battles in Africa, India, Egypt, Persia and the Sudan; displayed courage under inadequate commanders in two wars against the Boers of South Africa; showed rare endurance at Mons, Ypres, the Somme and Passchendaele; and twenty-one years later, had to do it all over again in the Western Desert, North Africa, Italy, North-West Europe and the Far East; and more recently, showed those same qualities in the Falklands and the Gulf.

Less taxing on the imagination is the civilised custom of setting aside annual periods of travelling to enticing corners of the world, seeking a complete change of environment, when hopefully every moment is passed in an enjoyable manner, even if only acquiring a painful sun-tan. Of course, it does not always work and, through sheer aimlessness and lack of purpose, the flight from reality is defeated by boredom and disappointment. However, it is becoming recognised that a growing number of holidaymakers are no longer content merely to rest or laze around; they seek diversion and activity rather than idleness, objectives which, without excessive financial or physical demands, results in a stimulating and different vacation. Among the increasing variety of 'interest holidays' currently on offer are Battlefield Tours, planned with professional precision and conducted by experienced military historians and soldiers, able to stimulate the interest and imagination required to people peaceful fields with long-dead warriors, re-creating in the mind's eye surging conflicts churning lush grassland into a littered and muddy waste.

Those major battlefields with names that are household words – Waterloo in Belgium and Gettysburg in the USA – are daily thronged with thousands of visitors, taking them in their stride as part of a holiday. The thorough manner in which America labels and signposts its battlefields turns them into places of pilgrimage and fascination to even the most militarily uninformed, with regular tours, trained guides and films. These are the factors which can give so much more satisfaction, and can be aided by the battlefield walker concentrating the mind, recalling all that has been read and said, then invoking once again the aid of our friend William Shakespeare:

> On your imaginary forces work,
>   Think, when we talk of horses, that you see them
> Printing their proud hooves into the receiving earth.
>   For 'tis your thoughts which must now deck our Kings,
> Carry them here and there; jumping over Time,
>   Turning the accomplishment of many years
> Into an hour-glass.
> (*Henry V*, Prologue, William Shakespeare)

Thus inspired, your patient pacing, binoculars, and a map can begin the weaving of a colourful and stirring tapestry, bringing to life those placid pastures and peopling them with the colourful characters who once immortalised their green acres. Following their footsteps is an interesting and memorable way of re-charging patriotic batteries!

2 *Battlefield Bonuses*

Heaven forbid that any self-respecting military historian will ever tire of walking historic battlefields! And yet, it gets dark, or it rains, or fatigue intervenes, the next scheduled field is too far to reach that day, or one has a few hours to spare on arrival or before departure from a country. All of these, and numerous other unmentioned reasons, are excuses for even the most fervent battlefield walker to cast the eyes at some of the other attractions in the area – and they need not even be of military interest! Every country, every area has many sites and sights that should not be missed, representing a MUST for visitors – but more than that, they can be classified as a BONUS to our battlefield explorations.

Considering, as this book does, many countries in three continents of the world, it would be optimistic to expect detailed lists and descriptions of the attractions of *all* of them, requiring about ten national guide-books under one cover! So, to set the tone and provide an example, here is a chapter dealing with battlefield bonuses in the Peninsular War 1808–14 countries – Portugal and Spain, which entitles it to the generic title of *Peninsular Plusses*. From it can be learned – in a general sense – what else there is to see, how to go about finding them, locations, opening hours and the like – all gleaned from books and pamphlets about the area to be visited, obtained from national tourist offices. For instance, London is well-stocked with such information centres for all parts of Europe, Africa and America, who can supply publications both of a general and a specific nature – so there is no excuse for ignorance of their existence!

The experienced battlefield walker must be prepared to face up to another scenario, to which this chapter is highly applicable and a possible life-saver! Here is the military historian in his home, some months before setting off for his target battlefields, announcing to his long-suffering wife that he intends visiting Portugal and Spain – again, with Tom, Dick and Harry as usual – at not inconsiderable expense. His wife displays no immediate incredulity, having been married to a military historian too long not to know the breed, but thinks it over, reflects that she has never been to either of these countries, that they are warm . . . and different . . . perhaps with nice towns . . . and shops – and drops the bombshell of saying that this year she will go with him! His defensive argument is quickly defeated, leaving him to give thought to how best he can work it out – it is too much to expect the lady to trudge over hill and dale by his side, gazing at a scenario of peaceful fields and hills over which she is quite unable to arouse any enthusiasm. So some other attractions have to be found, ideally in the company of other wives who have jumped on the bandwagon, so that he – and their husbands – can get on with the battlefields.

Peninsular Plusses are the answer to the problem, in the enticing form of the two fascinating capital cities – Lisbon and Madrid – both very civilised and abounding with shops and venues of notable interest. More than that, the battlefield walker, once he has got over the frustration of being within a few miles of an enticing military site, will more than likely find much that will interest him in the extensive streets and buildings – for instance, both cities offer fine military museums! That in Madrid is enticingly described in its publicity pamphlet:

> The Army Museum is located in an elegant area which has a history dating back to the times of the House of Austria. This museum is part of what was once the 'Palacio del Buen Retiro', a sumptuous mansion built in 1631 by the Conde-Duque de Olivares, when he learned that Philip IV was particularly fond of this area, which was, in those times, a beautiful and peaceful forest.
>
> The palace and park designed by the Conde-Duque were so sumptuous that the Spanish Court was known all over the world as the 'Court of the Buen Retiro'.
>
> Army Museums house some of the mementos which are the legacy of their country's history throughout the centuries: flags, trophies, paintings and commemorative sculptures, portraits of heroes and, in short, all of these are reminders of a most deeply-felt patriotism, with the essential purpose of these museums being the conservation of those things which are our legacy from those who preceeded us in their love of their Homeland.
>
> A visit to the Army Museum manifests and awakens the pride and glory of being Spanish, of having been born in a country which extended its culture throughout the world.
>
> The Museum contains numerous pieces of indubitable historical value and valuable works of art, such as a part of a tree from the 'Sad Night' of Hernán Cortés; a part of the cross that Christopher Columbus carried when he landed in the New World; pieces of Pizarro's shirt and both sides of the standard that he carried during the conquest of Peru; the field tent of the Emperor Charles I, in Tunisia; a fragment of the flag from the battle of Lepanto and many more, being of particular interest the famous sword of EL CID, called 'LA TIZONA', which was kept by Isabel la Católica and which is a gem of limitless worth.
>
> The Medinaceli Armour Room contains an extraordinary collection, which includes two 'half armours' which belonged to Gonzalo de Cordoba, the 'Gran Capitán', when he was a page.
>
> The weapons collections are of considerable value due to their variety, their age and the historical importance of some pieces, both regarding the

firearms and the steel arms, in addition to the artillery weapons.

There is also a room containing military miniatures, both in wood and in tin, which has approximately 16,000 figures.

Tapestries, such as that of the 'Santa Hermandad de Toledo', from the times of Philip II, and famous flags, the most outstanding of which is the one taken from the British on the conquest of Pensacola, that of the ship 'San Juan de Nepomuceno', of the heroic Churruca; the flags and standards with coats of arms of the glorious Old Regiments and Divisions, and the busts of some of their famous captains.

Numerous documents of unsurpassable historical value, such as some letters signed by Nelson, by Castaños, by Palafox, by Wellington; a warrant issued by the Catholic Monarchs and the original of the last communiqué issued in the Spanish Civil War.

It is estimated that the collections contain a total of approximately 30,000 pieces.

A visit to the Army Museum, which is considered to be one of the finest in the world, is a journey through the history of Spain.

In Lisbon, the National Army Museum, situated in the Alfama area of the city, contains a valuable collection of weapons and armour, military objects, prints, uniforms, artillery ranging from the fifteenth century to the present day. It is – or was on the author's last visit – a 'real' museum, an archaic and crowded place, housing in massed profusion a multitude of interesting military exhibits. At the other end of Lisbon, in the Belem area, is the Maritime Museum, a very comprehensive place containing a large collection of finely detailed model ships reaching far back into history to include models of 3,000-year-old Egyptian and Greek ships. Besides an interesting selection of beautifully carved and gilded state barges, it contains innumerable maps, maritime paintings, instruments and other relevant naval objects.

When planning to visit continental museums – any museums, not only those dealing with military collections – always remember that NONE of them open on Mondays, bearing this in mind obviates a lot of disappointment and frustration.

Perhaps unique in the world is Madrid's famed Prado, containing the incomparable works of Goya, depicting the horrors of the Peninsular War, and his masterpiece painting of the Duke of Wellington, besides the splendid Velazquez collection. If you have inbuilt objections to queuing, then do not visit the Prado on a Sunday! The seventeenth-century Plaza Mayor, now a colourful area of first-class bars and restaurants, was once witness to bullfights and public executions, and is well worth a visit.

Lisbon, capital of Portugal, Britain's oldest ally and staunch fighters by the side of the British infantryman during the long Peninsular War, is the ideal jumping-off place for travel to the battlefields in the north,

Rolica, Vimiero, Lines of Torres Vedras, Busaco, and thence to the Spanish border for Almeida and Fuentes de Oñoro. Lisbon is a colourful and pleasing city, bordered on north and south by the intriguing suburbs of Alfama and Belem, with museums in each of them. The Castle of St George, dating back past 1147, is in the Alfama district and from its ramparts can be seen a breathtaking view of the city and the River Tagus. It is said that Alfama breathes the true spirit of Old Lisbon, with its crowded streets, alleyways and tavernas, from which at night can be heard the melancholy lilt of the Fado. Belem houses the Presidential Palace, the Monastery of Jeronimos, the Coach Museum, the Maritime Museum, the Gulbenkian Planetarium, and the picturesque tower of Henry the Navigator dominating it all.

Madrid, the Spanish capital, is ringed with superb places for day visits – the walled city of Avila, Segovia, and the Valley of the Fallen – Valle de los Caidos, the monument to the dead of the Civil War of 1936–39 situated in a wild valley of the Guadarrama Range, with its granite cross 500 feet high and 150 feet across the arms. If one has never before seen a completely walled town then Avila, enthroned on a hilltop like a castle carved out of stone, resembles an enormous and unreal medieval stage with walls, rising to an impressive height, that are the oldest and best preserved in Spain. They are in the shape of an equilateral hexagon, strengthened by eighty-eight bastions and towers, crowned by 2,500 embrasures, and with nine gateways. Almost as impressive is El Escorial, the monastery-palace from which the fanatical King Philip II ruled much of the known world in the sixteenth century.

It has been said that if a traveller can spend only one day in Spain, then it should be used seeing the city of Toledo, a historic town silhouetted in sharp relief against a background formed by the crests of encircling hills and more distant mountains sprawling over a vast crag surrounded by the River Tagus in the bare Castilian plain. Standing out amid the buildings of the town is the great fortress–palace, the Alcazar, scene of a remorseless siege early in the Spanish Civil War. Here, on 26 July, the commander of the Red Militia investing the place telephoned Colonel Moscardo, commander of the Nationalist garrison, telling him he held his son Luis captive and, if the fortress was not immediately surrendered, he would have him shot. Asking to speak to his son, the Colonel said: '. . . commend your soul to God, shout Viva España and die like a hero'. In due course, the son was executed and the fortress held out until relieved by General Varela's Nationalist column.

Since the beginnings of time, it has been noteworthy that whoever controls these things has a knack of balancing bad with good, and the Alcazar siege in 1936 was no exception. Down in the stifling hospital beneath the citadel, a Spanish surgeon, Trueta, lacking drugs and medical supplies to treat the many wounded, despairingly devised a revolutionary treatment for gunshot wounds which, by any accepted line of reasoning, could only culminate in gangrene and death. Incredibly, it did the reverse, the immobilised wounds healed successfully; during World War Two which shortly followed, this method of treatment saved the lives of countless soldiers of many nationalities.

With some regret we left our Toledo hotel, the King Alphonse VII, an old and beautiful building where panelled corridors were lined with suits of armour and weapons, as befits a town noted throughout the ages for its skill in making those artefacts.

Memories abound from the hours, days and weeks spent rushing across Spain and Portugal seeking battlefields, museums and, last but by no means least, hotels (although on two tours we took a tent and achieved a high degree of pleasure sleeping on the fields of Roncesvalles, Sorauren, Vitoria and the Nivelle, among other places – there is nothing like it for bringing one truly close to the men who did the fighting on that hallowed ground). High among those nostalgic recollections is the long haul north-east across Spain, moving from Badajoz to Talavera de la Reina, on the NV E4, which is a good road running through the southern part of the ancient land of the Conquistadors – Extremadura, Spain's 'Wild West' littered with splendid castles and elegant cathedrals set in an atmosphere steeped in ancient echoes and ways. Coming upon the very old and intriguing town of Mérida, we chanced upon perhaps the most extraordinary hotel in our experience – the Emperatriz, an incredible building of great antiquity, its interior mounting skywards in an open, chandelier-hung space, encircled by great railed galleries from which led the bedrooms. A very old town, founded in 25 BC, called Emeritus Augustus and known as 'the Rome of Spain', today it proudly displays a Roman theatre in remarkably good state of preservation, together with sculpture, statues, columns and arches, all bearing witness to Mérida's glorious past.

Further along the road to Talavera, one passes through the old town of Trujillo, its remarkable colonnaded plaza is proudly surmounted by a large mounted statue of the town's famous son, the Conquistador Pizarro, conqueror of Peru, who was born there in 1471. The eye is then caught by a magnificent skyline landmark, the sixteenth-century monastery towering over the sleepy town of Guadalupe below. Truly these picturesque Spanish towns must be counted among one's 'Peninsular Plusses'!

At the north-eastern end of the Guadarrama Range about fifty miles from Madrid on N1 E25 lies the Somosierra Pass where, on 22 November 1808, Napoleon himself, at the head of 45,000 troops marching to Madrid, came upon an extemporised Spanish force 9,000-strong entrenched at the head of the Pass. Impatient at the halt, Napoleon ordered his personal escort squadron of eighty-seven Polish lancers to charge the Pass and clear it. Bravely they attempted to do so and were almost wiped out; quickly outflanking forces drove the Spanish from their position, and Napoleon's march to Madrid was resumed. Even today, on the modern road, with a little imagination, it is possible to picture this sanguinary action.

Last but not least, are the 'spin-offs' which can, with careful planning, be reasonably considered as Peninsular Plusses, certainly for those driving south through France from the Channel Coast ferries to the Pyrenees or, conversely, returning home by that route. The author has innumerable cherished memories of long hauls of over 600 miles to pick-up the ferry at Le Havre or Cherbourg, after battlefield walking in Spain as far south as Pamplona, when the three/four-day drive was enlivened by visiting the fields of numerous other wars of past centuries.

Driving through France *en route* to or from Spain, it is possible to plan routes that take in the following well-known battlefields of wars, given in their historic chronological order:

The 100 Years War (1336–1453)	Agincourt 1415
	Auberoche 1345
	Castillon 1453
	Cravant 1423
	Crécy 1346
	Formigny 1450
	Mauron 1352
	Patay 1429
	Poitiers 1356
	Verneuil 1424
French Wars of Religion	Arques 1589
Napoleonic Wars	Craonne 7 March 1814
	Laon 9/10 March 1814
World War I	The Argonne 1918
	Arras 1917
	Cambrai 1917
	Chemin-des-Dames 1918
	Somme 1916
World War II	Caen area 1944
	D-Day (Normandy) 1944
	Dieppe 1942
	Dunkirk 1940
	St Lô 1944

Then there are the 'off-beat' places of interest, far too numerous to list, but fondly recalled by the author are such places as: Château Gaillard, at

Les Andelys on the Seine (Richard the Lionheart's 'Saucy Castle'); Compiègne, where the 1918 Armistice was signed in a still-existent railway coach, where in 1941 Hitler danced a jig of joy, and where the *Hôtel de Ville* (town hall) has a remarkable display of model soldiers in a huge diorama of a French Army parade; Brouage, a medieval walled town, south of Rochefort; the Naval Museum at La Rochelle. Each place conjures up recollections of another one – the list could be interminable, and is perhaps far-removed from our Peninsular War terms of reference.

With a little pre-holiday research and study, any tourist can discover, 'read' and be stimulated by battlefields that may happen to be on or near his route. For example, the motorist drives off the cross-channel ferry at Cherbourg and speeds over the excellent roads of northern France, through the lush green fields of Normandy, along Route N13 to Bayeux. It is an area well known to British and American soldiers who landed on D-Day 1944, but it is doubtful if many of them were aware – or even more likely, cared – that on this very road inland of the infamous Omaha Beach and today's huge US Military Cemetery at St Laurent, a fierce battle was fought at Formigny that virtually ended the 100 Years War between England and France.

These pages will chart such places and describe in vivid detail the stirring events of the day so as to stimulate even the most unhistorically minded tourist.

Part Two

France – The Hundred Years War 1337–1453

3 An Introduction to the Hundred Years War

Famed for the immortal trinity of the battles Crécy, Poitiers and Agincourt, the Hundred Years War began in 1337 when English raiding parties carried out Commando-style raids at Cadzand and other French coastal towns, then came a sea victory at Sluys in 1340 and, at Morlaix in 1342 and Auberoche in 1345, two extraordinary battles were won that set the pattern for the competent command and fighting style of English commanders and their men for much of the long war. These two battlefields are easily accessible and so little changed that hindsight and imagination allows them to be stirringly re-lived. The War lasted 116 years, ending in 1453 at Castillon on the Gironde not far from Bordeaux when the legendary Sir John Talbot was killed at the age of seventy-one, leading repeated attacks on more than 200 emplaced French cannon.

Nevertheless, all the man-in-the-street knows of it probably comes from the colourful films of Shakespeare's play, *Henry V*. But Sir Winston Churchill, no mean warrior himself, provided one good reason for closer acquaintance when claiming Agincourt to be 'the most heroic of all the land battles England has ever fought!' With that in mind, add the enchantment lent by time of chivalrous characters whose ringing names conjure up a colourful cloak of medieval pageantry – Kings Edward III and Henry V, the Black Prince, Joan of Arc, and a host of names made familiar by Shakespeare's stirring words. Man's propensity to offer violence to his fellows causes many of the best-known names and faces of history to be warriors – kings, princes, marshals, generals and soldiers who have hallowed or made notorious – depending upon your outlook – those places where they fought. Political and geographical circumstances site many of these fields in highly accessible parts of France where, mercifully softened by the passing of time, the battlefields of the Hundred Years War – that long-drawn-out medieval conflict which actually lasted 116 years (1337 to 1453) lay less changed than perhaps any other historical areas of conflict. Small and compact, readily recognisable as the time-honoured arenas bestrode by prancing knights, dour men-at-arms and the incomparable English archer, they reveal at a glance where it all happened. To walk them is to re-live an exciting and glowing era when England, a young nation feeling her feet and still a trifle unsteady, won all her battles and in 1346, the heady year of the twin victories over the French at Crécy and the Scots at Neville's Cross, could not find room in the Tower of London for all her royal and noble prisoners-of-war.

Agincourt, best known of them all and said by Sir Winston Churchill to be the greatest of all England's land battles, remains almost exactly as in October 1415. Were Henry V to return, he would instantly recognise it as the place where, on a misty autumn morning, he immortalised himself in 180 minutes of fierce fighting. A most evocative experience is to begin from the edge of either Agincourt or Tramecourt Woods, on a line with the clump of trees by the side of road Route D104, which conceal the old calvaire, and pace steadily across the ploughed land towards the distant trees, halting on your 500th step. With awe, reflect that here the gallant King, positioned between the second and third lines of his dismounted knights and men-at-arms, stood over his brother's stricken body and fought off sixteen French knights pledged to kill him. At one point he was beaten to his knees by a blow that sliced off part of the crown encircling the helmet; that same battered headpiece can be seen today in Westminster Abbey. Only the dullest of mortals can stand on such a spot and remain unaffected!

At Poitiers, scene of the Black Prince's victory in 1356, it is still possible to find the hedge line defended by Salisbury and Warwick's soldiers; the modern beet-factory at Crécy conveniently marks where impatient French knights rode down their own mercenary Genoese crossbowmen in 1346. Shakespeare has Henry cry inspiringly at Harfleur: 'Once more into the breach, dear friends, once more! Or close the wall up with our English dead!' Today, it is a drab and dreary suburb of seaport Le Havre; those castle walls painstakingly besieged at Caen, Calais, Orleans and Rouen have long since succumbed to progress in the shape of roads, factories and flats whose inhabitants know nothing of the history around them. But Cravant, Falaise, Fougères, Verneuil and Vitry proudly display battered turrets, and at Beaugency the waters of the Loire foam around the ruined piers of the bridge over which Joan of Arc led a spirited foray.

The routes to these fields and places are also interesting. On their way to victory at Crécy, after landing at St Vaast de la Hogue, King Edward III and his 16-year-old son, the Black Prince, marched across the same area where their descendants were to fight the battle for Normandy in 1944; the route of the French to that same field was on the old road from Marchville, still marked on maps as Chemin de l'Armée. Few motorists rushing along the black ribbon of Route N. 13 from Cherbourg to Bayeux know that in 1450, just inland of Omaha Beach on this very same road at Formigny, was fought a desperate battle, the penultimate conflict of the Hundred Years War, when Sir Thomas Kyriell's small English force battled almost to the last man in the orchards that still lay on either side of the road, and lay buried in grave pits marked by grassy mounds.

But this is merely to whet the appetite, to encourage further ventures in search of those and other recognisable fields: Mauron, Morlaix and

Roche-Derrien in Brittany; Verneuil in Eure; Patay in Loiret; Cravant in Yonne; Auberoche in the Dordogne and Castillon on the Garonne. Truly, in those places one walks with the kings and commoners who were our ancestors – sturdy Englishmen, incomparable archers, later the British man-in-the-ranks who won a vast empire and was victorious in practically all his battles, winning the reluctant admiration of enemies at his rare defeats.

It requires an almost impossible stretch of imagination to be one with Henry's weary, hungry, dysentery-ridden army, trudging along muddy tracks to Agincourt, aware that a huge enemy army was remorsely marching to trap and destroy them. Kings, princes, earls and knights were spared for ransom and would eventually return home – although the Duke of Orleans was a prisoner in the Tower for twenty-five years, until his huge ransom could be raised – but the common soldier could expect only death on the spot, while archers had the thumb and forefinger of the right hand struck off.

Perhaps more than on most fields of war, stark courage abounded on medieval and ancient battlefields, where every combatant knew he faced personal hand-to-hand combat, survival depending upon dredging up every single drop of courage and sending it into battle to bolster skill and strength. There is no way for a modern man to know what it was like encased from head to toe in heavy steel armour, to clumsily cavort in a desperate face-to-face confrontation where a slip of the foot resulted in grotesquely sprawling on churned muddy ground, snatching a last look at blue sky above through narrow visor slits, awaiting oblivion by mace or axe, battering head and helm into a bloody mass, or the dagger slipped through an armour chink into throat or eye. Perhaps that was more merciful than to be left alive with a gaping wound far beyond the primitive surgery of the day, or to helplessly suffer through the chill hours of night until roughly stripped by plundering peasants, then put out of misery by a blunt knife sawing through the throat.

Far removed from today's vast impersonal and horrific conflicts the Hundred Years War was a series of small battles, now softened by the passing of time to spread a colourful cloak of medieval pageantry over the exploits of legendary heroes who displayed chivalrous attitudes in their savage combats where personal courage predominated. To walk these fields is to re-live those days when England won all her battles and was the most feared nation in Europe.

4 *The Course of the War*

The war was a series of eight major periods of conflict between England and France: four periods of military activity occurring in the fourteenth century, and four in the fifteenth century.

1   The Sluys Period 1337–43

English raiding parties went from England and Flanders in 1337/8 but the only decisive actions were:

1340	Naval battle of Sluys – English victory.
1342	Battle of Morlaix – English victory.

2   The Crécy Period 1345–52

1345	Minor actions in Brittany.
	Battle of Auberoche – English victory.
1346	French invasion of Gascony, held up by stubborn resistence of Castle of Aiguillon.

To forestall a possible French invasion, Edward III determined to advance his claims to the throne of France by landing a large expedition in Normandy and marching through France. Probably the largest and best expedition to leave these shores until the nineteenth century, they sailed on 11 July 1346 from the Isle of Wight area to land unopposed next day some eighteen miles east of Cherbourg and began their march. On 26 August 1346 at Crécy, they encountered and defeated a large French army.

1346	English besiege and capture Calais.
1352	The Battle of Mauron – English victory.

3   The Poitiers Period 1355–67

1355	Edward III leads raids across northern France.
	The Black Prince raids from Bordeaux into Languedoc.
	John of Gaunt raids into Normandy from Brittany.
1356	Black Prince raids into central France.
	The Battle of Poitiers – English victory.

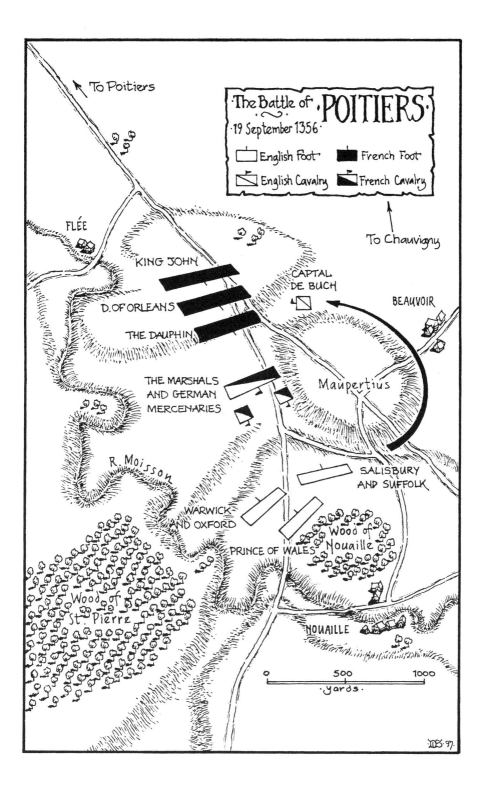

To Poitiers

The Battle of **POITIERS**
·19 September 1356·

English Foot French Foot
English Cavalry French Cavalry

To Chauvigny

FLÉE

KING JOHN

CAPTAL DE BUCH

BEAUVOIR

D. OF ORLEANS

THE DAUPHIN

THE MARSHALS AND GERMAN MERCENARIES

Maupertius

R. Moisson

SALISBURY AND SUFFOLK

WARWICK AND OXFORD

Wood of Nouaille

PRINCE OF WALES

Wood of St. Pierre

NOUAILLE

0   500   1000
·yards·

DS·97

1356/60	English raid throughout France.
1360	Edward III makes a final raid up to the walls of Paris.
1360–67	War of succession ('War of Liberation') in Brittany continues.
1364	Anglo-Breton army besieging Auray defeat French relieving army, and take town.
1360–67	French and English mercenaries take part in King Charles (the Bad) of Navarre's raids into southern France. French and English mercenaries continue Hundred Years War by proxy during Castilian Civil War.
1367	Black Prince leads army over Pyrenees to restore Pedro the Cruel to the throne of Castile; opposed by Castilian army under Henry of Trastamara aided by a French contingent led by du Guesclin. Battle of Nájera – English victory.

4   The du Guesclin Period 1368–96

In 1364, Charles the Wise came to the throne of France. Through his sagacity and the skill of Bertrand du Guesclin, an outstanding Marshal of France, the country is saved from collapse. Instituting far-reaching improvements in military organisation and reconciling chivalry with commonsense, du Guesclin follows a shrewd strategic policy. Within five years and without fighting a single major battle, the Marshal has pushed the English into a narrow strip of land between Bordeaux and Bayonne.

1368	Bertrand du Guesclin, Constable of France, leads French armies aiding Gascon nobles rebelling against Black Prince.
1368–77	Constable du Guesclin steadily pursues campaign of sieges in Gascony, reaching within twenty miles of Bordeaux in 1377. No real battles are fought.
1368	John of Gaunt leads an army in an unopposed march from Calais to Harfleur and back.
1370	Sir Robert Knowles marches with an army from Calais, via Arras, to Troyes, past Paris and on to Brittany. Internal quarrels break up the force and dispersed columns are destroyed by du Guesclin.
1370	Black Prince captures and sacks Limoges.
1372	Sea battle of La Rochelle, French/Castilian fleet defeat English fleet.
1373	John of Gaunt leads army of 15,000 to relief of Gascony, marching 1,000 miles from Calais to Bordeaux in five months, losing half his army through hunger. French consistently evade him and no major actions take place.
1375	Edmund, Earl of Cambridge, marches his army through Brittany from end to end.

The Earl of Buckingham leads an army from Calais on Knowles's 1370 route into Maine, then on to Rennes, capital of Brittany.

1375–83	Spasmodic fighting between French and English adherents.
1376	Death of Black Prince.
1377	Death of Edward III.
1380	Death of du Guesclin.
1380	Siege and capture of Châteauneuf de Randon – French victory.
1386	Combined French/Castilian fleet defeated off Margate by English fleet, causing abandonment of French invasion plan.
1389–96	Truce period interspersed with minor fighting.

5   The Uneasy Truce Period 1396–1413

Small-scale fighting, raids and revolts encouraged by rulers of both England and France.

1402	French support the Earl of Douglas's Scottish invasion of England, defeated at Homildon Hill by Lord Henry Percy ('Hotspur') – English victory.
1403	French raids on Plymouth and English Channel ports.
1405	French land in Wales to support Owen Glendower, but return home with little accomplished.
1406	Burgundians and Orleanists temporarily unite to attack English possessions in Vienne; operate against Calais.
1407–11	French civil war between Burgundians and Orleanists (Armagnacs); both seek aid from Henry IV of England.

In 1411 an English expeditionary force under the Earl of Arundel, sent to assist the Duke of Burgundy *against* the Armagnacs, has some easy successes and undoubtedly provides information for later campaigns. In the following years, King Henry IV sends his son, Thomas, Duke of Clarence, with a force to *aid* the Armagnacs in a profitable *chevauchée* into Anjou and the Orleanais. Eventually the two French warring parties make a truce and, as a necessary feature of late medieval warfare, pool their resources to pay Clarence to go back home again.

Henry IV dies in March 1414 and his son, Prince Henry, comes to the throne.

6   Period of Henry V, and the Regent Bedford, 1415–29

On 11 August 1415, Henry V sailed from Southampton with an army of 12,000 men to take possession of his claimed territory in France. Through the summer and early autumn they were held up outside Harfleur by the stout resistance of the besieged city and by disease. Harfleur fell on

22 September, and Henry decided to march over 160 miles by direct route through Normandy to Calais, his other secure possession in northern France.

October   8   Henry's army begins march to Calais.
          12   Skirmish at Eu on the Bresle, against Boucicaut's French force.
          17   Skirmish at bridge at Corbie.

Although the best known of his campaigns, Agincourt was Henry V's most reckless venture on French soil, with his cross-country march in the Edwardian-style finally becoming delicately balanced on the inescapable fact that, if the enemy blocked his path, the English army would be defeated through hunger. But the French, forgetting the lessons of Crécy and Poitiers and ignoring the subsequent successful tactics of du Guesclin, decide it would be humiliating to use their four-to-one superiority in anything but a direct attack. It is a disastrous mixture of faulty reasoning and chivalrous attitudes, and at Agincourt on 25 October 1415, the French are defeated through an attempt to perpetuate an 'unscientific kind of combat that resembled a huge tilting match'.

1417   Siege of Caen – English victory.
1417/18   Siege of Falaise – English victory.
1418   Action at Pont de l'Arche – English victory.
1418/19   Siege of Rouen – English victory.
1419   January   31 – Surrender of Lillebourne.
          February   3   "   " Vernon.
                       5   "   " Mantes.
                       8   "   " Dieppe.
                       9   "   " Gournay.
                      15   "   " Eu.
                      25   "   " Honfleur.

By the end of February practically the whole of Normandy is in English hands, except five great castles: La Roche-Guyon; Gisors; Ivry; Château Gaillard, and Mont St Michel. All but the last fall after sieges of varying length.

	July	English storm and capture Pontoise.
	September	9th Duke of Clarence's column at gates of Paris.
1420	March	Battle of Fresnay, against combined French/Scots army – English victory.
	May	Siege of Sens – English victory.
	June	Storming of Montereau by Anglo-Burgundian army.
	July–November	Siege of Melun – English victory.
1421	March 21	Battle of Baugé – French victory.
	June	Henry V returns to France with a new army.

	July 18	Siege and capture of Dreux.
	September	Siege of Beaugency. Sickness forces army to move. Villeneuve attacked and taken.
1422	October ⎱ May ⎰	Almost all northern France in hands of Anglo-Burgundians.
	August 31	Death of Henry V.
	September	Period of sporadic raids and sieges. French take Meulan, Salisbury re-takes it. Sir John de la Pole raids into Anjou, cut-up and captured by French under the Count of Aumâle. In the west, Warwick captures Noyelles, then Le Crotoy besieged by Sir Ralph Boutellier – with its fall ends resistance in Picardy of Jacques d'Harcourt.
1423	July	Battle of Cravant (Anglo-Burgundian army versus Franco-Scots). English victory. Salisbury, Sir Thomas Rempston and John of Luxembourg 'tidy-up' in eastern regions, many towns taken. Burgundians lose Compiègne, retaken by Bedford in early 1424.
1424	August	Battle of Verneuil – English victory. Bedford defeats Franco-Scots army. Maine and Anjou overrun. Campaign in the Loire. Remaining French strongholds in Picardy and Champagne surrender. Duke of Burgundy campaigns South to Mâcon.
1425	Summer	Salisbury drives into Maine, captures Étampes, Rambouillet, Le Mans and Mayenne.
1426	January	Sir Thomas Rempston invades Brittany, basing his small force on St James. Besieged by Richemont, Constable of France. Breaking out in March, Rempston attacks French in rear and routs them at Battle of St James.
1427		Warwick captures Pontorson. Warwick and Suffolk besiege Montargis, where French relief force defeat them – French victory. Talbot relieves Le Mans. Talbot captures Laval.
1428	July	Salisbury's army enters Paris.
	August	Salisbury begins Orléans campaign, taking Chartres, Puiset, Janville, Meung and many other towns.
	September	Sieges of Beaugency ⎫ Jargeau and Châteauneuf ⎭ English victories

October 12	Siege of Orléans begins.
24	Salisbury killed.
1429 January	Siege continues.
29	Battle of Rouvray – English victory.
	'Battle of the Herrings'; Sir John Fastolf defeats Franco-Scots force.

7   The Period of Joan of Arc, 1429–44

1429 February	Emergence of Joan of Arc.
April 27/29	Joan leads relief army to Orléans.
May 3	Joan involved in French sortie that captures important Fort St Loup.
5/6	Joan leads successful attacks on Tourelles and Augustins Fort.
	English raise siege of Orléans.
June	Jargeau, Meung and Beaugency re-taken by French.
19	Battle of Patay – French victory.
July	French capture Troyes, Châlons and Rheims.
September	Joan captures St Pierre, but has to abandon siege of La Charité.
1430	Burgundian army with English support besiege Compiègne, where Joan is captured in a skirmish.
1431 May	Joan of Arc executed.
	Warwick defeats French in minor battle at Savignies.
Autumn	Louviers taken by English after three-month siege.
1432	Chartres falls to French.
	English besiege and then retreat from Lagny.
1433	Successful Burgundian campaigns in Eastern theatre of war.
	Sporadic minor fighting elsewhere.
1434	Earl of Arundel is killed while conducting very successful campaign in Maine and Anjou.
	Talbot, released from captivity in exchange for Poton de Xantrailles, carries out extensive operations north of Paris, capturing many towns.
1435	English alliance with Burgundy ends.
	Talbot carries out successful operations in Isle de France and with Bedford, makes unsuccessful attack on St Denys, which is later surrendered.

	The Regent Bedford dies.
1436	French recapture Paris.
	French leaders La Hire and Xantrailles, raiding to Rouen, are totally defeated by Talbot, Lord Scales and Sir Thomas Kyriell at Ry – English victory.
1437	Talbot captures Pointoise, and then makes unsuccessful attempt to recapture Paris.
	Talbot relieves La Crotoy, defeating Burgundians at Blanchetaque ford over the Somme; then ravages their country.
1438/9	French attempt to drive English out of Acquitaine with small success; in following year are driven back by Earl of Huntingdon.
1439	French beseige Meaux, Talbot drives Richemont's army off but is unable to relieve town, which surrenders.
	Talbot re-takes towns in area between Rouen and Dieppe.
	Richemont, Constable of France, besieges Avranches, Talbot's relieving army scatters the French.
1440	English besiege Harfleur, which surrenders after French relieving army is thrown back.
1441	French besiege Pointoise; Talbot's army repeatedly enter town, which remains under siege.
	Talbot and Duke of York conduct brilliant Seine and Oise campaign. French go back to besieging Pointoise. Talbot again repeatedly replenishes town but is unable to effect relief. French artillery cause surrender.
1442	Successful French campaign in Gascony, with many sieges.
	La Reole surrenders to French after fierce resistance.
	Talbot returns to France and takes towns in Normandy.
	Invests Dieppe but, in his absence, French relieving force pen British and eventually defeat them.
1443	Somerset takes army on aimless expedition into Maine and Brittany.
1444	Truce of Tours.

8   The Period of French Professional Superiority, 1444–53

1449		French re-conquest of Normandy.
		Rouen surrenders; Talbot taken as hostage.
		Harfleur taken by French.
1450	January	Harfleur falls to French.
		Most of eastern and south-eastern parts of Normandy in French hands.
	March	Sir Thomas Kyriell with small English army lands at Cherbourg.
		Reinforced in Normandy, captures Valognes, but is brought to bay at Formigny.
	April 15	Battle of Formigny – French victory.
		French take Vire, Bayeux and Caen.
		Avranches falls to combined French/Breton army.
		Falaise surrenders to French in return for release of Talbot.
	August 11	Cherbourg, last English town in northern France, falls.
1451		French invade Gascony and occupy Bordeaux.
1452		Talbot (now over 70) sails for Gascony. Re-occupies Bordeaux, takes back most of western Gascony, some towns by force.
1453		Three French armies march on Bordeaux, and lay siege to Castillon. Talbot goes to its relief but is defeated and killed when attacking strong artillery defences.
	July 19	Battle of Castillon – French victory.
		Gascony lost to France.
	October 19	Fall of Bordeaux – virtually ending Hundred Years War except for minor English and French coastal raids during following years. France achieves both internal stability and a substantial technical and tactical superiority over the English that sweeps them out of France within four years, save for a single tiny foothold at Calais.

5 *The Battle of Crécy*
26 August 1346

Milestoning nearly a century of English military supremacy in France, the ringing names 'Crécy!', 'Poitiers!' and 'Agincourt!' are linked together in an immortal trinity of victories that have moved the hearts of Englishmen ever since. It is a stirring story, because on these green fields lying before you was fought one of the most decisive battles of military history – it was here that the infantryman, the foot soldier, commenced his centuries-old reign as the basic battlefield element.

To counter a rumoured French invasion of England and to advance his claims to the French throne, Edward III decided to land in Normandy and march through France. At last an army of at least 15,000 men – the largest force up to that time ever assembled by England for an overseas expedition – were packed in ships laying off the Isle of Wight. Sailing on 11 July 1346, they landed unopposed on the following day in the St Vaast de la Hogue/Barfleur area, some 18 miles east of Cherbourg. After six days' consolidation, with the 16-year-old Black Prince commanding the vanguard, they marched unhindered southwards, to plunder St Lô, before turning east to Caen, capital of Normandy.

The long, colourful column of armoured men, spear points glittering and lance pennons fluttering, must have marched very close to the village of Ste Mère Eglise, to be the centre of the dropping zones of US Airborne forces 600 years later, where Private John Steele of 505 Airborne Regiment hung helplessly in his parachute harness from the steeple of the church. Doubtless many of the ancient buildings sacked by Edward's soldiers were finally destroyed during bitter fighting in the summer months of 1944. Caen's garrison and citizens resisted too fiercely to be given quarter, and the town was savagely sacked; then the army marched to Lisieux, where the King refused to treat with a pair of Cardinals, who carried the French King's offer of the entire province of Acquitaine. Next, the Seine was crossed, and the line-of-march veered towards Paris, following the south bank of the river, through Pont-de-l'Arche, Louviers, Vernon and Mantes, unable to cross because all bridges had been destroyed. After covering 215 miles in 27 days, they came to Poissy, where the engineers spent three days building a crossing on the piles of the old bridge.

While this went on, the King sent parties raiding to the very gates of Paris, while King Philip of France desperately tried to gather together an

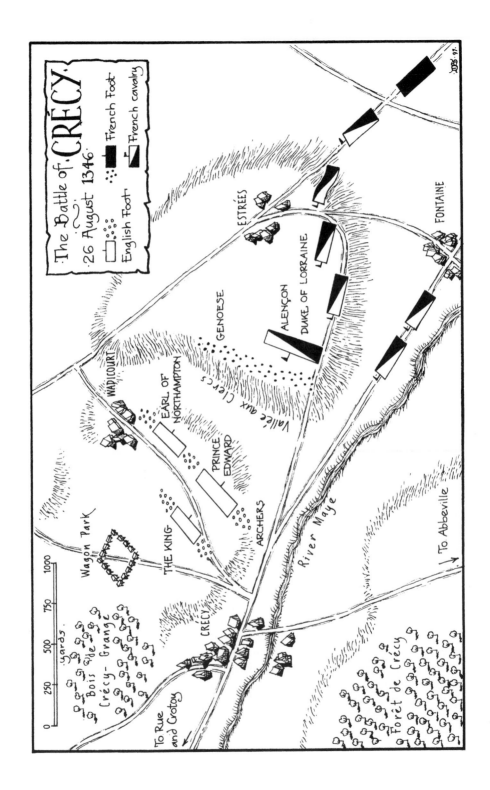

The Battle of CRECY.
26 August 1346.

French Foot
English Foot
French cavalry

ESTRÉES

FONTAINE

GENOESE

ALENÇON

DUKE OF LORRAINE

WADICOURT

EARL OF NORTHAMPTON

Vallée aux Clercs

PRINCE EDWARD

Wagon Park

ARCHERS

THE KING

River Maye

CRÉCY

To Abbeville

Bois de Crécy-Grange

1000 750 500 250 0
yards

To Rue and Crotoy

Forêt de Crécy

army at St Denis. Across the river, the English now turned north towards Beauvais and Amiens, following the line of today's Routes D981 and D901, through Grandvilliers and Poix, to Airaines in Edward's own inheritance of Ponthieu. Many towns were deserted and undefended, and Poix was spared on payment of a ransom, but after the army had marched on, townsfolk attacked the small party that remained behind to collect the money. They had to be rescued by a hastily returning rearguard who then burned the town and razed its two castles to the ground. The two daughters of the Lord of Poix were saved from molestation by Sir John Chandos and, at the King's command, escorted to Corbie. Although living off the land with legitimate booty was permissible, the conduct of the army was strictly controlled and wanton assaults on women of gentle blood, or clergy, were forbidden; twenty men were hanged for setting fire to the Abbey of St Messien near Beauvais.

Halting at Airaines, Edward gave thought to the critical position he was now in – out of touch with his fleet and lacking contact with Flemish allies, he knew that their whole future depended upon the outcome of a single pitched battle that could lose the entire war. His army, although tired, were in good spirits despite worn-out boots and lack of food so that

Charge of the French cavalry on the English bowmen at the Battle of Crécy

many men suffered gripes through eating unripe fruit; horses were flag-ging and clumsy farm animals were pressed into service. Harassed by local levies and with an enemy at least twice their strength behind them, it was imperative to advance across the River Somme, but it was unfordable and all bridges were destroyed or strongly guarded. Seeking crossing places, two marshals were sent out with 1,000 men-at-arms and 2,000 archers to follow the course of the river – at Longpré the bridge was down, at Pont Remy they fought hard but unsuccessfully for a well fortified and guarded bridge, reaching Picquigny they found the town, castle and bridge too well garrisoned to assault. Hearing this, Edward led his army out onto the Abbeville road; the French, their numbers daily increasing, marching from Amiens, entered Airaines two hours later. By-passing Abbeville, the English arrived at Boismont where they rested; again the marshals went out to find crossing places, to return unsuccessfully that evening after overrunning the country between the well-guarded gates of Abbeville and St Valery.

Prisoners taken from the districts of Ponthieu and Vimeu were brought before the King who asked if they knew of a ford below Abbeville where his army could cross without danger, offering liberty to the informant and his comrades plus a purse of 100 nobles. After some hesitation Gobin Agace – 'a common fellow' – said: 'Sir, I promise you, under peril of my life, that I will conduct you to such a place where . . . you may pass twelve men abreast twice in the day and not have water above the knees, but when the tide is in, the river is full and deep and no one can cross it. The bottom of this ford is very hard of gravel and white stones, it is called Blanchetaque.'

The English army rose at midnight to be marshalled into a single column, the advance guard with a large force of archers led by Warwick, then the men-at-arms, followed by the baggage wagons, lastly the King's Division. They marched out of Boismont before dawn on 24 August and, guided by Gobin Agace, reached Blanchetaque just before sunrise to find the tide beginning to ebb but the water too deep to attempt the crossing. Throughout the four-hour wait men anxiously scanned distant horizons for the approaching French as they closed up on the wagons heavily laden with tents, armour, weapons and plunder so that the marshals could despatch the long narrow column across the ford.

It was ten o'clock in the morning when Hugh Despenser led the vanguard of archers into the running water to splash their way waist deep in a compact group across the causeway that stretched before them for a mile and a half; Warwick and his mounted knights and men-at-arms followed closely, then the wagons, and soon the river was more than half spanned by a colourful foam-bordered ribbon rippling with movement. Two-thirds across, those at the head of the column saw men moving on the far bank to assemble as a formidable force lining the water's edge.

Advised of the English approach, Godemar du Faye, a Norman baron, led a force of more than 3,000 knights, squires and men-at-arms with a contingent of mercenary Genoese crossbowmen, from St Ricquier in Ponthieu, to Crotoy and thence to Blanchetaque, gathering armed townsmen from those places and Abbeville.

The tightly packed English came within range and the crossbowmen sent showers of bolts into their massed ranks causing men to stumble and slip from the causeway into the deep churned-up water on either side. The English archers, despite difficulties in wielding longbows to avoid wetting strings, returned a hail of five or six clothyard shafts for every crossbow bolt. The Genoese fire began to slacken, and Warwick ordered the men-at-arms to advance, then Edward himself spurred his horse through the press crying: 'Let those who love me follow me!' and knights plunged and splashed forward, forcing archers to the edges of the causeway.

Drawn up in battle array at the narrow pass leading to the ford, the French sacrificed much of their advantage when impetuous honour-seeking knights dashed forward to clash with the English in a confused, splashing mêlée at the water's edge. Many gallant feats of arms were performed on both sides before unceasing hails of arrows and increasing numbers of English knights and men-at-arms gradually forced the French back until finally they broke and fled in confusion, being pursued towards Abbeville and St Ricquier for more than a league. The unfortunate infantry and levies could not escape and most of them were cut down – there were no ransoms for insignificant French foot soldiers.

At the other end of the causeway the last wagons were trundling into the rapidly deepening water, protected by a small rearguard, when the King of Bohemia and Sir John of Hainault came dashing up at the head of the light horse of the French advanceguard to kill or capture a few of the English remaining on the bank and take some wagons. However, the river had risen too high for pursuit and the French stood gazing in frustration at the rear of the English army as it moved towards safety; turning, they rejoined the main army and retraced their route to Abbeville.

Edward, after giving thanks to God, rewarded and freed Gobin Agace and his comrades, then resumed the march, despatching Hugh Despenser and a force to take the town of La Crotoy. Its capture, after a short, sharp assault, provided provisions in plenty for the army in the field, and, together with the mouth of the Somme, made it possible for Edward to transport his army back to England. But the King, being in Ponthieu, by right his own fief, was determined to stand, saying: 'I have good cause here to abide them.' So the army pushed forward through the Forest of Crécy and before evening on Friday 25 August were encamped around the little town of Crécy-en-Ponthieu where the King and his marshals selected an advantageous position to offer battle.

Immediately north-east of the town was a windmill-crowned ridge extending about 2,000 yards to the hamlet of Wadicourt, fronted by a depression (later known as the Valley of the Clerks) with a slope on the right flank of about one in twelve where the village and the River Maye served as a protection against cavalry attack. On the left and weaker flank, where Wadicourt was the only bastion amid open country, the slope was almost imperceptible. A few hundred yards to the rear backing onto Bois de Crécy-Grange was the site of the wagon leaguer, guarded by the pages; the horses were tethered within.

The English army, about 12,000–13,000 strong, was deployed in three distinct divisions. The Black Prince's division on the right, placed well down the slope within 300 yards of the valley bottom, consisted of 800 dismounted men-at-arms flanked on either side by 2,000 archers and 1,000 Welsh spearmen. Edward was determined that his 16-year-old son should prove himself on this day, so, although under the personal protection of Godfrey Harcourt, he was given command of a division with the Earls of Warwick and Oxford as his chief officers. About 300 yards off, on his left extending to the village of Wadicourt and somewhat drawn back to be higher up the slope, was the rearguard commanded by the Earl of Northampton – 500 dismounted men-at-arms with 1,200 archers flanking them on both sides. Drawn up in solid herces or wedges, the archers on the flanks blended with each other, so that only bowmen held the centre of the position between the two divisions – but it was fronted by semi-concealed terraces too high to be surmounted by cavalry. The King's division of 700 dismounted men-at-arms, 2,000 archers and 1,000 Welsh spearmen formed up as a reserve on a plateau fronting the wood of Crécy-Grange, a few hundred yards behind the Prince's division.

When every man was in his allotted position, the King, on a white palfrey, rode slowly down the line studying the dispositions with an experienced eye, frequently stopping to give his soldiers words of cheer and encouragement. He finished his inspection at about midday when, as there was no sign of the enemy, he ordered the men to fall-out and eat, enjoining them to quickly resume their positions when the alarm was given. Armour and helmets were removed and archers marked their places by laying bows carefully alongside sheaves of arrows pushed point downward into the ground. The summer afternoon dragged on without a warning cry from the lookout in the windmill, chosen as the King's command post because of its clear view of the entire position. Then, at four o'clock the sky darkened and a brief but fierce rainstorm rudely awakened sleeping soldiers, archers rushed to unstring bows, coiling the string inside helmets; then the storm passed over as quickly as it had come and more than 5,000 archers worked as one restringing their powerful bows. Fresh with the scent of rain, the clear air hummed with the deep resonance of a multitude of male voices.

Suddenly, rising above all, the alarm was given by a hastily loud clear call from the windmill; the King climbed the rickety wooden steps to verify that it did indeed indicate the coming of the enemy and gave the signal for the trumpets to sound. Armour and helms were quickly donned and all stood motionless at their posts, silent and confident; everything was as ready as it could be – pot-holes had been dug in front of the position to hamper the enemy horses, the archers had checked distances and knew that shafts could reach the bottom of the valley. Nothing had been overlooked. Not an English eye saw anything other than the approaching mass of horse and foot descending the gentle slope into the valley of the Maye, armour and weapons glittering, flags and pennons rippling in a cascade of colour.

The French, marching out of Abbeville after sunrise that morning, had covered about twelve miles when ordered to make some semblance of forming into battle order; four knights went out to find the English

The Black Prince at the
Battle of Crécy
From a picture by Wal Paget

position. Returning, they counselled King Philip to halt, allowing the army to group and rest so that they could go fresh into battle on the following morning. Marshals went along the massive column crying out: 'Halt Banners! In the name of God and St Denis!' Those in front came to a standstill but were pushed forward by the press from the rear; neither the King nor his marshals could stay them, so the vast shambling mob again rolled forward until suddenly the vanguard came in sight of the waiting English to their left forefront. Approaching the field from Marchville, the French had to turn sharply left to face their enemies, a sudden change in the direction of march that caused confusion and disorder made worse by their habitually ragged march discipline. Massed tightly together, this uncohesive army formed of the King's regular troops, foreign contingents, German mercenaries, Genoese crossbowmen and a multitude of fearful provincial levies, jostled and crowded each other so that units became inextricably mixed until the army was almost out of hand long before a blow had been struck.

There were 40,000 of them – three times as many men as in the English army – formed in three divisions: Antonio Doria and Carlo Grimaldi led 6,000 mercenary Genoese crossbowmen; the King's brother, Count d'Alençon, commanded another, with three crowned heads serving under his banner – blind John of Luxembourg the King of Bohemia, his son the King of the Romans, and the King of Majorca; the third division was led by him who had failed at the ford, Godemar du Faye.

Alarmed and surprised by the sudden dramatic sight of the English drawn-up in battle array, Philip sought indecisively for his best course of action – his men were weary, hungry and in considerable disorder, better to wait and attack on the morrow. He gave the order to halt. Outraged French knights at the head of the column could see troops in the rear still advancing and, believing that they were to be deprived of the honour of opening the battle, impulsively pushed ahead. Seeing this and confident in the knowledge of their superior numbers, the main body followed until the bulk of the French army had stumbled so close to the English position that battle was unavoidable. In their impatient shuffling progress the French knights had forcibly propelled before them those men who formed the advance-guard – the luckless Genoese mercenaries, consisting of heavily accoutred, drenched and bedraggled Italians with weighty weapons, weary after marching six leagues and fearfully aware that their wet crossbow strings virtually disarmed them. Their reluctant dragging feet affronted the sense of militancy that the inevitability of action had thrust upon the King so that he cried loudly: 'Make the Genoese go in front and begin the battle, in the name of God and St Denis!'

The mercenaries muttered and complained to their constables: 'We be not well ordered to fight this day; we be not in the case to do any great deed of arms, and have more need of rest.'

The constables conveyed their men's complaint that they were being unfairly treated. Count d'Alençon was scornful: 'Truly, a man is well at ease to be charged with these kind of rascals, who are faint and fail us now when most at need!'

The Genoese, competent professional soldiers under normal conditions, were stung by these words and sought to salve pride by forgetting useless weapons and marching against the enemy formed on the ridge ahead. It was a difficult procedure for such a large force whose disorder was much aggravated through being roughly hustled forward by the French knights in their rear. Despite their experience and training, they advanced in an uneven line that was hopelessly ragged and out of dressing, halting to re-form three times. Slowly they progressed across the valley plaintively whooping and shouting, waving arms and stamping feet to bolster up flagging spirits. At the foot of the gentle slope leading up to the English position they halted to rally, then gave three loud ordered warcries before loosing off a ragged hail of bolts that all fell short, because of the rain-relaxed cords of their clumsy weapons. From the blue sky behind the English position the sun shone brilliantly full into their eyes, outlining them to present conditions ideal for archery. Squinting apprehensively at the English archers ominously flexing bows, the Italians found fingers fumbling as they went through the laborious process of winding-up arbalests. Failing to shake the silent statuesque posture of their waiting foes, Genoese screams, shouts and whoops trailed off despondently until dramatically overwhelmed by a loud cry of command on the ridge.

As one man, thousands of English bowmen stepped a pace forward, drew bowstrings back to ears – then loosed. The summer air was filled with an unending twang and hiss, the bright sunlight shut out by black swarms of shafts wailing down to quiver in faces and bodies of men reeling and staggering as though drunk. Their discomfort was increased by a series of belches of flame and roaring resembling thunderclaps as heavy iron or stone balls cut bloody swathes through the ranks and stampeded horses behind them. It was Edward's 'secret weapon' – crude iron tubes laboriously borne across France in the bottom of ammunition wagons to be the first cannon ever fired in open warfare. Surprising as they must have been, these crude and noisy innovations to the art of war do not seem to have had as much physical or morale effect as might have been expected. The chroniclers report the battle in terms of the devastating results of English archery rather than rough 2lb stone and iron balls sent on their way with such a spectacular gush of flame and smoke.

The savagely belaboured Genoese sought desperately to leave the nightmare scene but could not fall back through the packed French knights belligerently pressing upon their rear. Resentful that these foreign mercenaries had done them out of the honour of opening the battle and convinced by their reluctant advance that they were treacherous, feelings came to a head when the sorely tried patience of the hot-headed d'Alençon vanished, causing him to cry as he clapped fierce spurs into his charger: 'Slay me these rascals! They do but hinder and trouble us without reason!'

Plunging convulsively forward into the disordered Genoese, his maddened war-horse was closely followed by a great mass of the nobility of France, all shouting and cursing as they trampled down their allies. Beset on all sides, the crossbowmen furiously discharged bolts at the horsemen, adding fierce internecine fights to the confusion. The heavily armoured French knights could not be withstood and relentlessly they battered their way forward towards the Prince of Wales's division, leaving a trail of arrow-pierced men and horses floundering among the cross-bowmen they had ridden down. Other formations brushed past the luckless Genoese and deployed into position until a continuous line was formed roughly equal in length and parallel to the English position.

Now began a desperate series of fruitless charges by heavily armoured horsemen lumbering uphill in the face of remorseless plaguing by needle-pointed arrows whistling in from front and sides. Men-at-arms, hunched forward with heads bowed, belaboured reluctant steeds with cruel medieval spurs, shuffling painfully towards formed and fully armoured men-at-arms who grimly hefted weapons as they awaited the onslaught. Mad from the pain of keen barbed shafts, great stallions went out of control, neighing and screaming wildly as they pushed, reared, swerved and plunged, striking and lashing out hideously. Count d'Alençon and his surviving knights reached and engaged the Prince of Wales's division, and other groups managed to close with Northampton's division – these were not concerted efforts but irregular spasmodic surges that did not cause the English line to yield even a yard of ground. Their numerical superiority allowed the French to persist in these efforts: whenever a man fell another lurched forward to take his place as though from an apparently inexhaustible supply. At varying intervals and without continuity, wave after wave of French chivalry bravely and characteristically lumbered clumsily up to the English position without ever effecting a penetration before being killed or beaten back.

At least fifteen attacks were put in by the French, who never understood at Crécy, nor at Poitiers ten years later, and still did not comprehend sixty years after at Agincourt, that to force by frontal attack a line of bowmen supported by men-at-arms was an almost hopeless task for cavalry. Their casualties rose rapidly and the trampled blood-soaked ground became heaped high with the bodies of men and horses. Distraught panting men drew apart like boxers regaining their breath, and Welsh and Irish foot soldiers crept forward to thrust great knives into joints of armour worn by men-at-arms wallowing like upturned turtles amid the press of battle, others slid beneath horse's bellies and nimbly circled groups of battling men to stab, slash and gash. In the pauses, archers ran forward from the line to search for arrows, wasting no time trying to pull from bodies barbed arrows that could only be removed from soft flesh by major feats of surgery or extensive crude carpentry.

Throughout the Hundred Years War, the French main assaults were invariably directed against men-at-arms formations and not against archers – this was because they became 'channelled' in their efforts to get away from the hissing shafts. In this manner the pressure on the English line increased, particularly on the right, and at one critical stage the Prince was felled to the ground, being saved by his standard-bearer, Richard de Beaumont, who stood over him. Godfrey Harcourt, anxious for the safety of his royal charge, ran clumsily across to the nearest unit of Northampton's division – that commanded by the Earl of Arundel – begging him to counter-attack in the flank those enemy assailing the Prince's division. Harcourt also sent a messenger to the King asking for reinforcements. From his command post high in the windmill, the King could see that Arundel's counter-attack was taking effect; that it was not yet the opportune moment to throw in his precious reserve. Without taking his eyes from the surging, heaving battle spread out before him like a colourful carpet, he said: 'Let the boy win his spurs. If God be pleased, I will this journey be his and the honour thereof, and to them that be about him.' The experienced soldier-King was right in his judgement – when the messenger arrived back, the Prince and his men-at-arms were sitting resting after beating off the attack, surrounded by more than 1,500 dead Frenchmen.

Restlessly mounted on their chargers about a quarter of a mile behind the battle, a group of armoured knights clustered around their leader, King John of Bohemia, his sightless head held high to catch every nuance of the noise of battle that assailed his ears. Repeatedly, the old man asked after its progress until it became too great to be borne: 'Sirs, ye are my men, my friends and companions. I require ye to lead me so far forward that I may strike one blow with my sword.'

On either side of their monarch, knights linked chargers to his and the chivalrous trio trotted across the valley, horses excited by the tumult being forcibly wrenched into line until brought to a standstill by the struggling press. Shepherded forward by his guides, the aged king struck out valiantly with his heavy sword, encountering arm-jarring resistance or employing his innate skill-at-arms to balance when blows fell on thin air. Next morning, all three warriors were found dead, still tethered together.

Throughout the evening steadily decreasing numbers of French and allies successively injected themselves into the welter or were carried forward regardless in a helpless choking mass by those pushing from the rear. Night fell, and under a rising moon fighting continued until at about the hour of vespers, the last attack shattered into fragments, then the cacophony of combat gave way to an uneasy half-silence broken only by cries and groans of wounded and those half-dead.

King Philip of France, refusing to believe all was lost and that only three score knights remained, was prevented by Sir John of Hainault from personally leading a last charge: 'Sire, depart while there is yet time. Lose not yourself willingly. If this field is lost, you shall recover it again another season.'

Taking the King's bridle, he led him from the field of battle as King Edward of England, who had not even worn his helmet, descended from the windmill and embraced his son: 'Sweet son, God give you good perseverance; you are my son for most loyally you have acquitted yourself this day . . . you are worthy to be a sovereign.'

The English, having won the day without stirring a foot from their position as the enemy conveniently came to them to be killed, lit great fires and lay down to sleep where they had fought, weary with slaughter, satiated with victory – and supperless. The King forbade rioting or celebration, and all rested save Irish and Welsh spearmen combing the battlefield finishing-off without quarter those wounded or unable to offer ransom. There was no pursuit, the vanquished melted away singly and silently into the night in any fancied direction, there being none left to give commands or orders. The flower of the chivalry of France had been wiped out, including the King's brother, Count d'Alençon, his brother-in-law, King John of Bohemia, his nephew, Count de Blois, and most leading knights and commanders. The allies from Bohemia, Heynault and Flanders dispersed to their homes – in a few fatal hours the most powerful monarch in western Europe had lost an entire army.

The morning brought a thick fog to blanket mercifully the green and pleasant little valley, now patterned by hideous heaps and mounds of torn and battered dead. Edward sent Lord Reginald Cobham and Lord Stafford, with three heralds to check arms and bearings, and two clerks to write down the names of the fallen. Throughout the day the party methodically traversed the valley that, marked by a modern beet-factory, lies today just as it did more than 600 years ago and is still called 'the Val aux Clercs'. Returning as the King was sitting down to supper, they presented a most circumstantial report telling of finding 80 banners, the bodies of 11 princes, 1,530 lords and knights, and approximately 20,000 'common men' – sergeants, crossbowmen and infantry, besides many thousand carcasses of horses. They also confirmed what had already been reported to the King – that the English losses were about 200 dead and wounded, including 2 knights, 40 men-at-arms and archers, and a 'few dozen' Welsh and Irish infantry.

Edward ordered the bodies of the principal knights to be carried to the nearby monastery of Maintenay to be interred in consecrated ground; the remaining bodies were shovelled, along with the horses, into vast burial pits. Then, the English marched on.

Its political significance eroded within a hundred years, nevertheless in a purely military context, Crécy was one of the most decisive battles of world history, marking the onset of the infantryman as the basic battle-field element.

6 Crécy Today

Maps Required:
Michelin 1:200,000 Nos. 54 and 236

The field of Crécy lies within the triangle Crécy-en-Ponthieu/ Wadicourt/Estrées and can be reached from Abbeville on Route D928 (Hesdin–St Omer road), turning left on D10 about 5.5 kms after Canchy, through Marcheville to Crécy-en-Ponthieu. Bear left in the Town Place, up the hill following direction signs to the 'Moulin Edouard III', where the road D111 runs along the ridge past the mill, just as it did in 1346. A more interesting route follows the probable path of the English after crossing at Blanchetaque, north from Abbeville on the N1, turning right after about 6 kms onto D105 (to Lamotte–Buleux) through the Forest of Crécy onto the D111. The French army marched along the old road from Marchville; still vaguely traceable, it is known locally as le Chemin de l'Armée.

An almost completely unspoilt battlefield, Crécy has hardly changed at all in 650 years so that it is possible to stand on the exact site of Edward's windmill command post and visualise the battle sprawling over the peaceful fields below. The sole anachronism is the beet-factory at the lower end of the Val aux Clercs, and even that serves to pin-point the area where the Genoese crossbowmen began the battle, being shattered by English arrows, then ridden down by their own knights. The windmill was standing as recently as 1898 when, in a wave of anti-British feeling resulting from the Fashoda Incident, it was patriotically pulled down. Its grassy mound remains with a water tank built into it and there is a small memorial plaque in French. Crowning the summit is a recently erected observation platform, from which a complete view of the battlefield can be obtained. In fact, just as the battlefield walker can stand on the exact spot where Henry V fought at Agincourt, so can he (or she) place their feet where Edward III stood on the 26 of August 1346 gazing out at what was later to be called the Valley of the Clerks. It was given that name because, after the battle, an elect little company of men who could read and write were sent out to list the dead of the French warrior class.

The precise location of the Blanchetaque ford, crossed by the English on their way to the field of Crécy, is not known other than through its place name; nor is it accurately known how the army reached it from the north, although there remains an access path from the south. Edward moved away from the river and reached the town of Crécy early in the morning of 26 August; here, realising that now his way to the coast and possible re-embarkation was clear, he decided to turn and fight, so sought a good defensive position. He decided upon a ridge facing east and west, its southern end sloping sharply down into the town of Crécy-en-Ponthieu; its eastern slope levelled out after about 275 metres into what was to later be known as the Val aux Clercs, rising again to a second broad ridge. Between the two ridges, the Val aux Clercs petered out as it progressed northward; on the southern end of the ridge nearest to the town stood a windmill from which a view of the whole of the ridges and valley could be obtained – so Edward naturally selected it as his command post.

The English position, on the eastern slope of the western ridge, faced eastward across the Val aux Clercs in two main divisions, the ground between them being marked by half-concealed terraces of land, a stepped embankment which still exists and served as a position for the English reserve around the King. On one visit to the field, members of our party stood below these terraces and were out of sight of people above their heads and conversely, anyone standing on the higher ground above cannot be seen from below. Close by, after ploughing and before new corn has risen to any height, white chalk smears can be seen and reveal mass graves of the charging French cavalry, buried *en masse* where they fell. Between the little village of Wadicourt on the English left flank and Crécy

Observation Tower on Crécy Ridge

itself, the traces of boundaries between fields which existed in 1346 are no longer apparent.

About 1.5 km from the battlefield itself, by the side of the D56 – the Crécy–Fontaine-sur-Maye road – an impressive monumental cross was erected after the battle to the memory of the blind King John of Bohemia, mortally wounded when charging into the fray, his two faithful retainers' horses tethered on either side of the King's mount and leading him into action. It is probably the only authentic monument of the battle; allowed to fall into disrepair, it was painstakingly repaired during the nineteenth century. It is improbable that this is the actual site of the deaths of King John and his squires from Bohemia, Henri de Rosemberg and Jean de Leucstemberg, being well away from the scene of action and quite out of range of English bows. It is more likely that King John was grievously wounded and picked up by the advancing English, who were told by Edward to carry the stricken monarch to the King's tent, where he died. From the rich clothing of the Bohemian King was taken the ostrich plumes tied with gold braid above the helmet, and the motto '*Ich Dien*' (I serve) and awarded to the young Prince by Edward; subsequently all succeeding Princes of Wales to this day have retained the motto and the three-feathered plume.

Today, the town of Crécy-en-Ponthieu is a charming little place, lying peacefully around a large and impressive battle monument standing in the Grande Place. Within the past few years, the local authorities staged a series of commemorative events, involving French, British and Czech (Bohemian) troops. Re-enactments were staged showing the daily life of the fourteenth century soldier, with exhibitions of the use of arms and armour, archery and jousting.

7 *Mini Memories of Walking the Battlefields of the Hundred Years War*

Maps Required
Michelin 1:200,000
Mid-Brittany 58, 59, 230 Le Havre–Amiens 52
Flanders–Artois–Picardy 236 Arras–Charleville–Mézières 53
Cherbourg–Caen–Rouen 54 Caen–Paris 55 Le Mans–Paris 60
Angers–Orléans 64 Nantes–Poitiers 67
Niort–Châteauroux 68

It needs imagination and interest to people peaceful fields with long-dead warriors, to re-create in the mind's eye surging conflicts churning lush grassland into a littered and muddy waste. It requires background knowledge of the soldiers themselves, how they fought, their weapons and leaders; without details of the field itself and an awareness of those spots where decisive actions occurred, reconstruction is guesswork. Detailing how the armies reached these fields and what happened on them, these pages provide sufficient information – in layman's language – to give an accurate picture of the period. Thus armed, the battlefield walker can achieve a high degree of satisfaction from his historic expeditions.

Every field considered in this chapter is covered by the Michelin maps stated above. They can be obtained at any major stationers or bookshop. On them can be followed the footsteps of Edward's army on their way to victory at Crécy – with them we can share their desperate search for the Blanchetaque ford across the River Somme; or drive over the roads once plodded by Henry's sick and weary army as they also sought to cross that river on their way to a date with destiny at Agincourt. Each route abounds with interesting features: the first part of the Crécy march has since been immortalised by the events of D-Day and the Normandy landings; approaching the actual field it is interesting to trace the old road from Marchville, still known locally as le Chemin de l'Armée, marched on by the French host; and are those Somme crossings which Henry V so thank-fully discovered at Bethancourt and Voyenne still causeway roads as they were in 1415? Great satisfaction can be obtained from tracing these recognisable links with stirring medieval events.

Each battlefield described in these pages remains much the same as it was over 600 years ago, allowing credible reconstruction of the battles fought over them. Only the dullest will fail to sense the aura around these places where, in a cruelly wasteful manner peculiar to man, soldiers fought each other. Is it unreasonable to assume they reluctantly departed from earth as though never existing, or should it be believed that their proud spirits reproachfully linger at the scene of their final curtain?

These old fields give rise to a privileged sense of being close to kings and commoners – our ancestors – who stoked the fires of our national consciousness to forge a pride that has bolstered the nation for 600 years. To be aware of the background to this stimulates the imagination and arouses contemplation; the physical effort of actually walking the fields themselves can be so satisfying that most people will plan to do it again another year!

Most of the battlefields mentioned in this section were extensively walked by day and camped upon by night – a Spartan refinement allowing the provocative pall of darkness to lend enchantment to sleeping on ground where history was made. It is difficult to contain one's emotions when lying in a tent pitched where stood the English right wing at Agincourt, on the edges of the Tramecourt Woods, separated only by a thin groundsheet from that very earth soaked by the blood of Guillaume de Saveuse, knight of France, brought down and killed when his horse was impaled upon an archer's protective wooden stake.

How tremulously we peered out from the leafy wood of Piseaux at Verneuil on the night of 16/17 August exactly 550 years to the day after Suffolk's advance patrols lay in that exact spot watching the French and Scots form-up on the plain beyond for the following day's battle, said to have been even harder than Agincourt by those who had fought at both. Did we imagine that we saw ethereal men-at-arms moving silently in the misty moonlight?

In the Val aux Clercs at Crécy on the morning following the battle in 1346, Edward's clerks tallied the bodies of more than 20,000 kings, princes, lords, knights, sergeants, men-at-arms and common soldiers – the imagination works overtime in the darkness, laying there gazing up at the star-speckled sky.

Even the balm of daylight brings its own mind-boggling surprises, as at Patay on a sultry afternoon much like that of the day of the battle in June 1429. Languidly trudging up the old Roman Road towards the crest of St Peravy ridge, breasted by hard-riding French cavalry cascading down upon the unprepared English, the hum of insects was replaced by the swelling cadence of drumming hooves. Staring incredulously at the ridge above, we awaited the phantom onslaught as horses and riders, shimmering as in a mirage, came into view. Was it La Hire, Poton de Xaintrailles, Dunois, d'Alençon, the Constable Richemont, Joan of Arc, Gilles de Retz (later to achieve notoriety as Bluebeard) and the rest – hot in pursuit of the retreating Talbot and Fastolf? They thundered down until close enough to exchange salutations with a dozen children from the local Pony Club, cantering down the dusty track once trod by Romans, to cross the Janville road to the low ridge where stood Fastolf at bay all those years ago, and vanished from sight.

It was but a brief encounter, yet for one irrational moment it aroused the same upsurge of alarm that must have convulsed the small English force retreating from Meaux, who knew the drumming hooves could only be hostile. Reflecting on the apprehension aroused by a dozen ponies, we tried to conjure up the sheer terror produced by the ground-shaking approach of hundreds of mighty war-horses, bits between their teeth! In truth, it was not an entirely new experience – once, walking in the dusk over that part of the field of Waterloo where Wellington's infantry squares had withstood Ney's cavalry hordes all day, we were startled by approaching horsemen galloping hard up slopes once carpeted by fallen cuirassiers, dragoons, hussars, lancers and their horses. As at Patay, it was only a handful of youthful riders, but similarly it lifted a curtain to expose us to apprehensions known to no living man.

Far removed from the clangour and tumult of battle, even after 600 years, these fields still carry an unmistakable aura, causing them to be viewed with a certain mixture of admiration and awe. Incredibly, considering their age, they have changed far less than better-known areas of World Wars I and II and are still readily recognisable as fields bestrode by armoured knights, men-at-arms and archers. This owes much to their compactness, for the armies that fought over them were small in number and used close-quarter weapons that did not allow sprawling belligerently over vast areas of countryside.

Very conveniently, these medieval fields were small and compact so that the viewer can stand and see where everything occurred; no need to tramp over ploughed fields, up hill and down dale. Fields of recent wars are far more extensive and it is difficult for the untrained eye to understand what went on, much of the action taking place beyond the range of vision. Even Waterloo, considered an extremely small arena for a major battle involving about 300,000 men, extends over a frontage of three miles, taking a day to satisfactorily walk. Fields of the Middle Ages were not large, simply because the armies fighting over them were small, even the biggest being only of 10,000–15,000 men.

It might seem optimistic to assume that were these men to return to those peaceful green fields they would recognise them as the arena where brilliantly bedecked knights clashed to a backcloth of whistling arrows, shouting men, squealing horses and the clash of steel. Yet today a re-incarnated Henry V could gaze around at Agincourt and, save for the metalled road bisecting the field, see it as it was on that misty morning of 15 October 1415 – the Feast of St Crispin and St Crispianus. Perhaps less changed than any major battlefield in the history of warfare, the placid ordinariness of the roughly rectangular wood-bordered arable French farmland quite belies the 180 minutes of violent drama that immortalised its muddy acres.

The poet Wolfe, writing of the burial of Sir John Moore, said:

> We carved not a line, and we raised not a stone,
> But we left him alone in his glory.

This would appear to be the case on the majority of battlefields where British arms have triumphed; lying outside our shores, rarely is there any commemoration of the victory and the brave men who achieved it – at Waterloo the uninformed tourist can be forgiven for assuming it to be a French victory!

Jealously proud of their brief military history, the Americans do these things better: the battlefields of their War Between the States are National Parks, lavishly signposted and marked by monuments, museums, dioramas and displays, backed by guidebooks, picture postcards and other literature. Yet, the much older battles of the Hundred Years War did just as much to form and mould the English nation as Gettysburg and other conflicts did for the United States. On the other hand, when walking battlefields in France, one soon becomes aware of that characteristically chauvinistic memory nurtured by the French, in these circumstances marked by a dogged reluctance to publicise those fields where battles were lost! Monuments are often in the wrong place, like that for the blind King of Bohemia at Crécy; monuments to French dead are erected in seemingly irrelevant places at Formigny and Verneuil, the last named being a plaque in the stone wall of a farm in the lane off the Breteuil road (Route D840) which does not even mention that the Scots fought with the French, incurring by far the heaviest losses! At Agincourt, a rough granite pillar lies well behind the English position, near the Maisoncelles crossroads, where the local Syndicat d'Iniative have erected a glass-fronted case containing a map of the battle – alas, usually too moisture-condensed to allow the map to be read! However, there is now quite a reasonable, if small, museum in the village of Agincourt where, in a bar, one can obtain stylised postcards of the battle, and a six-page narrative (in French).

Monuments in and around Poitiers seem to bear what could be termed a somewhat purposefully vague resemblance to topographical reality. In Mauron there is a colourful town name plate bearing references to the battle of 1352, and Patay is said to have a Rue Talbot, the English Paladin taken into the town after being captured in 1429 in the battle of that name.

Singularly, few people living on or near a battlefield appear to be aware of its existence or to know anything of the course of events. Like the farmer's wife at Morlaix in Brittany, curious to know why four middle-

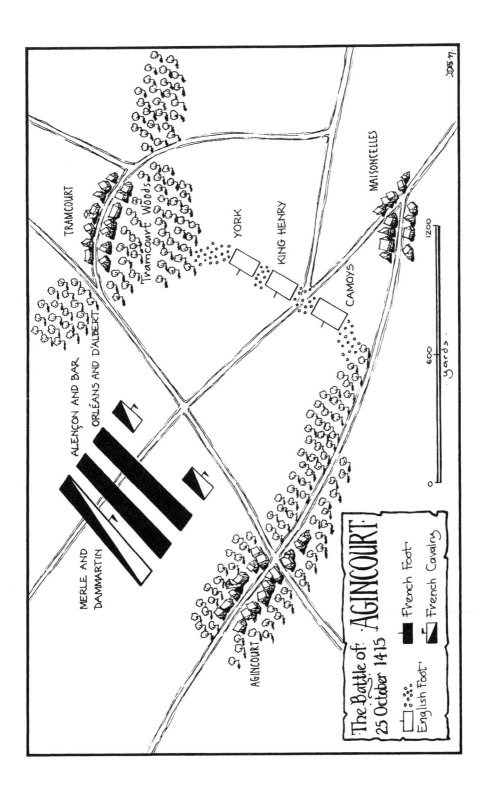

The Battle of: AGINCOURT
25 October 1415

English Foot
French Foot
French Cavalry

TRAMCOURT

Tramcourt Woods

ALENÇON AND BAR
ORLÉANS AND D'ALBERT

MERLE AND
DAMMARTIN

YORK

KING HENRY

CAMOYS

MAISONCELLES

AGINCOURT

0   600   1200
yards.

aged Englishmen should ask permission to walk over her fields, and what did they expect to see?

'We are military historians and wish to view the battlefield.'

A puzzled frown crossed her homely tanned face: 'What battlefield?'

'The Battlefield of Morlaix, Madam, fought in that field and the wood behind!'

She gazed over our shoulders, gaping at familiar pastures as though expecting to see fighting men emerge from the muddy plough: 'Who was it between?'

'The French and the English, Madam.'

'Did we win?'

'Afraid not, Madam, the English beat you.'

Her brawny arms raised high in despair: '*Quel dommage!*'

On one memorable occasion it seemed that the French might have unconsciously achieved revenge for a military rebuff, arising from our Battlefield Walking Party's 'ritual restaurant prowl' involving circulating around a town's eating places, surveying menus, until deciding upon the favoured establishment. Over the years, an unerring eye for quality arose, so that it is not unusual for memorable meals to be fondly recalled years later! Over many years, only ONE occasion can be recalled when we went to bed supperless!

It was an August evening in the pleasant little town of Romorantin, in Loir et Cher, when all restaurants were closed! Philosophically, we took it as a belated reprisal for that occasion in early September 1356 – some 640 years earlier, when the Black Prince's Army of Gascony, marching inland from Bordeaux, besieged the castle of Romorantin, property of the Counts of Blois. Battlemented and with tall towers roofed in pepper-pot style, standing on the Ile Marin in the middle of the Sauldre, it was said to be one of the first castles of the War to be defended by guns, which roared loudly and scared the horses but were as much danger to gunners as attackers. When Bernard, a favourite squire, was killed by a boulder hurled from the walls while standing next to the Prince, he swore by the soul of his father – the most solemn oath – he would not quit until the place had fallen. After three days of abortive assault, cannons were wheeled up – great clumsy iron-hooped tubes hurling earthenware vessels containing Greek Fire that ignited on impact. With the lower courtyard ablaze and greedy yellow flames licking at a thatch-covered tower, the castle became uncomfortably warm and full of smoke and ashes; soon the defenders preferred surrender to being grilled alive.

Going to bed hungry was made easier to bear by such knowledge!

Battlefield walkers are often adventurous and imaginative people, responding to the evocative accounts of battles to the extent that they wish somehow to become involved, to see new dimensions by bringing history to life, through the feel of battlefields underfoot. They are aware that, armed with imagination, hindsight, and a little knowledge of the soldiers, their weapons and tactics, it is possible to step from today's prosaic and sometimes taxing existence into a new and stimulating world. Girded with such a shield and buckler, they know they can step back, not only into the shoes of such immortal leaders as the Black Prince and Henry V, but that they can don the tattered mantle of Nicholas Blakethorne or the Welshman Richard Ap Gruffyd of Ceso, who were archers with Henry at Agincourt. Of course, this transition to a harsh and violent period soon ends, but not before arousing in the breasts of ordinary twentieth-century mortals a nostalgic admiration for our brave ancestors whose deeds in a cruel and crude period of warfare added colour and lustre to the age in which they lived, and to our nation's history.

Our group of battlefield walkers never tire of returning to the fields of the Hundred Years War in northern France, now easier and less expensive to reach than at any other time. Full of colour and interest, the principal fields of Crécy, Poitiers and Agincourt carry an unrivalled charisma, repeatedly drawing our footsteps in their direction. Thus, it can be said that these pages recapture years of reading and research, of exploring and tirelessly walking in perhaps a foolishly romantic and modern version of the many expeditions made by the Black Prince – his *Grandes Chevauchées*!

Part Three

Belgium – Waterloo 1815

8 *Prelude to Waterloo*

In April 1814, Napoleon was banished to the Isle of Elba, but escaped and returned to France on 1 March 1815. Troops sent to apprehend him rallied to his cause and, on 20 March, he entered Paris in triumph and the Bourbon King Louis XVIII fled. The Allies – Great Britain, Russia, Austria and Prussia – hastily met and agreed to each put an army of 150,000 men into the field so that, as in 1813/4, Napoleon would be overwhelmed by sheer weight of numbers. Commanded by Wellington, the Anglo-Belgian-Dutch forces, plus the Prussians led by Blücher, would invade France from the north; the Russians were to attack across the middle Rhine, and the Austrian army across the lower Rhine. First to be ready, Wellington and Blücher were advancing from the Netherlands and the lower Rhine by early May, and Napoleon planned to commence operations by attacking them, as they were already in the area of Brussels and Liège, so that they most directly menaced Paris.

By the end of May, Napoleon had nearly 300,000 men under arms, 125,000 of them formed the Army of the North under his personal command, with which he planned to tackle Wellington and Blücher, striking them at the point where their armies joined. At this time, the Prussian lines of communication lay north-east via Liège to Cologne; Wellington's lay north-west on the line Mons to Ghent, south-west of Antwerp and east of Brussels. Therefore, Napoleon decided to advance along the axis of the Charleroi–Brussels road, leading directly to where Wellington's left wing joined the right wing of the Prussian army, whose advance-guard was at Charleroi on 14 June, but the army as a whole were spread over the area Charleroi–Liège.

By 14 June, the French Army had concentrated in the area Maubeuge–Avesnes–Rocroi–Chimay, and on 16 June attacked Blücher's Prussian army – not yet fully concentrated – at Ligny, ten miles north-east of Charleroi. Although driven back, the Prussians withdrew in reasonably good order in a northwards direction, towards Wavre, instead of moving eastwards away from Wellington's army, so fulfilling their part of the agreement not to lose contact with each other. Mistakenly, Napoleon assumed that Blücher was actually moving away from Wellington, an error compounded by his Marshal Grouchy, who failed to adequately pursue Blücher.

Taken by surprise by the speed of Napoleon's movements, Wellington had advanced his force towards Quatre Bras, where contact was made with Marshal Ney on the afternoon of 15 June, whom Napoleon had

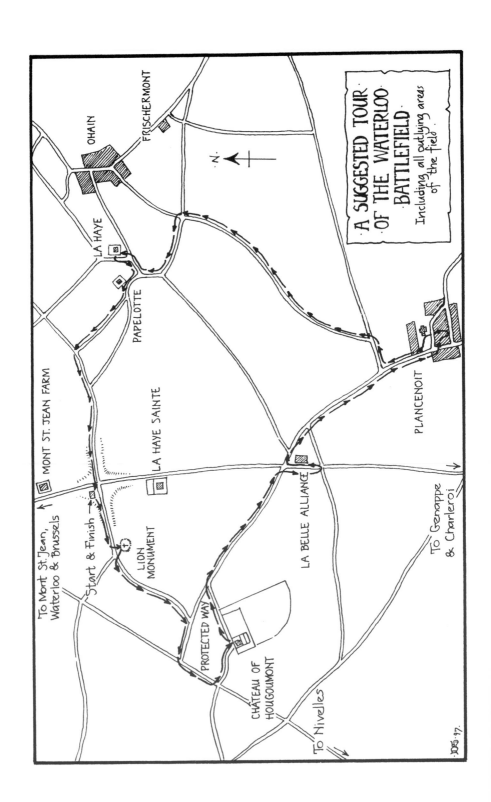

A SUGGESTED TOUR OF THE WATERLOO BATTLEFIELD
Including all outlying areas of the field

·N·

OHAIN

FRISCHERMONT

LA HAYE

PAPELOTTE

MONT ST. JEAN FARM

To Mont St. Jean, Waterloo & Brussels

Start & Finish

LION MONUMENT

LA HAYE SAINTE

PROTECTED WAY

CHATEAU OF HOUGOUMONT

To Nivelles

LA BELLE ALLIANCE

PLANCENOIT

To Genappe & Charleroi

·DES ·97·

ordered to contain Wellington's forces. Subsequently these two commanders watched each other at Quatre Bras on 16 June, with some
indecisive action taking place, with Ney losing the opportunity of
defeating Wellington before he was ready to fight by failing to strike
swiftly. On the next day, hearing of Blücher's temporary reverse and
movements, Wellington ordered a withdrawal to the Waterloo position,
which he had noted in past days. On 18 June, Napoleon and Ney had
concentrated their forces, and lay facing the Allied army on the field of
Waterloo. Both were intent on battle, Wellington because he now knew
that two Prussian Corps would march at daybreak to join him, coming in
on Napoleon's right flank.

Divided by the Charleroi–Brussels road, the chosen field was comparatively small, extending two and a quarter miles from north to south,
with an extreme width of no more than four miles. Wellington's main line
ran along a low ridge about a mile from the village of Mont St Jean, it
extended about a quarter mile west of the road, and a mile and a quarter
east of it. As he had done so often in past battles, Wellington positioned
his regiments protected by the dead ground behind the ridge, from where
they would move forward when the action began; his centre-front was
strengthened by the farm of La Haye Sainte and a sandpit, his right by
the forward-placed château of Hougoumont. To the south of the field was
another low ridge; the ground between this and the northern ridge did not
dip anywhere more than fifty feet. On this southern elevation Napoleon
drew up his army, stretching from the Brussels–Nivelles road – from a
point about a mile and three quarters south of Mont St Jean, north of
Hougoumont, to the hamlet of Frischermont.

During the afternoon of the previous day, 17 June, there broke a storm
of an intensity to match the occasion, which continued as a torrential
downpour throughout the long night, said to be the most miserable one
soldiers could ever recall, as they bivouacked under its chill and remorseless onslaught. The Duke of Wellington rested in Widow Bodenghien's
inn opposite the church in the village of Waterloo (today the Musée
Wellington). Six miles to the south, up the long straight road running
through the Allied position, from Mont St Jean to the farm of La Haye
Sainte, Napoleon was resting at Le Caillou, a comfortable farmhouse
(which is now a museum with a strong Napoleon bias).

And so, at daybreak when the opposing armies stood-to, the stage was
set and the players in position; the weather began to improve and fires
flared-up; the first notes of the overture hung on the air as irregular fusil-
lades proclaimed the cleaning and drying of muskets.

9 *The Battlefield Walker's Waterloo 18 June 1815*

Any man who survived the Battle of Waterloo could live the remainder of his life with the knowledge that never again would he have to face anything quite so awful. Even in these days of deadly weapon systems there are precious few modern soldiers who would exchange the Falklands, World War II, or even the Flanders trenches of World War I for what soldiers faced on 18 June 1815. Probably the most dramatic event of the nineteenth century – along with Gettysburg it is the most widely studied battle of the western world – it has been discussed extensively in English, French, German and most other languages and still inspires in the military historian those same ambitions that the role of Hamlet is supposed to raise in the breasts of actors. Possessing all the ingredients of conflict that have fascinated man for centuries, Waterloo represents to the romantic the war as it really was – colourful uniforms, prancing horses, flags, drums and trumpets, all parading before a stupendous background cacophony of musketry and artillery, with the outcome in doubt until the last minute.

In 1815 the accustomed noise level was minimal to that regarded as normal in this age of motorcycles and jet aircraft, so inexperienced young soldiers must have found it a nightmare, this discordant symphony of war compounded of the roar of guns, the rattle of muskets, the neighing of horses and the cries of men. Much of the artillery was actually within sight of its target and men could see the menacing monster belch out flame and smoke, and the black cannonball looming steadily larger. Almost any act of heroism was possible on this amazing field and nothing like it will ever be seen again – and yet not a single man among the thousands present realised it was to be the last great action of the accepted traditional kind; the typical pitched battle with its lines, columns and squares, met its Waterloo at Waterloo, when the participants turned a page of history with the bloodiest hands Man could so far remember. Officers were in no doubt they had been part of something unique, and even the most unimaginative private soldier became convinced he had survived an extraordinary event when, for the first time in British military history, he was told he was to be awarded a commemorative medal and to be known in future as a 'Waterloo Man', and that the single day of service on 18 June 1815 was to count as two years for his pension. Even the French, by some strange but characteristic interpretative process, managed to make

WATERLOO

1   2

BRAINE-L'ALLEUD

1 · Royal Chapel (Commemorative chapel of the Battle)
2 · The Wellington Museum (HQ of the Duke of Wellington)
3 · Mont Saint Jean Farm
4 · Saint-Etienne Church
5 · The Waxworks Museum
6 · The Panorama
7 · Butte du Lion & Visitor's Centre
8 · Hougoumont manor farm

Mont St. Jean

4   3   5   14

26   13   LASNE

Chapelle · St.- Lambert

6   9

7   La Marache

10   11

12

Hougoumont   18

8   17   PLANCENOIT

19   16

20   15   21

27   22

9 · Memorial to Belgians who fell on 18 June 1815
10 · Gordon Memorial - Wellington Tree
11 · Hanoverian Memorial
12 · La Haye-Sainte farm
13 · La Papelotte farm
14 · Monument von Schwerin
15 · Saint-Catherine's Church
16 · Prussian Memorial
17 · Napoleon's vantage point
18 · La Belle Alliance farm
19 · Victor Hugo Column
20 · The Wounded Eagle
21 · Chantelet Farm
22 · The Ferme du Caillou Provincial Museum (Napoleon's final headquarters)
23 · Former 'Au Roi d'Espagne' Inn
24 · Tomb of General Duhesme
25 · Chapel of Notre-Dame de Foy
26 · Picton Monument
27 · Chapel of 'le Caillou'.

Vieux-Genappe

23   24

GENAPPE   25   WAYS

an epic out of a defeat and there is little on show at Waterloo today to confound that claim!

On a huge stage with a cast of nearly a quarter of a million, this colourful battle combined both pageantry and theatre way beyond the finances of film-makers – not even Sergei Bondarchuk's film *Waterloo*, costing over twelve million pounds, with 20,000 soldiers of the Russian Army, filmed over forty-eight days by five Panavision cameras from ground-level, from 100-foot towers, from a helicopter and an overhead railway traversing the 'field', on a battlefield in the Ukraine with two hills bulldozed away, five miles of roads laid, five thousand trees transplanted, and four historic buildings reconstructed. Nor could the wardrobe department ever hope to match the fashion-conscious soldiery of the Napoleonic period: light infantry in brilliant green; cuirassiers in gleaming breastplates and burnished helmets with flowing horse-hair tails; and the Imperial Guard in blue and white with red epaulettes, bearskin shakos making them look nine feet tall. Pants were tight with richly embroidered stripes; there were innumerable buttons and loops, sabretaches, pelisses, busbies, flapped cuffs and spangles; facings were pink, primrose, sky-blue, scarlet, yellow; there were furs, feathers and leathers; curly black lamb, white sheepskin, dyed marmot, leopard skins, and shiny black leather or white buffalo hide; black ostrich plumes curled

La Haye Sainte, as it is today

over Scottish bonnets, and a single upright white plume topped the lancer's czapska, already dangerously overloaded with padilon, soutache, turban, peak, hooks and rosettes; infantry uniforms were scarlet, blue, grey, white, and rifle-green, a colour capable of saving more soldier's lives than the burnished cuirasse, eagerly purchased as souvenirs from Belgian peasants who had taken them from dead French cavalrymen. All this gorgeous apparel was worn by soldiers scrambling, slithering and sliding in the clinging embrace of the sticky muddy slopes, fighting for their lives in fancy uniforms that restricted and encumbered them. As the deadly game ran its course one feature became common to all ranks on both sides as unwashed and unshaven faces were made indistinguishable and uniform glories invisible by a liberal coating of mud. The many colourful and inspiring paintings of the battle were born in the artist's romantic imagination!

To allow cavalry and guns to be brought up on roads, infantry regiments had to march in flooded fields, through ankle-deep mud, slipping, sliding, struggling and cursing; shoes were pulled off by the quagmire and some men fought barefoot that day. The battlefield was covered with wheat in strong luxuriant soil made heavy by incessant rain. This soon churned into a gluey liquid morass that clung to wheels, feet, hoofs and bodies; as late as a month after the battle, holes measuring twelve to eighteen inches deep made by horse's hooves could still be seen.

Hougoumont from British lines

Napoleon spent much of the battle on high ground behind the inn of La Belle Alliance (on the main road south of the farm of La Haye Sainte) seated before a table bearing maps; Wellington's style of command was to personally see everything and he continuously moved about the field to points of stress, giving orders and encouragement; no man exposed himself more and most of his staff were killed or wounded at his side. Armed with a 1:8,000 map purchased locally, today's visitor need not be so mobile and can best see the whole battlefield by climbing 226 steps to the top of the Lion Monument, raised at the order of the Prince of Orange. In later years, when Wellington visited the field, he cried: 'They have ruined my battlefield!' He spoke with justification for Netherlands labourers had taken the earth for the mound from the ridge that gave the Duke his victory. In 1815 the road now running behind the mound was lined with hedges and sunk below the level of surrounding land, concealing Allied infantry from French sight and artillery fire, except when they stood to form a square against cavalry. The visitor should try to view the area with imagination, peopling its peaceful acres with colourful combatants; above all, they must visualise the naked face-to-face quality of the fighting, the offering and delivering of death over the distance from one side of the road to another, in congested conditions resembling a crowd at a cocktail party.

Over the bare slope to your front, extending for 1,000 yards from the

Ferme du Caillou – Napoleon's final HQ. Today it is a museum

road on the left to the buildings of Hougoumont half-left, from four to six o'clock in the afternoon the French launched at least eight major cavalry attacks, with as many as 10,000 cavalry coming up that slope at a steady trot in lines of 500 men and horses, each following the other, tightly packed together. It was said to resemble a stormy wave at sea catching the sunlight; the earth vibrated beneath thousands of thundering hooves. Then showers of grapeshot and canister from British guns and volleys of musketry, held until the horsemen were within thirty yards, tore the gaudy array with fire until it resembled the shattered ranks of brightly coloured toy soldiers trampled upon by a spoilt child. The effect was magical: helmets fell, riders convulsively sprang from saddles, tormented horses plunged and reared, spinning round in agonies of fright and pain as hissing missiles sliced through their sleek sides.

Coming up to the squares, some horses baulked at the hedge of bayonets and halted and quickly a tidemark of carcasses piled up on the edges of each square's killing zone. Huge in breastplates and crested helmets, cuirassiers rode up to the squares, their very appearance inspiring dread as they cavorted and caracoled, fired pistols, slashed with sabres or prodded with lances; secure behind the gleaming bayonets, infantry poured deadly musketry fire into them, balls pounding into breastplates sounded like heavy rain on a leaded roof. The heavy jack-booted men crashed down to lie sprawling and kicking like turned turtles;

Looking through a loophole in wall of orchard – Hougoumont

those dying instantly were fortunate, the wounded lying amid heaps of thrashing horses were kicked to death. Each charge became more painfully slow than the last as horses were too weary to even trot over the thick churned mud, picking their way through mounds of dead men and mounts high enough to form a breastwork. Not a single square was broken throughout the day; the infantry, gaining confidence at each repulse, began to scorn the cavalry's useless perseverance, growling: 'Here come those damned fools again!', but they were relieved when cavalry approached because then French guns ceased firing on them and it became the turn of British guns to spew out canister and grape.

Now look down at the area to the right and left of the base of the mound – that was where the squares stood and where, at the last stage of the battle, the French Guard were turned back. All that afternoon the infantry were in and out of square, the only formation to save them being cut down; it took thirty seconds to make a square four ranks deep, front two extending bayonets, rear ranks firing one round per man at fifteen-second intervals, reloading in turns. At Waterloo, Wellington placed his guns in front of the infantry and they continued firing until the cavalry were almost upon them; then the gunners ran to the cover of the squares, lying under the bayonets of the front rank; when the cavalry retired gunners rushed back to their guns and poured fire into the retreating backs. In a deadly game, cavalry threat forced infantry into square, to be

La Belle Alliance, as it is today

flayed by enemy guns, the hurtling roundshot carving bloody corridors in the close formation, the dead thrown out and wounded brought into the square, officers and sergeants thumping and pushing dazed men into the gaps. An officer, asking why a square was lying down, was told that the 30th and 73rd Regiments had just moved from that position, leaving more than 300 dead and wounded in formation on the ground where they had just stood, in an area churned ankle-deep in mud, made worse by men not being able to leave the ranks to relieve themselves.

Turn the gaze half-right, to the château of Hougoumont, a group of buildings and a walled enclosure which formed one of Wellington's key-positions, strongly fortified and garrisoned by British Guards. Opening the battle, the attack on Hougoumont lasted most of the day and 10,000 men of both armies fell in and around the château, yet it remained in British hands throughout. The giant French Lieutenant Legros, nick-named 'L'Enfonceur', smashed the door with an axe only for his small party to be trapped within when it was forced shut; all were hunted down and killed save a small drummer boy whose life was spared. Open to visitors, within the ground of the château can be seen a monument to the French killed there, and two graves – Captain Blackman of the Coldstream Guards buried the day after the battle, and Sergeant-Major Edward Cotton of the 7th Hussars, who died in Waterloo in 1849 after many years as a professional battlefield guide and museum keeper.

Look ahead, down the main road, to La Belle Alliance, from where Napoleon watched the battle, and where Wellington and Blücher had their historic meeting after the Prussians had arrived to save the day. Nearer, on the right of the road is the enclosed Belgian farm of La Haye Sainte, exactly as it was in 1815 when it formed a key position; it can be viewed and proudly displays musket-ball holes still. All day it was stoutly defended by Major Baring and 376 men of the King's German Legion and fell in early evening when they ran out of ammunition – the only tangible French success of the entire day.

Beyond the farm, over the open expanse of sloping ground beyond the crossroads, the British Heavy Cavalry went out of control after destroying D'Erlon's Division of 18,000 men; trying to return up the muddy rise on exhausted horses they were badly cut-up by French lancers. General Ponsonby, their commander, lost his life here through false economy – knowing the government would not fully compensate him if he lost his best charger, he rode an inferior hack, was ridden down and speared to death.

Because it came more easily off the English tongue than did Mont St Jean or La Belle Alliance, Wellington called his battle Waterloo, and subsequently a London railway station was named after it to preserve it for posterity. But such as William Hewitt, last surviving officer who died in 1896 and whose grave can be seen in Southampton Cemetery, never forgot the two square miles covered at early morning by standing crops and by nightfall with the bodies of 40,000 men and horses. It takes imagination to visualise it thus from the top of the Lion Monument.

Waterloo

Date:	18 June 1815
Location:	Waterloo village is situated nine miles south of Brussels on the road to Charleroi via Genappe. The battlefield lies a further three miles south.
War and Campaign:	The Hundred Days – or final campaign of the Napoleonic Wars.
Object of the action:	Napoleon, having defeated the Prussians at Ligny, was intent on crushing Wellington's Allied army, thus opening the way to Brussels.
Opposing sides:	(a) The Duke of Wellington commanding an Anglo-Dutch army. (b) The Emperor Napoleon in command of the French army.
Forces engaged:	(a) Allies: 50,000 infantry; 12,500 cavalry; 5,600 artillerymen; 156 guns. Total: approximately 68,100. (b) French: 49,000 infantry; 15,750 cavalry; 7,250 artillerymen; 246 guns. Total: approximately 72,000.
Casualties:	(a) The Allies lost 15,000; the Prussians suffered a further 9,000 casualties in the later stages. (b) The French lost 25,000 killed, wounded and prisoner.
Result:	Complete victory for the Allies and the final defeat of Napoleon, leading to the firm restoration of the Bourbon dynasty on the throne of France.

10 *Waterloo Today*

Maps Required: Michelin 1:200,000
Ostend–Brussels–Liège No. 213

So far as the area surrounding the actual field of conflict is concerned, this battle has been adopted as a major local industry. From that day in 1815 after the battle, the curious have flocked to the area, continuing to do so ever since and it is estimated that more sightseers visit Waterloo than the fields of World War I. Thus, there are numerous shops selling souvenirs, cafes and restaurants, besides innumerable memorials, monuments, exhibits and pictures, all designed both to commemorate the immortal martial happenings and to make a living out of it.

The most eye-catching of them all is, of course, the towering Lion Monument, 40.5 metres high, surmounted by a 29¾ tonne iron Lion of Brabant, gazing out across the battlefield from his stone plinth; taking three years to build in 1823–26, the climb up its 226 steps is a physical exercise well worthwhile. Whether or not that is attempted, the New Visitors' Centre, erected in 1990 at its base is a MUST. Its attractions and aids are described thus in its colourful leaflet 'Gateway to History':

> The 'Bataille de Waterloo 1815' non-profit association has opened a reception and information centre for visitors to the battlefield. It is open seven days a week, all year round. Here, you can explore and learn about more than forty historic and commemorative sites through a series of interactive screens. Direct enquiry of the centre's database calls up photographs and descriptions of any and all the museums, monuments and events around the battlefield. A wall-map with locations indicator lights helps you to identify and understand where the momentous engagements took place. The staff of the Visitors' centre are on hand to answer questions, and a vast number of publications on the issues, people and battlefield itself are also on sale.

The Centre's electronic maps are very helpful, and the short film show is interesting. Also sited below the mound is the Waterloo Panorama, providing a 360-degree view of what took place in this part of the field. Erected in 1912, it is a striking composition by the painter Louis Dumoulin. Opposite the panorama is the waxworks museum, with life-size models of all the major participants in the events of the day.

Few fields offer a bigger abundance of battlefield bonuses than Waterloo, where all the major buildings that played a role on 18 June 1815

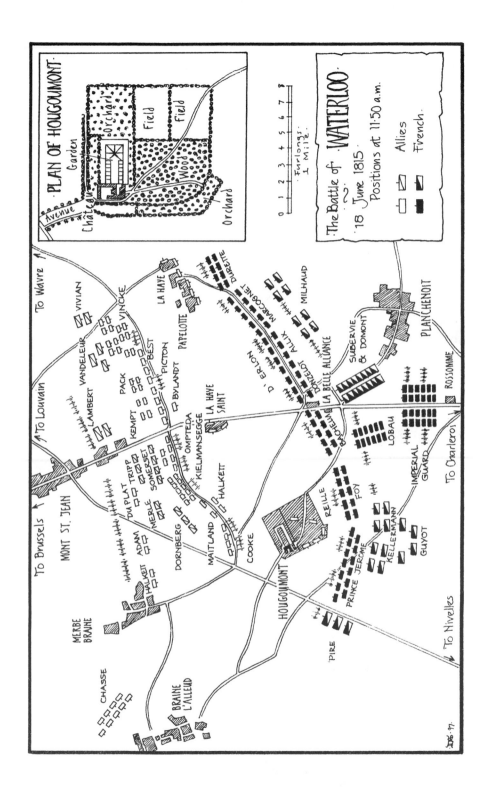

PLAN OF HOUGOUMONT.

Garden

Orchard

Field

Field

Wood

Avenue

Château

Orchard

The Battle of WATERLOO
18 June 1815
Positions at 11:50 a.m.

☐ Allies
■ French.

· Furlongs ·
0 1 2 3 4 5 6 7 8
1 mile.

To Wavre

VIVIAN

VANDELEUR

VINCKE

LA HAYE

PAPELOTTE

DURETTE

MILHAUD

PLANCHENOIT

To Louvain

LAMBERT

PACK

PICTON

BYLANDT

KEMPT

LA HAYE
SAINT

D'ERLON

DONZELOT

ALLIX

LA BELLE ALLIANCE

MARCOGNET

SUBERVIE
& DOMONT

ROSSOMME

To Brussels

MONT ST. JEAN

DU PLAT

TRIPP

SOMERSET

OMPTEDA

KIELMANSEGGE

HALKETT

REILLE

FOY

LOBAU

IMPERIAL
GUARD

To Charleroi

HALKETT

HALKETT

ADAM

MERLE

DORNBERG

MAITLAND

COOKE

HOUGOUMONT

PRINCE JEROME

KELLERMANN

GUYOT

MERBE
BRAINE

PIRE

CHASSE

BRAINE
L'ALLEUD

To Nivelles

are still in existence and can be viewed, although it must be appreciated that in most cases they are still 'working' farms and sheer courtesy demands that the owner's permission be obtained before tramping over their historic confines. Thus, one can see and closely inspect: Hougoumont; La Haye Sainte farm; La Belle Alliance (now a restaurant); Ferme de Mont St Jean; Ferme du Caillou (now a museum to Napoleon) with an Ossuary, containing bones of those who fought in the battle, in the garden behind the house; Ferme la Papelotte; and the former Hôtel Boderglieu, where Wellington spent the nights of 17 and 18 June (now a Wellington museum). Here Wellington wrote his Waterloo despatch; and Colonel Gordon died in Wellington's bed, while the Duke used a pallet on the floor.

There are a number of excellent 'official' museums, while in the shopping area behind the mound are some small 'private' affairs. Just south of Le Caillou is a small museum commemorating Dutch–Belgian participation in the campaign, whilst at the farm itself is the Napoleonic Museum, the farm having been acquired in 1950 by the Belgian Society of Napoleonic Studies. The exhibits are displayed in four rooms and among them are Napoleon's campbed, his telescope and travelling mug and the hat he wore at St Helena. In the town centre of Waterloo itself, in the house occupied by Wellington before and after the battle, is a museum containing many Wellington memorabilia, including unique pieces taken from the wonderful tableware presented to him by the Allied Sovereigns. Besides a micro-panorama and an electric plan of surrounding farms, it houses a wooden leg worn by Lord Uxbridge who lost his own late in the battle. Behind the house, the coachhouse displays illuminated maps tracing the progress of the conflict.

Across the road is St Joseph's Church, the interior of which has been converted into a temple commemorating the battle, with plaques bearing epitaphs to the memory of English, Dutch and Belgian officers who lost their lives, plus busts, bas-reliefs, and marble sculptures.

As would be expected, there are innumerable memorials and monuments dotted throughout the area. At Quatre Bras near Gemioncourt, on the western edge of the main road stands a lion-topped monument to William, Duke of Brunswick, who was killed while rallying his cavalry on 16 June 1815; nearby is another monument to Belgian soldiers who also fell on that day. At Ways, a village on the route between Quatre Bras and Waterloo, in the old cemetery surrounding the church of St Martin de Ways, is a handsome memorial, erected by his widow, to General Duhesme, mortally wounded leading the Young Guard in the battle. Towards the crossroads, where the Braine Alleud–Plancenoit road crosses the N5, is the Wounded Eagle Monument, marking where the squares of the Old Guard checked the Allied pursuit towards the end of the battle. Nearby is the Victor Hugo column, carrying a remarkable effigy of the author of *Les Misérables*, in which he included a not-too-accurate account of the battle. Next can be seen a Gothic Monument; erected in 1819 on the spot where an artillery battery of Bulow's Corps fought, it commemorates the Prussians killed in the battle.

A short distance down the road, still going towards the crossroads, is a hillock marked 'L'Observatoire de Napoleon' (Napoleon's Vantage Point), which was used as the Emperor's forward command post during the conflict; it is about 150 yards away from La Belle Alliance and affords a good view across the eastern part of the field. On the right of the road lies the truncated pyramidal monument, erected in 1818, to the defenders of La Haye Sainte; on the other side of the road is the Gordon Monument, a fluted column resting on a mound, erected in 1817 to the memory of Sir Alexander Gordon, aide-de-camp to Wellington, mortally wounded on this spot.

At the crossroads north of La Haye Sainte there is a small tree marking the site of the large elm tree under which Wellington spent most of the battle. Immediately behind the crossroads, on the north-western corner, some years ago there was a small – typically Belgian – hotel where the author and a party of military enthusiasts stayed when we first visited Waterloo; it was abandoned and semi-derelict when the author was last in the area. Back to the crossroads – on the left of the N5 is a prominent monument, erected in 1914 nearly a hundred years after the battle, in memory of the Belgians who fell.

The Lion Monument at Waterloo

Moving west from the crossroads, past the Lion Monument along a minor road leading to Nivelles, one comes to the area where Maitland's Guards Brigade repulsed the French Grenadiers, and where Mercer's guns flayed the French cavalry with canister. Here are memorials to Cavalie Mercer and to Lieutenant Augustin Demulder of the 5th Cuirassiers. From here it is possible to walk across to the Château of Hougoumont (now known as the Château de Goiumont), which played such a vital part in the battle. It has not changed a great deal and bricked-up loopholes can still be seen in the garden walls; there are memorials to both Allies and French combatants; the ruined chapel is still there; and, among an assortment of memorials, the grave of Sergeant-Major Cotton of the 7th Hussars, who settled in the area after the battle and, for many years, guided battlefield walkers (early nineteenth-century models) around the battlefield.

Moving east from the crossroads, towards the direction from which Blücher's Prussians came, along the road past the farm of Papelotte, it is possible to find a memorial stone marking the spot where Sir Thomas Picton fell. On the road to Plancenoit, the church (much rebuilt later) fought over by the Prussians on the French right flank still stands. The verger (or whatever) took our party over an old house whose timbered ceilings still bore holes made by musket-balls in 1815.

If the battlefield walker were restricted to visiting but one battlefield in his lifetime, then the field of Waterloo would surely be among the strongest contestants for that honour!

Part Four

*Portugal and Spain –
The Peninsular War
1808–14*

11 *The Course of the War*

Napoleon, pursuing his ambitions, sent Junot with a French army into Portugal in December 1807, and in March 1808, Murat led an army of 100,000 into friendly Spain and forced the Spanish king to abdicate. Napoleon's brother Joseph was placed on the throne, alienating the Spanish people and peasants who rose in anger against French garrisons throughout the country.

The French army in Spain largely consisted of recent conscripts completing their training under service conditions, and in July 1808, some 20,000 of these raw troops under Dupont stunned Europe by surrendering at Baylen to a force of Spanish regulars and guerrillas.

The British sent arms, equipment and money to the Portuguese and Spanish people, and an expeditionary force under Sir Arthur Wellesley landed in Portugal. Before taking the field, Wellesley reorganised his army by allocating a Portuguese infantry battalion, armed and arranged in the British style, to each British infantry brigade, giving the local troops experienced backing so that by Busaco they had become first-class soldiers.

On 1 August 1808 Wellesley's army landed north of Lisbon; Junot marched out to meet him with 14,000 men. On 17 August, Wellesley skilfully manoeuvred from two strong positions at Rolica, a smaller French force. It was a small but significant battle because Delabord's force of veterans fought stubbornly and for sixteen years the French had rarely been defeated in the field even when fewer in number. On 20 August, Wellesley positioned his 16,500 men on two long hills at Vimiero, where they were attacked by 13,000 French in two columns shielded by tirailleurs, supported by mobile field artillery and with cavalry protecting their flanks. The tirailleurs were so troubled by the riflemen that they were unable to adequately protect the columns and the French gunners were harassed so that their fire was light and ineffective. The British line was using all its muskets as its flanks wrapped around the columns, who found it impossible to deploy into line under fire, finally breaking and fleeing, taking artillerymen with them so that the guns were stranded and captured. Similar events occurred on at least five more occasions during the battle, forming a pattern to be repeated in every British success in the Peninsula. This defeat amazed the French army and astonished the rest of Europe, who were unaccustomed to a veteran French army being beaten, even if outnumbered 13 to 17, when using the invariably successful Napoleonic tactics in the open field.

In September 1808, Sir John Moore with 22,000 men marched from Portugal to aid the Spanish armies, hoping to join up with Sir David Baird's 18,000 at Corunna, but had to change his plans because of Spanish defeats and the fall of Madrid, plus the fact that Napoleon himself, disgusted with the showing of his generals, had arrived in Spain and with 194,000 men was advancing towards him. Sir John Moore skilfully retreated, outwitting and out-marching three French armies under Napoleon, Soult and Junot, fighting rearguard actions under appalling winter conditions in the mountains of Galicia, until his decimated, exhausted and ragged army of 15,000 men reached Corunna on 11 January 1809 with Soult and 20,000 men at their heels.

Moore's force consisted of about 15,000 infantry, nine 6-pdr guns, but no cavalry. They were positioned on high ground with the village of Elvina on their right/centre repeatedly changing hands. After Sir John Moore was mortally wounded, the battle tailed-off to a quiet end with both armies occupying their original positions, having lost about 1,000 men each. The British force were able to embark without leaving a man behind.

After Corunna, the French overran the Peninsula and beat the Spanish armies in four battles until, on 12 May, Wellesley, after days of marching, feinting and manoeuvring, made a daring crossing of the River Douro and threw the French out of Oporto with surprising ease; retreating into the mountains, the French lost several thousand men. In June 1809 Wellesley invaded Spain hoping to unite with some 100,000 Spanish regulars and guerrillas, but found them poor allies.

One tactical formula brought continual success to Wellesley in the Peninsular War, the pattern being set at Talavera on 28 July when he was attacked by 46,000 men under Victor and King Joseph Bonaparte. His Spanish allies were so ineffectual that Wellesley placed them behind fortifications, supported by both British and their own cavalry so that they were in an almost impregnable position. Nevertheless, this meant that he had to take on 48,000 French with more or less 20,000 British, Portuguese and King's German Legion positioned behind and protected from artillery fire by a low ridge. On the forward slopes a screen of British riflemen engaged enemy skirmishers and harassed the French columns, steadily advancing up the hill, while shrapnel shells burst over and among them. The French advanced in columned divisions, each composed of three battalions with two companies formed abreast, sixty men wide and twenty-four ranks deep, making 4,300 men in a three-column attack.When the columns neared the crest of the ridge, the riflemen fell back and the two lines of British infantry went forward to the crest where they met the French with platoon volleys fired at 50- to 100-yards range. In less than three minutes they fired ten platoon volleys before the French broke and ran. Successive column attacks were thrown back with most of their artillery captured before firing a shot.

Even so, after one attack had broken down, the pursuing British infantry (including the Guards and two King's German Legion brigades) went out of control and, with unloaded muskets, came up against overwhelming numbers of French infantry who roughly handled them before pursuing them back to their own lines. There, four British battalions (totalling about 3,000 men) opened out to let their comrades through and then closed to beat back the French attack. The British cavalry also took unnecessary punishment when the 23rd Light Dragoons and KGL Hussars hit a small ravine at speed, causing losses and disordering them so that the 23rd lost half their original strength when they encountered a brigade of *chasseurs-à-cheval*.

At Talavera, Wellesley lost 5,365 men, a quarter of his entire force, while the French losses of 7,268 represented only 18 per cent of theirs. His rear menaced by Soult and Ney, Wellesley withdrew back into Portugal.

During the winter of 1809–10, the Spanish, defeated in the field, carried on a most effective guerrilla campaign, while Wellington (made Viscount Wellington after Talavera) constructed north of Lisbon, the Lines of Torres Vedras, stretching for 30 miles from the Tagus River to the sea, by fortifying two low ranges of hills mounting some 600 guns. French troops, including Guard units, crossed the Pyrenees and poured into Spain throughout the winter. In May, when Massena was ordered to take Portugal, there were 300,000 French soldiers in the country. By mid-July he had taken Ciudad Rodrigo, but on 27 August at Busaco, his 65,000-strong army was soundly beaten by Wellington's 48,000 (including 24,000 Portuguese) by the same tactical methods of line versus column that had triumphed at Talavera. The French fought as courageously as they had ever done but their artillery and cavalry accomplished nothing and the tirailleurs, far from disordering the Allied line, were not even capable of defending their own columns. French casualties of nearly 5,000, including four generals, provided the highest casualty percentage of officers to men suffered by the French in the entire war. The Allies lost 1,250. At Busaco Wellington avoided any massive concentration of fire, siting his guns in small numbers in line with his infantry and using them at effective ranges. The ratio of artillery to infantry in the Allied army seldom exceeded 1 gun per 1,000 men while the French armies in central Europe had 3 guns per 1,000 men and 4 guns per 1,000 in Spain.

In October 1810 Wellington withdrew into the Lines of Torres Vedras, and Massena, after fruitlessly probing the defences, settled down to blockade the lines, living precariously in a devastated area so that 25,000 French were lost through wounds, disease and malnutrition. In early March 1811, the French withdrew to Spain, harassed by Wellington and by guerrillas, reaching their base at Salamanca in early April after

Massena had skilfully extricated his army from a number of critical situations.

In March 1811, Soult attempted to advance into Portugal and captured Badajoz, but was prevented from proceeding further when his force under Victor was well beaten at Barrosa on 5 March 1811 by a smaller British force under Sir Thomas Graham. On 3 May, Massena, marching with 48,268 men to relieve Almeida, came up with Wellington's 37,000 positioned behind the village of Fuentes de Oñoro. There were two days of hard fighting with desperate hand-to-hand contests in the village; at one stage the Light Division with Cotton's British cavalry were isolated on an open plain surrounded by large numbers of French cavalry, three divisions of infantry and several batteries of artillery. Craufurd handled his command with great skill, keeping the line battalions in mobile squares while using his riflemen as skirmishers, not allowing himself to be pinned down by enemy cavalry, so that infantry and artillery could pour their fire into his formations. Slowly retiring, the riflemen, behind cover of low rock outcrops, kept up a galling fire on the enemy cavalry and artillery at about 250 yards range, running to the cover of squares whenever the cavalry approached. When the French artillery came near, the danger of being charged by Cotton's cavalry forced them back. As the squares formed by the three line battalions moved alternately back, Bull's horse artillery positioned themselves between the formations and kept off the French cavalry, artillery and infantry. In their two-mile withdrawal the Light Division, showing the highest discipline, courage and confidence, lost only 35 men. A British Army tradition began here when Captain Norman Ramsay's two guns of Bull's troops, completely enveloped by French cavalry, cut their way through the encircling mass at a gallop, with mounted gunners surrounding the limbered pieces and caissons.

At Fuentes, the British open-order fighting was far more effective than the French mass system, even within the confines of the village, where the light companies and riflemen showed more aptitude for street fighting than the French, accustomed to attacking in column. The British cavalry surpassed themselves and, working in small units, did not get out of hand in charges.

Soult advanced to relieve Badajoz, besieged by Beresford, who marched to meet him at Albuera on 16 May with 20,000 men, including British, German and Portuguese brigades and a Spanish force of 14,650. After early skirmishing, the French made the most massive single attack of the entire war, against four battalions of Spanish infantry on the Allied southern flank. There were about 8,500 men (two full infantry divisions) in an almost solid column with only a light skirmish line in front; artillery accompanied the mass, whose left flank was protected by 3,500 cavalry and more guns. The Spanish infantry fought unusually well but would have been broken had not a British division come up on their right flank, with Colborne's brigade attacking the flank of the French column. A sudden thunderstorm with sheets of rain swept across the field, allowing two regiments of Polish Lancers to approach unseen and hit one end of the British line, whose muskets had been put out of action by the sudden downpour. The first three of Colborne's battalions were practically annihilated under the lances wielded by skilled horsemen in tight formation. Breaking into the Spanish rear, the French cavalry almost caught Beresford and his staff besides sweeping over a battery of King's German Legion guns. Rallying, the Spanish infantry came back to the front, reinforced by two British brigades and the remaining battalion from Colborne's brigade; muskets were now fireable as the rain had ceased. Seven British battalions (3,700 men) in a two-deep line, now began a close range fire-fight with the two French Divisions (8,000 men) formed in one huge column about 200 men wide and 40 ranks deep. Occupying an area about the size of a cricket field, this contest dragged on for nearly an hour, with several French batteries, less than 300 yards back from the head of the column, enfilading and cross-firing through the centre of the British line with grape and canister. Losses would have been astronomical but for the smoke and heavy clouds which obscured targets.

Torrents of rain brought the fighting to an end; armies remained in position until late on the following day when the French retired covered by horse artillery and cavalry. The Allies lost nearly 6,000; the French about 7,000. The British, German and Portuguese soldiers missed Wellington and did not have the same confidence in Beresford, who, although brave, loyal and talented, did not employ Wellington's successful tactics, and if Soult tactically out-manoeuvred him, then he would have done the same to any other British commander in the Peninsula, bar Wellington himself.

Wellington stormed Ciudad Rodrigo on 19 January, where Craufurd was killed, and Badajoz in April, when he lost more men than in any major battle except Talavera and Albuera. Then Wellington thrust boldly into northern Spain with an allied army of some 48,000 British, Portuguese and Spanish troops, with fifty-four guns. In mid-July Wellington and Marmont (who had taken over from Massena) at the head of similar-sized armies, marched parallel for several days with each commander keeping his army well in hand, seeking a tactical advantage. At midday on 22 July, at Salamanca, Marmont had extended his left flank, and Pakenham's 3rd Division with Portuguese cavalry, hidden behind a range of hills, were able to drive into the leading French column before they knew what had hit them. The 2nd French Division formed into a square but were slaughtered in three volleys by a two-deep infantry line, and the survivors broke and fled. Le Marchant's cavalry charged the disintegrating French infantry and smashed five battalions, then charged into the French 3rd Division, who had double-marched for a mile and, although in squares, were unable to withstand the heavy dragoons and were scattered. A French counterstroke of 12,000 men in columns, lacking artillery and with fewer riflemen than the Allies, were stopped in their tracks and completely broken in five minutes. Five of the originally eight French divisions were now dispersed, Marmont and General Bonnet being among the casualties. To cover their retreat Clausel, for the first time in the Peninsular War, formed the seven battalions of a complete French division in a continuous, three-deep line with a single battalion at either end in square, to be dispersed by artillery. The French army, having lost 14,000, were now in full retreat, but the physically exhausted British army, with 5,000 casualties, were unable to pursue.

During the winter 1812–13 Wellington trained his army hard and every battalion was capable, even in rough country, of moving from line to open column or square in 30 seconds. Some veteran French units were withdrawn from Spain, but their conscript replacements were good soldiers and did all that was asked of them. The total French force south of the Pyrenees still exceeded 200,000 men. Moving with great secrecy and speed, Wellington had his entire force north of the Douro by 3 June, and the out-manoeuvred French streamed north in disorder, constantly harassed by Spanish guerrillas.

On 21 June 1813 the French (66,000 men under Joseph) took up defensive positions around Vitoria, formed in three lines with artillery and cavalry supporting them. Wellington divided his force (27,000 British, 27,000 Portuguese and 9,000 Spanish) into four columns that came into the valley at various points while cutting the French line of retreat. All went as planned and by late afternoon the French, out-fought and out-manoeuvred, were streaming away in small groups. Although suffering fewer casualties than at Salamanca, the French abandoned everything and saved only two guns so that they required complete reorganisation and re-arming before resuming as a fighting force.

Joseph retired across the Pyrenees; the Allies did not pursue because Napoleon himself was in France (having signed an armistice with Russia and Prussia) and might well bring an army of overwhelming strength against them. Soult, replacing Joseph and Jourdan, reorganised the French forces which were more numerous than the Allies, who had fewer than 60,000 Anglo-Portuguese on a front of forty miles, positioned in depth to take advantage of the road system. On 25 July, with Wellington away, Soult sent strong forces to partially force the passes at Maya and Roncesvalles, where 13,000 British troops held 40,000 French until withdrawing at nightfall; four Portuguese guns were lost, the first and only guns ever taken from Wellington in any action. It is said that British soldiers had rarely fought so courageously but had seldom been worse commanded. With Wellington back in command, the Allied army took up defensive positions on ridges at Sorauren, to be attacked on 28 July by

Soult with a considerable numerical advantage, when Spanish troops backed by British infantry fought well to beat Soult back, causing 4,000 casualties. The Allies lost 2,650. On 30 July the numerically weaker Allied columns stormed down from their ridges with all the precision and impetuosity of Salamanca against strong enemy positions, but French morale was low and the second battle of Sorauren was soon over. The French streamed back across the border into France, more disorganised and defeated than they had been after Vitoria.

In October 1813 Wellington attacked at Vera, where the French, immobilised in static field fortifications, were out-flanked by the Light Division and forced to retreat when the 5th Division, after crossing the river by little-known fords, appeared on their flank and rear. Thus, the line of the Pyrenees was broken. Along the Nivelle, Soult had some 63,000 men in naturally strong positions, heavily fortified with numerous artillery redoubts. Wellington's army totalled 80,000, including some doubtful Spanish units. His attack on 10 November 1813 included some excellent work by the Light Division in capturing the Lesser Rhune, an area so rugged that only three small mountain guns could move up to support them. By the end of the day, the French had lost 4,300 men and fifty-nine guns and Soult had been forced back.

All the Spanish, with the exception of Morillo's experienced force, were sent home following atrocities committed in looting a village, so that Wellington had under his command in France 36,000 British, 23,000 Portuguese and 4,000 Spaniards – 63,000 men exclusive of cavalry. Soult had about the same number (but without cavalry), National Guards and the garrison of Bayonne. Crossing the River Nive at dawn on 9 December, Hill's corps, formed of troops from three nations with twelve guns, were cut off when the river suddenly rose, and were attacked by heavy French concentrations at odds of 3–1. After fighting for four hours Hill, unaided, defeated Soult and caused him 3,300 casualties against 1,775 of his own. On the same day three whole German battalions, complete with officers, colours and baggage, deserted to the Allies.

In the early days of 1814 Soult, with a total force of 62,500 men, still held Bayonne with his field army of 36,000 in position on a ridge at Orthez. Wellington divided the Allied army into a siege force of 18,000 under Hope around Bayonne, and a field force of 48,000 under Hill, Beresford and himself. In an amphibious operation which included the first use of Congreve's rockets, Hope got a force across the Adour to completely surround Bayonne. On 27 February Wellington, with 31,000, attacked in five columns and drove the French from strong positions largely because of the decline in French morale through an unbroken series of defeats.

By mid-March Wellington had driven Soult halfway across southwestern France and on 10 April made a strong assault on Toulouse which, although not apparently successful at the time, forced Soult to abandon the city. A few hours later it was learned that Napoleon had abdicated and after almost six years the fighting was over. British cavalry and artillery proceeded across France to Calais, while Anglo-Portuguese divisions marched to Bordeaux, both conscious that they had been equal partners in many hard battles.

Napoleon called the Peninsular War 'the Spanish Ulcer' and there is little doubt that it played a big part in his downfall. A classic example of guerrilla warfare, the war also emphasised the value of English sea-power.

12 *The Battle of Salamanca* 22 *July 1812*

Following a visit to the fields of Salamanca, military historian Kenneth Brooks wrote what must be the model formula for obtaining the most benefit from one's battlefield.

> In April last year we left the coach at the foot of the Lesser Arapile, having already visited the village of Calvarrasa de Arriba where Foy's advance guard had arrived the night before the battle on 22 July 1812. Whilst there we had walked forward to the site of the convent of Nuestra Señors de la Pena around which skirmishing had taken place during the battle. It was both useful and very interesting to start by looking at the British position from a French viewpoint, and to see the reverse slope of the Greater Arapile.
>
> Many accounts have been written about the battle and the battlefield, but none have given a really living picture of it. Only a visit can do this. By coincidence we arrived at the time when the battle was in fact being fought, and I thought of this as I climbed the steep grassy side of the Lesser Arapile. Small rocks and outcrops both helped and hindered the ascent. I took a beeline to the top – arriving breathless and thankful I was not in full kit with musket.
>
> The top of the hill is flat, harsh tussocks of grass and rock break the harsh outline – already yellowing and dry. After photographing the entire field I started to study the ground. One could imagine the tension of the day, caused by the frustration of retreating and impatience of waiting to see if a battle would be fought or not.
>
> Half an hour earlier Wellington had galloped off to the north-east to fetch Pakenham's 3rd Division and D'Urban's cavalry. In the interval before his return I could look around and see what was going on.
>
> The battleground can be described as two reversed 'L's formed by broken ridges and hills. The two 'L's are anything from 1,200 to 1,800 yards apart, with the western one fitting inside the eastern feature. The Lesser Arapile where I stood is at the south-eastern point of the British, or western feature. The Greater Arapile stands about 800 yards away from the Lesser in a south-westerly direction, and is forward of the main eastern ridges. Hot bright sun illuminates the area of rolling ridges, flat or gently sloping fields with woods visible in the distance.
>
> Through my spyglass I can see to the north of me the Light Division, the

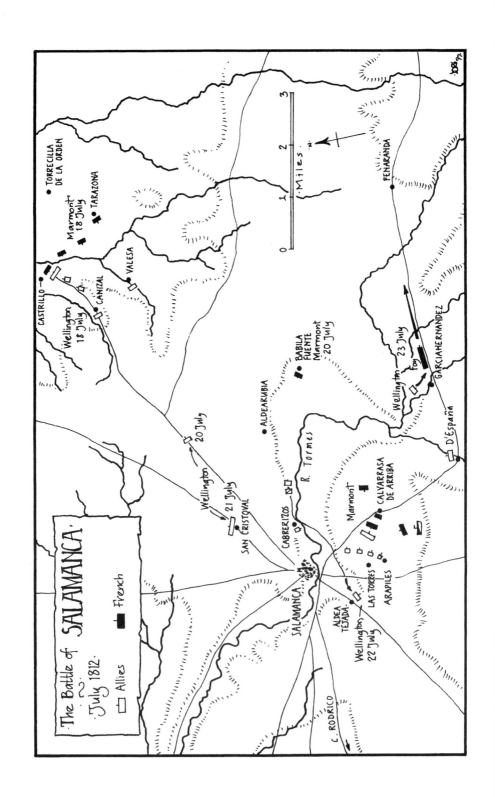

The Battle of SALAMANCA.
July 1812.

☐ Allies
■ French

TORRECILLA
DE LA ORDEN
TARAZONA
Marmont
18 July
CASTRILLO
Wellington
18 July
CANIZAL
VALESA
20 July
Wellington
21 July
SAN CRISTOVAL
SALAMANCA
CABRERIZOS
ALDEARUBIA
BABILA
FUENTE
Marmont
20 July
R. Tormes
Marmont
CALVARRASA
DE ARRIBA
ALDEA
TEJADA.
Wellington
22 July
LAS TORRES
ARAPILES
Wellington
23 July
Foy
GARCIAHERNANDEZ
D'España
PENARANDA
C. RODRIGO

0 1 2 3
Miles

1st Division and Bock's Heavy Cavalry Brigade. Some elements can doubt-less be seen by the French, but most are in dead ground. All face east where Foy bickers with the troops in the convent. Ferey's division can be seen in support of Foy and further round, nearer to the Great Arapile, can be seen another division. This turned out to be Sarrut's division. Although the Greater Arapile is in fact twenty feet higher than where I stand, it is easy to see French guns and battalions on it. More French battalions are formed up behind it.

Sweeping my glass around until I am looking due south I can see the reason for Wellington's rapid exit. On the ridge opposite stands a solitary division facing us while to its left another division is striking out westwards. In the rear of these divisions are two more divisions – not yet in supporting distance. Later on we discovered it was Maucune facing us while Thomières was busily trying to outflank our right.

Looking towards our right rear I can see the dust-clouds of our bag-gage-train moving from Salamanca to Ciudad Rodrigo. Nearer to us, however, can be seen the massed infantry of Leith's, Cole's, Clinton's and Hope's divisions. Their red and white contrasts with the blue of their Portuguese infantry, and the infantry of Pack's and Bradford's Indepen-dent Portuguese brigades. Movement among them heralds Wellington's return! Shouted orders and movements taking shape indicate something is to happen shortly. Stirs of expectancy among the 40th and 27th Foot of Cole's division, who share the Lesser Arapile with me, gradually die down

Salamanca – This is the area where the four British divisions assembled before moving forward into the battle. In the background is the village of Aldea Tejada

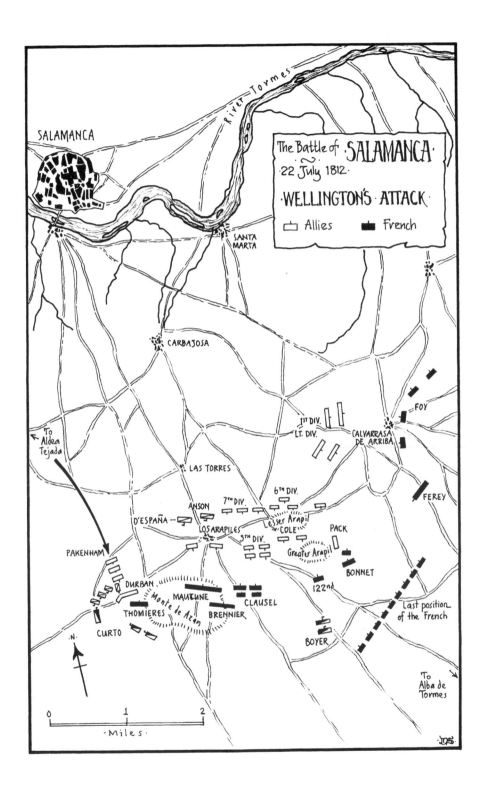

The monument on the top of the Greater Arapile, taken from some 50 feet below it, just where the terrace rises from the lower slopes

Taken from the top of the Lesser Arapile, with the village of Los Arapiles over on the right. This is the area over which Clausel made his counter-attack, fought back along the line of today's road by Clinton and other British divisions.

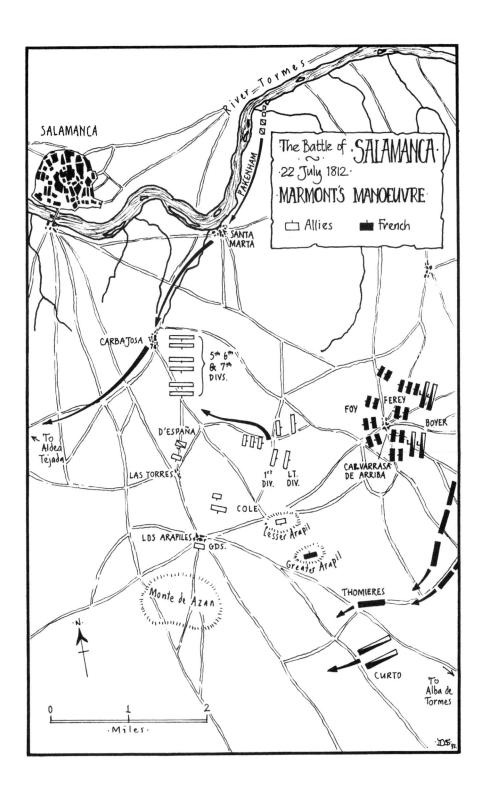

SALAMANCA

River Tormes

PAKENHAM

SANTA
MARTA

The Battle of · SALAMANCA·
· 22 July 1812 ·
MARMONT'S MANOEUVRE
▢ Allies   ◼ French

CARBAJOSA

5ᵗʰ 6ᵗʰ
& 7ᵗʰ
DIVS.

← To
Aldea
Tejada

D'ESPAÑA

FOY   FEREY
            BOYER

LAS TORRES

1ˢᵗ   LT.
DIV.   DIV.

CALVARRASA
DE ARRIBA

COLE

Lesser Arapil

LOS ARAPILES

GDS.

Greater Arapil

Monte de Azan

THOMIERES

·N·

CURTO

To
Alba de
Tormes

0   1   2

·Miles·

DS
97

as no orders are received by them. Down on the plain to my right I can see Leith's division moving out and forming in two lines, with Hope forming to his rear. Nearer at hand Cole's two remaining brigades stand-to and Clinton's division appear in their rear. Something is certainly going to happen.

As though by pre-arranged signal a roar of cannon and musketry to our right announces the clash of Pakenham and Thomières. It is now 5.00 pm and battle is to be joined at long last. Pakenham had advanced three miles from Aldea Tejada in our right rear and had approached unseen to within

The area west of the Greater Arapile over which Cole's division attacked, going towards the French massed on the ridge beyond it. Taken from the Lesser Arapile.

The Greater Arapile taken from the top of the Lesser Arapile. Up those slopes Pack's Portuguese Division attacked and were repulsed.

five hundred yards of Thomières's leading column. Spirited action by Portuguese dragoons had halted them and Pakenham's leading brigades – the veteran 74th, 88th and 45th – are attacking without halting. The division is deploying for action on the march before achieving overwhelming success. Thomières's division has been destroyed before our eyes – it seemed almost in a flash.

In the meantime it is as though Leith had shouted '5th Division will advance in review order – by the centre – quick march'. As steadily as on the parade ground the front line of red coated bayonets advances, checking their dressing, while supported by the second line of Portuguese infantry. The village of Los Arapiles around which British light companies had been skirmishing with French tirailleurs has been passed. After an advance of 1,200 yards swept by French artillery the front line – still in perfect order – breasts the ridge and Maucune's division is lost to our right in clouds of smoke and dust.

Now here is a most stirring sight – in some ways the climax of the battle. Bradford's Portuguese brigade had been advancing on the right of Leith, while on their right again was Le Marchant's brigade of dragoons followed

The Lesser Arapile taken from the top of the Greater Arapile. The town of Salamanca is in the left background behind the Lesser Arapile. The ground between the two Arapiles is that over which Pack's Portuguese charged and were repulsed, when they attacked the Greater Arapile. The ground all around here is far less flat than it gives the impression when you look at it from the top of the two Arapiles; it contains a lot of dead ground, and was probably fairly heavily wooded.

The area to the east of the Greater Arapile where, at the last stage of the battle, Foy's division formed-up with the infantry in line with infantry squares at either end. Wellington broke it up by enfilading them with artillery brought up from the Light Division and other sources

by Anson's light dragoons. Le Marchant is now breaking into a canter, riding up on to the ridge and the sound and milling dust-clouds tell us that great things are happening. Where Maucune had stood is now thronged with red coated figures – but beyond them billowing dust-clouds and fresh musket smoke suggest a further clash has occurred. This was in fact Brennier's division being destroyed by Le Marchant's cavalry before it could enter the battle effectively. The time is now 5.40 pm and three French divisions have been destroyed. The triumphant divisions of Leith and Pakenham have joined forces and can be seen reforming to sweep east-wards along the known ridge to our southern front.

It is difficult to choose between the spectacles claiming our attention. Cole has now been dispatched by Wellington to assault the eastern end of the ridge south of us – on which we can see a fresh French division forming. The 1,400 British bayonets form the right of the single two-deep line with 2,400 Portuguese on the left. Their job must be the toughest one so far. Advancing over 1,600 yards of reasonably flat, sun-parched glacis – enfiladed by artillery from both flanks and heavily outnumbered – the men of the 7th and 23rd Foot must surely be thinking this is Albuera all over again. The divisions meet, muskets belch and the French front line recoils on their second line supports. The British stand firm until nine French battalions come out from behind the Greater Arapile and take them in the left flank. The brazen helmets of a division of French dragoons can be seen gleaming dully through the smoke. Cole is down! Not even British Peninsular infantry can do more. They break and retire. The dragoons are charging in for the kill – but discipline and the will to survive triumph and *ad hoc* squares form as though by magic. Around me the 40th Foot are tumbling down the steep slope to re-form at the foot and advance as a bastion behind which the survivors of Cole's division can concentrate and retire to safety. Beaten but unbowed they return to fight again later that day.

The other competing spectacle is Pack's assault on the Greater Arapile with his Portuguese brigade. What a grandstand view we have! Pack has decided to attack as though assaulting a fortress – which in effect he is. There go his storming party of four grenadier companies followed by four line battalions in two columns. His approach is over clear ground with no smoke to blind us, and I see his cacadores skirmishing forward and up the steep slope. Artillery fire has damaged but not stopped his columns. Our climb up the Lesser Arapile was difficult but theirs is worse. Up they go with bayonets flashing. But something has checked the cacadores! Ragged musketry continues as they spread out and start to climb some obstacle in company with the leading grenadiers. The scene is clouded by a sheet of smoke and the crash of musketry tells us the French battalions are counter-attacking. Through the smoke hurtle blue-clad figures and the French firing overthrows the grenadiers and the line battalions, tumbling them in a broken heap at the foot of the hill.

But more important events are taking place before us. The triumphant French battalions – nineteen of them – who defeated Cole are now advancing to the centre. The dragoon division covers their right flank, eager to avenge the slaughter by Le Marchant's cavalry. A mounted staff officer clatters up to the 27th Foot and they are moving down to join the 40th already on the left of Clinton's division, 2,700 British bayonets form the first line with 2,500 Portuguese in close support. The rolling thunder of musketry is incessant, smoke and dust must be choking and blinding the fighting men. The French dragoons are threatening the British left, but the 40th and 27th are standing firm. A Portuguese brigade can be seen coming down from the far ridge and is taking the French in the left flank. They are still fighting but swirling eddies of figures say the end is near – and off they go in a broken, stumbling mass. Darkness is beginning to add its difficulties to smoke, dust, blood and fatigue. Clinton reforms his division and the battered remnants move after the French shattered masses. In the far distance to the south-east stands yet another ridge – wooded this time. Bitter fighting is taking place on the final ridge, but presently the last gun fires and it is all over. Small grass fires spring up over the fields and I fear that many wounded will suffer the same fate as many of their comrades at Talavera three years ago.

I wondered as I left the Lesser Arapile whether any survivors thought – as I did – that Wellington's iron resolve not to be tempted into doing something rash contrasted sharply with Marmont's overconfidence and underestimation of his adversary. I expect that their only wishes were for a drink and a chance to lie down in peace and quiet.

13 *Walking the Field of Salamanca*

Map Required
Michelin Map No. 447
Centro-Oeste de España. Madrid-Extremadura 1/400000 (1cm=4km)

The tales arising from three visits to this incomparable battlefield are a saga in themselves, arousing nostalgia for days long past. This must truly be among the best of all battlefields to explore, and a delight to walk.

1973 Arrived in town of Salamanca in late afternoon, hastily checked bags into hotel and then rushed coach out to battlefield, where first surveys indicated enough dead ground to hide an army – as the French found out to their cost. Negotiating a barbed wire fence, we climbed to the summit of the Lesser Arapile, where we encountered a bitterly cold gale-force wind as doggedly we turned binoculars in all directions. Sheltering in the lee of a clump of rocks, we listened to one of David Chandler's fascinating battlefield discourses and soon we had a pretty fair idea of the course of this somewhat complex battle. In the gathering dusk we began to imagine cavalry charging across the plain and columns of infantry pressing forward. It was almost dark as we drove on narrow dirt tracks to Aldea Tejada, but gave best to a truculent Spanish farmer driving a very big tractor. Re-entering the town of Salamanca, we were held up by a picturesque procession of candle-bearing penitents, garbed rather as one imagines the Ku Klux Klan, marching to the measured beat of drums, crosses held high above, it brought to mind tales we had heard of the Inquisition of the Middle Ages.

1974 On first arriving in the town of Salamanca, a very pleasant civilised and colourful city, we lunched outdoors in the impressive colon-naded Plaza Mayor under a hot sun. Then we drove out to the battlefield where, last year on a much colder day, we had ascended the Lesser Arapile; this time we walked the area between the two Arapiles, halting to listen to David telling us a concise but colourful account of the events that had occurred over the ground on which we were standing.

1990 On a hot day without a cloud in the sky, we were on the immortal field of Salamanca by nine in the morning and stayed there until late after-noon, eating a picnic lunch on top of the Greater Arapile. Quite unchanged and unbuilt on, except for a wispy railway line and a minute halt, it is a field where everything falls into place, and from the summit of

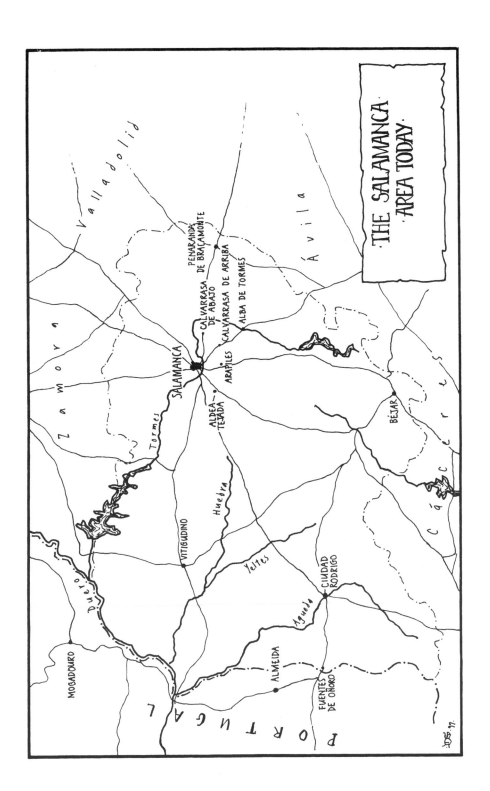

THE SALAMANCA
AREA TODAY

Taken from the top of the Greater Arapile. The ridge in the far distance along by the trees is where the French were marching, with Thomières in the lead, then Maucune, before they were hit, by Packenham's division coming round from Alva Tejada, out of the picture over on the right. The area leading up to the Greater Arapile, the scene of Cole's unsuccessful attack, is today covered with extensive growths of bright scarlet poppies.

The village of Los Arapiles, taken from the Lesser Arapile. Beyond is the ridge along which Packenham's division marched to hit Thomières's leading divisions, which were hit somewhere near a line of dark trees to the left of Los Arapiles.

the Lesser Arapile it can all be placed in its chronological sequence, as the landscape's seeming flatness begins to reveal folds and dips in the ground that answer all the unspoken questions one might have on the battle. We left with reluctance, each of us ruminating on Wellington's incomparable military genius.

September 1991 In the company of Todd Fisher and John Brewster of the Emperor's Headquarters in Chicago, a long drive was made from Badajoz, through Cáceres, Plasencia and Beja lying somnolent in the wild regions of central Spain, to arrive in the region of Salamanca. Tired and thirsty, we stopped at a Modal Hostal for a drink, and seeing from it an excellent view of both Lesser and Greater Arapiles, made a snap decision to book-in and begin exploring the area. Hardly pausing to dump baggage, we set off for the famed field and were soon cogitating on a series of grassy ridges, until deciding on which of them Packenham hit Thomières's division, to put a match to the fuse that flared up into the Battle of Salamanca, on 22 July 1812. Then onto the Lesser and Greater Arapiles, where imaginations were given full rein to people the bare and lonely grassland with the warring forces of Cole, Pack, Ferrey, Bonnet and the rest. Seeking the scene of operations on the Allied left, we drove to Alba de Tormes, and determined where the Light Division were engaged, and the movements of Foy's force.

14 *Mini Memories of Walking the Battlefields of the Peninsular War*

Maps Required:
Michelin 1:200,000
Portugal and Spain No. 990
Portugal 37
Centre and Eastern Spain 447
Burgos-San Sebastián 42
Midi-Pyrenees 235
Pau-Bayonne 69 (Inst. Geog. National)

The hills on which the Battle of Rolica was fought can be seen from the ramparts of Obidos, and a short drive brings one to the roads bordering the position. After that, it is out of the car and, map in hand, either a climb up one of the gullies, or a less arduous path from the rear of the position. As the area is quite unchanged, one can adequately employ a contemporary map of the actual battle to locate salient points. It is possible to get close behind Delaborde's second position, where one comes upon a mouldering stone memorial half hidden in relatively dense undergrowth, dedicated in English to Colonel Lake, who fell there when leading part of the 1/29th too far into the French lines. To find it, seek the village of Columbeira and go through it up the ravine, on the road, to the village of Zambugeira; continue past an ancient tree and the church, and take the road to the left until reaching a dirt-track; then proceed through orchards through the rear of the French positions, until arriving at the memorial at the head of Lake's gully.

Try making for the monument on Vimiero Hill, which has been considerably 'tarted-up' in recent years. From this commanding elevation it is easily possible to identify East and West Ridges. This is another relatively unchanged field so far as its topography goes, and it is possible to discover all salient points if one is working from a detailed map of the battle. It is only a short drive from the monument to where, for the first but not the last time in this war, British riflemen destroyed French columns.

As with most of these Peninsular fields, it is impossible to view it without becoming overawed at the sheer size of the area – Vimiero was a

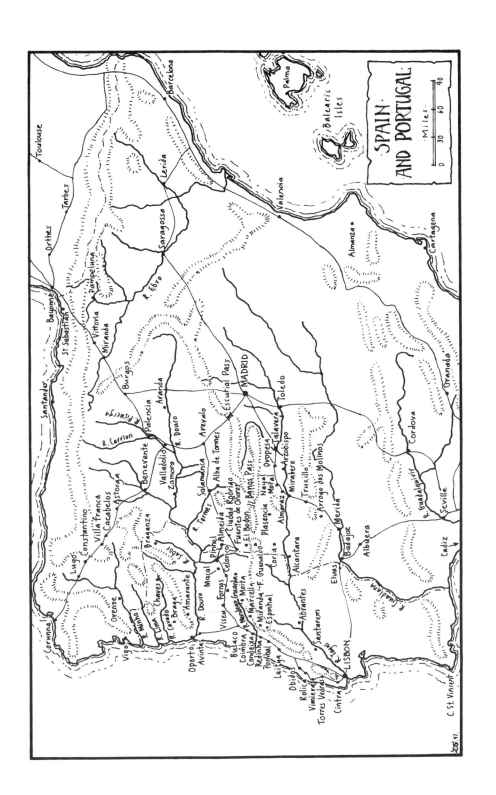

SPAIN·
AND PORTUGAL·
Miles
0   30   60   90

battle involving much tactical manoeuvring over a succession of hills, providing a lasting impression of the sense of ground shown by the respective commanders, and feeling for the unfortunate soldiers who had to march every yard of it.

And so to the historic battlefield of Talavera de ia Reina, and today perhaps the greatest disappointment of all Peninsular fields – if Wellington himself was moved to ask what had they done to his field of Waterloo, then he would surely be brought to the verge of apoplexy by Talavera field today!

Our respect for the Duke increased as we contemplated positions by no means as perfect as expected, showing that he had made the best out of very little.

Later trips were made in the knowledge that a well-publicised national scandal had been caused in Spain (and to a lesser extent in Britain) when it was revealed that a motorway had been built through the centre of the battlefield, disturbing gravepits and the general topography.

On the left flank now there is a sheet of shining water held in check by an impressive dam at the foot of the Medellin. That hill still exists but can only be ascended for a small part of its heights: the high railings of a

Guadalupe and its 16th century monastery towering over the town
(Extremadura area)

The Walled city of Avila

private dwelling on its summit bar further access. The whole area is a mass of wheel tracks and dumps of road-making material; so, after studying maps and reading notes, we gained what could only be a sketchy impression, before crossing the busy motorway and walking the flat area by the Portina, between the Medellin and the town itself, accepting that it was something to even be in the general area of one of Wellington's great triumphs.

Of course, one never visits Talavera without taking in the Casa de Salinas from the towers of which Wellington was watching through a spyglass the approach of the French columns. So intent was he that he failed to realise that enemy skirmishers were in the courtyard below. The Duke made a hasty retreat with his staff, narrowly escaping from a volley of French fire. Partly in ruins, the house had not changed since last visited, indeed probably not over the past 180 years, still looking peaceful and serene, a valuable piece of property. However, it might seem that things were not exactly as history relates, for Bernard Cornwell, when researching his book *Sharpe's Eagle*, encountered five independent sources in the town of Talavera who told him that the Duke was actually occupied in the Casa by a conquest of an entirely unmilitary nature!

It is known that, prior to moving on to the area outside Almeida, Craufurd's Light Division had positioned themselves in and around an

From outside the walls of the fort, showing interior with gun emplacements on the right. In background is the chapel – the reverse side of that shown below.

The old chapel used as a magazine at the fort of St. Vincente, the principal fort of the Lines of Torres Vedras. The fort is very large and extensive and had room for about 5,000 men and numerous guns. It is surrounded by deep stone-faced moats, and has many gun emplacements, most having an extensive field of fire.

isolated eighteenth-century Spanish fortress, Fort Concepción, just inside the Spanish border facing the Portuguese fortress-town of Almeida, with the River Thuronnes between.

Within sight of the Customhouse and barriers at the frontier, there is a small signpost pointing to the right, labelled ALDEA DEL OBISPO,

Taken from inside the fort near the chapel, looking through a gun emplacement behind which can be seen the stone-faced wall of one of the ditches which can be enfiladed by fire from this emplacement. Beyond it, higher up, can be seen stone walls of other parts of the fortification.

some ten kilometres away – Fort Concepción HAD to be somewhere to the left of that road or village! On our first visit two false trails over rough tracks proved useless until, working in a field, we encountered a labourer who spoke French (we spoke no Spanish) who directed us into the village of Aldea del Obispo, turn left on a track marked 'Private' and the fort lay ahead on the ridge! Last time there it had been made easier by a direction sign showing the route to the Fort, which we approached in some awe! It is an extensive, desolate place, massive outworks and main buildings, a huge gate still surmounted by the Spanish Royal crest carved in its stonework, now in ruins through Craufurd blowing it up on 21 July 1810 on Wellington's orders as it was too remote to defend and had to be denied to the French.

Over the frontier the fortress-town of Almeida stands compact and picturesque, completely surrounded by low fortifications and earthworks. Seemingly it has changed little since being levelled by the vast gunpowder magazine explosion of 1810, the ruins of the cathedral (Oman says it was a castle) wherein was situated the magazine can be walked, and around it the ramparts and embrasures are being repaired and dummy guns point threateningly from them.

Among the easiest of all Peninsular War fields to visit, Busaco is probably more forested than it was at the time of the battle. The village of Sula lies under the hot sun, and it does not need too much imagination to people

Area at Fuentes de Oñoro over which Craufurd's riflemen and Ramsay's Horse Artillery troop retreated. This is in Spain, although the photo was taken from Portugal, the border lying a yard in front of where I am standing.

it with fighting soldiers; indeed, it is possible to still find walls pock-marked by missiles fired in 1810. The convent, later a royal palace, is now a luxury hotel and its imposing baroque appearance is reflected in its charges for accommodation, food and drink! Using a battle-map, it is easy to find the exact spot where Craufurd stood, in solitary splendour, awaiting the French onslaught before ordering his infantry to come forward; Wellington's command post at the southern end of the ridge is marked by a memorial stone (in Portuguese), and Massena's command post is signposted and similarly marked (on the squat circular stone building). There is a small but interesting museum (closed on Mondays); a monument to the battle on the hill overlooking the ridge (near the museum); and one can see the cell(?) in the convent where Wellington is said to have slept on the night of the battle.

Although every hilltop in the area of the town of Torres Vedras bears signs of crumbling fortifications, it is only San Vincente to the north that has been restored so that it is now much as it must have been when Wellington's army moved into the famous Lines. Work is continuing there; currently the roof of the magazine is being re-tiled. Recalling that San Vincente must have been one of many such forts, it is truly impress-ive to consider how much work must have been done in a relatively short time, and how much military foresight was shown by Wellington and his chief engineer, Major Richard Fletcher (later killed in 1811 at San Sebastián).

In many ways the battlefield of Fuentes de Oñoro fully lives up to expectations. The village itself seems little changed over nearly two centuries, and if the tumbledown buildings, scattered stone walls and enclosures are not those which figured so significantly in the fierce fighting of 5 May 1811, then they must greatly resemble them. The churchyard in which the Highlanders fought hand-to-hand with the Grenadiers of the Imperial Guard has been vanquished by a modern road, but the church still stands ruminatively there, with a memorial for all to see. Imaginations working overtime, we wandered through the deserted streets, found the dried-up stream with its stone-slab footbridge, across which the French attacked, before moving up above the village to where Picton's 3rd Division and other allied formations had been positioned.

But, of course, the aspect of this battle that tends to stick in the memory is the fighting retreat of the Light Division and Cotton's cavalry across two miles of open ground against greatly superior numbers, and where Norman Ramsay's troop of Horse Artillery performed their legendary charge.

It was found best to drive slowly along rough tracks bordered by inter-valled frontier signs, with the ground of Portugal within touching distance on our right hand. With three minds actively considering the problem, finally we agreed upon the area, and the car was halted while each of us painted a mental picture of green-clad riflemen in square and behind sparse cover, with the mounted General Craufurd exhorting and ordering, as fast-moving Light Dragoons of Cotton's cavalry force swooped hither and thither, while Ramsay's guns and limbers thundered on!

Not a strong or well-marked position, the battlefield of Albuera was situ-ated on a long rolling line of low hills which extend for several miles along the Albuera stream. Fordable more or less anywhere by infantry or cavalry, here and there the banks drop ten to twelve feet, so are impass-able to wheels. The French side gently slopes upwards and numerous olive groves prevent other than vague impressions of troop movements; on the north-west (English) bank the rolling slopes are completely bare of trees. There are many 'dips' on the summit of the position and the main battle spot was on the two slopes of one of these dips.

The Albuera stream is formed by two small brooks – the Nogales and the Chicaperna – which meet a little south of the village; there is a low wooded hill between them which conceals from an observer on the British position the upper course of the Nogales and part of the woods beyond. The French formed their order of battle in these woods and Soult hid his main attacking column behind this long low knoll, covered by the more distant woods. Beresford drew up his army in the assumption that, by capturing Albuera village and storming the heights beyond, Soult would

Just inside the entrance gate of fort San Cristobal. Taken to show the outer defences by the side of the main gate.

attempt to penetrate his centre. The slopes are so gentle that nothing can be concealed, except by the woods on the French side; but a dip in the skyline of the English position meant that the French had an imperfect view of the English line near the village of Albuera.

The relatively featureless expanse over which Albuera was fought gives little help when attempting to picture the truly stirring events that took place there. But painstaking study on the ground and considerable map-reading acumen while pacing its deceptive undulations provided a pin-point of the spot where Colborne's battalions were smashed by French cavalry, and the attack area of what was claimed to be the biggest French columnar formation of the entire war.

The field is approached over the bridge beyond the town (village) of Albuera, marked by a huge rectangular white building of some antiquity. The bridge lies unused, having been replaced by a more modern construction and a mini bypass, but standing on the old bridge allows the battlefield to stretch out before the eyes. A road moving off at an angle to the right takes one to the Allied right-flank area. A marked feature of the field is how its shallow undulations must have been adequate to hide formations from each other, so that a group in one hollow would have scant idea of what was befalling their comrades perhaps only 75–100 yards distant.

Unique and unchanged, Ciudad Rodrigo is a National Monument with a strict Preservation Order placed upon it that precludes any major work that might impair it retaining its original appearance. Passing over the bridge spanning the moat and through the heavily fortified gates set amid Vauban-style defence works, it is not hard to believe that were both besiegers and besieged to return to Earth, they would readily recognise the ramparts and vaulted gateways, the narrow winding streets with over-hanging buildings, and the dominating Moorish castle towering over this crowded walled enclave. We were fortunate to see this impressive building both from outside and in, as it is now a state-run Parador. Standing on the ramparts near the castle, one can see to the left the bridge over the river, crossed by Colonel O'Toole's Portuguese, who met up with Mackinnon's Brigade inside the town.

Leaving the town by one of the many gates, one can walk around its outskirts, with the still existing deep moat and out-works between one and the walls still rearing defiantly skywards. Then down into the ditch, gazing upwards at the church and city walls still pockmarked by the roundshot hurled at them from Wellington's siege guns, and note the different masonry that indicates where the breaches were and later filled-in. Climb up onto the Tetons (not without difficulty as it is now a housing estate) and note the relation between the siting of the siege guns

Badajoz. Porta das Palmas

and the walls they were battering. From these parallels where the guns stood, it is possible to trace the flight of their shot to the Greater and Lesser Breaches, tracing grooves made by glancing shots and ricochets on the opposite wall to the original hit-mark. It is all as it must have been on that dreadful dark night of January 1812 and it is here, with the aid of a little imagination, that one can really catch the spirit of the stirring events that occurred. Perhaps the greatest stimulus lays in standing in the Lesser Breach with the awareness that here Black Bob Craufurd was mortally wounded and later buried by a sorrowing party of his men.

If one does not go to any other Peninsular War site, then one MUST see Ciudad Rodrigo, which is satisfying, stimulating and a historical site one is proud to have visited.

We came into Badajoz across the bridge over the River Guadiana, with Fort Cristobal on our left, to the area where, behind the high city walls, the castle ruins loom over the area traversed by Picton's 3rd Division in their attack.

In the heat of mid-morning we traversed the ramparts and into the castle area, found and studied the breaches, and paused to gaze sightlessly

Taken on the site of the breach at Trinidad, looking up towards the town and the castle, in the far background, towards which the attackers, bursting through here, would be surging. I am standing right over or on the site of the centre breach as I take this picture.

The walls of Badajoz. This one is taken from the foot of the wall where Picton's 3rd Division attacked, after crossing the Picturina Brook which is behind me. Also behind me, across the river is Fort Christobal.

into the eye-narrowing bright sunlight as we imagined the turbulent events of the escalade in the fearful darkness of the night of 5/6 April 1812. Then a detailed study of the major breaches, identifiable by areas of obviously repaired wall, into which cannonballs had been imbedded to spell out the year '1812'.

Next we walked right round the outside of the town walls, and studied that part of the defences where Picton's 3rd and Leith's 5th Divisions made their entrance, to take the breach in the rear and capture the town. It was all so clear and so understandable on this unchanged ground, hallowed by the memory of the courage and fortitude of our ancestors, 180 years ago.

Back to the car and across the bridge again, over the River Guadiana and up to Fort Cristobal, laying opposite Badajoz so that a panoramic view of the city walls could be seen – and duly photographed. Fort Cristobal is in ruins yet sufficiently intact for one to get a pretty good idea of its size and importance, enough to resist Wellington's assaults twice, in May and June 1811 – it finally raised the white flag on the day following the fall of Badajoz.

The author has lodged in the pleasant town of Vitoria on more than one occasion, viewed the impressive Peninsular War monument and visited the town museum which displays a very large relief model of the battlefield, among many other military artefacts. The field has been driven over and around at least three times and, on a memorable occasion, it snowed very hard overnight, and we drove out to the field in a veritable blizzard and there was about a foot of snow underfoot when we recklessly decided to ascend the Knoll of Arinez, carried by the 3rd Division and two brigades, under personal command of the Duke, at one stage of the battle. Arinez was no stranger to battle for, on that same hill on 22 March 1367, a small English force of about 100 knights, men-at-arms, and archers, under command of dark foppish Sir Thomas Felton and his stout brother William, fought almost to the last man against some 6,000 French and Aragonese, commanded by Don Tello and the French Marshal D'Andrehen. Today, the hill is known locally as *Alture de los Ingleses* – Englishman's Hill. In his wonderful book *The White Company*, the writer Conan Doyle has his hero, Sir Nigel Loring, fight on the hill with the Feltons, and be taken prisoner. However, back to the present, from

Vitoria. The bridge at Tres Puntes over which Picton attacked.

The Hill of Arinez at Vitoria, taken from a knoll in the loop of the river by the bridge at Nanclares.

the summit of the knoll a good view of the field is obtained, and salient points can be orientated from the map.

The bridge at Nanclares is still there, presumably just as it was on 21 June 1813 when Wellington rode over it at the head of Lowry Cole's 4th Division; so is Trois Puntes, albeit in ruins and replaced by a more modern bridge, where the impatient Picton aggressively led his 3rd Division into the fray. The heights of Pueblo, where Hill's men performed wonders, and the hills north of the town of Vitoria from which Graham's flanking force came, are still there, unchanged and waiting to be walked.

There was a memorable occasion when folders, maps, binoculars and cameras set up a frightening confrontation in Spain, when visiting Wellington's 1813 battlefield of Vitoria. The picnic lunch was unwittingly set-up on a wooded ridge overlooking a high-security prison holding numerous Basque terrorists, which gave rise to a dramatic invasion by soldiers bearing automatic rifles, guard dogs, and police cars at the base of the ridge, with crews of stony-faced Garda, made awesome by dark glasses and unbuttoned pistol holsters. Fortunately, commonsense eventually told them that four middle-aged Englishmen were unlikely to be bent upon 'springing' Basque prisoners from their barbed-wired and watch-towered prison. However, it remains a memorable item in our annals!

Nostalgically, the author recalls visiting Roncesvalles one April when the snow lay on the ground, so much so that the Spanish driver of the coach took one look at the snowplough working on the icebound road, and refused to go any further! So, leaving the coach in the village at the foot of the Pass,we trudged up the slippery road to the mist-enshrouded summit where, nearly a thousand years before, Roland the Paladin had held the Pass for Charlemagne. In 1813 there was considerable action in the area, amid a countryside so rugged, torn and heavily wooded that one achieved an increased respect for the men who fought over it and for their

The land-bridge at Sorauren over which Maucune or Reille attacked onto Cole's right flank and were then attacked themselves in the flank by Anson.

commanders, who were able to keep a perhaps tenuous hold on operations far beyond their range of vision.

Marshal Soult personally accompanied Clausel's three divisions on the march over the old Roman road from St Jean Pied de Port to the Pass of Roncesvalles. Here the allies were out-numbered about seven to one but the terrain favoured them, as was discovered by the French near the Altobiscar Pass, where they were halted in their tracks by three light companies of Byng's Brigade plus a company of 5/60th Rifles and some Spanish light infantry. This force, not more than 500 strong, deployed on a front of 300 yards with deep flanking valleys falling away on either side, held them off.

The other flank lay west of the modern road and we struck off it by the chapel, to begin a steady climb on narrow rocky paths through what appeared to be a game reserve with shooting boxes concealed in the undergrowth. Eventually reaching the foot of the Linduz Peak (1,065 metres above sea-level) we began the climb until reaching the plateau atop the Linduz. Here, high above the Pass, lies a very well-preserved and defined earthwork, with ditch, walls and entrance gates area.

On all sides, the terrain spread out until vanishing in mist, with the Bay of Biscay gleaming distantly to the west. We looked for and found the ridge-top mule-track running back towards France on which the 20,000 men of Reille's three divisions painfully worked their way forward, sometimes in single-file or two-abreast and so stretched that when the leading troops made contact with Ross's troops the rear of the French column was eleven miles back! At first fighting was confused, then, between four and five o'clock in the afternoon, a thick mist began rolling in from the Bay of Biscay – forcing both sides to cease fighting. They bivouacked within hearing distance of each other.

Leaving our base at Sare in the French Pyrenees, we crossed the border into Spain near Vera and, travelling at a speed far faster than the Duke's fine horse, moved south on the same road as used by him in 1813, through

Cole's centre at Sorauren, held by Campbell's Brigade with Stubbs in support. Picture taken from the position.

Almandoz – where he spent the night 26/27 July 1813 – and over the Pass at Velate. Here we branched off on a side road, taking us to the little village of Lizaso where, throughout the evening and night 26/27 July, 14,000 weary and hungry men of Pack's 6th Division had tramped in, soaked to the skin by the thunderstorm that had been raging for hours. We pictured them, grousing as only the British soldier can truly do, stumbling around in the darkness, huddling together against walls and in alleys of this small Spanish village, where the old houses still cluster around the dominating church – it is possible to distinguish old from modern by the markedly contrasting roof styles.

Aware that we were travelling on the same road as the Duke and Fitzroy Somerset (QMG Murray had been left at Lizaso) we hastened, as he did, to the little stone bridge over the River Ulzama at Sorauren, where we halted to savour the emotion of knowing we were standing on exactly the same spot as the Duke when he unhurriedly wrote his message and despatched Somerset back to Lizaso with it. The Duke, aware that French light troops had entered the village to his left, had seen above him, crowning the rocky ridge, the red and brown tunics of British and Portuguese.

Owning no fine mount like that of the Duke's, it was hard climbing the rough track leading up from the bridge to the east–west ridge – 2,000 feet high and 1.5 miles long – where, on the Allied left, five brigades of Cole's Division were thrust well forward, the chapel at the end being garrisoned by the 7th Portuguese Cacadores. It was these Portuguese troops who, seeing the familiar figure of the Duke breasting the steep slope, had raised the echoing cry 'Douro! Douro!' Alone on the hillside, and meriting no such greeting, we raised it ourselves – our dual cries, albeit somewhat breathless, resounded on the still, warm air! By the time we reached the crest of Cole's Ridge, we had acquired a wholesome respect for any horse that could gallop up that slope. Regaining our breath in the ruins of the little chapel that had been held by the Portuguese, we surveyed the rugged ridges and the mountainous terrain surrounding us on all sides.

In truth, the author recognises Sorauren as a battle possessing so much interest and stimulation as to vie with the Coa, Roncesvalles, and Agincourt as being among the most evocative battlefields he has ever walked.

Today, San Sebastián is a pleasant seaside town fronted by a picturesque bay; it is a fascinating mixture of narrow old streets and modern boulevards with smart shops and hotels. Most interesting is the old town below the castle, rebuilt after the siege, a maze of alleys and courts abounding in colourful bars and restaurants.

It is an arduous climb to the summit of Mount Orgul, on which is perched the impressive castle which dominates the town, as it has done for centuries. But the effort is well worthwhile if only to see the panoramic view across the beautiful bay. But more important, because one is looking down from the lofty height it is easy to visualise the assault of 31 August 1813 – that same day on which Soult chose to make his abortive attacks across the River Bidassoa, when Captain Dan Cadoux immortalised himself on the bridge at Vera. It is clear that the only feasible assault approach was over the low sandy isthmus bordering the front of the forti-fied town which was small and compact then, about 400 yards square, and some 600 yards from the mainland on a promontory bordered by the River Urumea on the east and a land-locked bay on its other sides; nestling around the foot of lofty Monte Orgul, it had about 10,000 inhab-itants. In 1813 it was encircled by a high wall backed by new earthworks, part being an older massive wall rising sheer from the river, which was fordable at low tide; above the town the fortified rocky mountain was crowned by an old castle. There is no trace of the walls today, but other-wise this part of the town is much the same; the castle is in good condition and houses an interesting military museum that was closed for repair on this occasion, but had been visited in the past when with the Military Historical Society party. From the castle high on the mountain the limits of the old town can be detected, having been rebuilt on the same site after being burned down in 1813; different architecture and roof styles reveal where the old town ends and new town begins. The local museum in the old monastery of St Elmo contains a large model of the town in the eigh-teenth century which confirms this.

Not far from Fuentes de Oñoro is the small village of Freinada where, in 1811, Wellington and his staff had their headquarters in a house that still stands and is lived in. On one occasion thirty British battlefield walkers descended upon the place, to create considerable tumult but also to be welcomed effusively! Taken into the house, we were invited to view the connecting residences of three families and to crowd into Wellington's personal room. Discussions ensued between the local schoolmaster, who lived in part of the house, and those in the party connected officially with the British Military Historical Society, as to the chances of having a commemorative plaque installed. Revisiting Freinada some years later, the author was both gratified and proud to find just such a plaque set in the wall of the house!

Crossing the Spanish frontier at Hendaye, we drove along the side of the ravine in which flowed the River Bidassoa until we came to the village of Vera. Hearts in mouths, the party walked along the pavementless street with huge trucks thundering past throwing up clouds of dust, so that we were glad to branch-off to the right, down a hedge-bordered track between houses that led to the banks of the river – and the bridge.

We stood in the centre of the bridge, gazing at the commemorative plaque set in its wall, which read:

> To the Glory of God and in memory of Captain Daniel Cadoux and his gallant riflemen of the 2nd Battalion 95th (Rifle Brigade) who, on 1st September 1813, fell gloriously defending this bridge against the fierce attacks of a French division – 'His fame can never die', Sir Harry Smith.

In Spanish, the wording is similar until the end, where it says: '. . . died defending this bridge . . . for the independence of Spain and allied to his heroic Spanish companions'.

On a very hot afternoon, the party set out for the battlefield, managing to climb a high ridge on which lay the main French defence, the Star Redoubt. We knew where it was but could not actually find it because the whole area is now covered with a quite impenetrable forest of prickly conifers – however, we explored an extensive modern defence system without knowing whether it was mid-twentieth-century French against possible invasion from Spain, or the reverse, or perhaps connected with the Spanish Civil War.

Gazing into the misty distance, we saw the Battlefield of Vera spread out before us; immediately to the front was the two-mile-long Bayonet Ridge, extending almost back into the village of Vera, and to our left the unmistakeable high-humped Hog's Back; all surmounted by the Lesser and Greater Rhunes on the skyline.

On another occasion, we did discover the Star Redoubt, its conifer-covering seemingly having been cut down; it needs imagination to achieve satisfaction because all that remains are shallow pits, about two feet deep, but covering sufficient ground in the right place to unmistakably be the Star Redoubt.

There can be little in the way of battlefield walking that approaches those grim rocky fortifications perched on the summit of the Lesser Rhune, nestling under the protective shadow of its big brother, the Greater Rhune. Three times has the author ascended the little rack railway, and then tramped past herds of wild ponies, up the slope to where the Light Division lay-up during the night of 9/10th November 1813 – and three times has the all-enveloping mist rolled in from the sea and made descending a hazardous business! But what memories it conjures up!

Never a general to miss a chance, Soult noting that the Duke's forces were divided by the River Nive, decided to try and defeat each separately by refusing battle WEST of the river while hurling 60,000 men (nine infantry divisions, cavalry and forty guns) against Hope to the East.

Directed at Wellington's bridge of boats at Urdain, four French infantry divisions advanced at dawn against Light Division picquets and outposts; in the running fight that followed in wooded valleys and enclosures, the battle-hardened and confident 95th Rifles, 43rd and 52nd Regiments supported each other by firing and running, then forming-up on every open area to throw back advancing French columns with rolling volley fire. Finally they reached the ridge at Arcangues where they occupied the walled church and a château, against which French attacks sputtered out like waves against a sea-wall.

Quite unchanged and still marked by battle scars, the church at Arcangues is stimulating ground to tread. It is built in Basque style with two balconies above the nave; as the wall around the churchyard is lower than the nave, the 43rd were able to pack into the church and its yard to fire from FOUR protected levels – the wall, the floor and both balconies. Their massed musketry so demoralised a French artillery battery *400 yards away* that the gunners eventually abandoned their pieces.

Part Five

South Africa – The Zulu War 1879

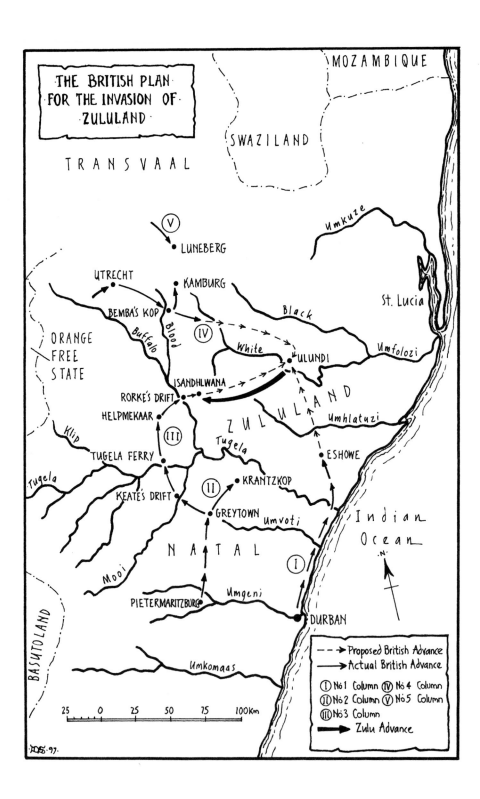

THE BRITISH PLAN
FOR THE INVASION OF
ZULULAND

MOZAMBIQUE

SWAZILAND

TRANSVAAL

Ⓥ
LUNEBERG

Umkuze

St. Lucia

UTRECHT
KAMBURG

BEMBA'S KOP
Black

Buffalo
Blood
Ⓘⓥ
White
ULUNDI
Umfolozi

ORANGE
FREE
STATE

ISANDHLWANA

RORKE'S DRIFT
Z U L U L A N D

HELPMEKAAR
Umhlatuzi

Klip
Ⓘⓘⓘ
Tugela
ESHOWE

TUGELA FERRY

Tugela
KEATE'S DRIFT
Ⓘⓘ
KRANTZKOP

GREYTOWN
Umvoti
Indian
Ocean

N A T A L

Mooi
Ⓘ

PIETERMARITZBURG
Umgeni

DURBAN

BASUTOLAND

Umkomaas

25   0   25   50   75   100Km

- - - → Proposed British Advance
———→ Actual British Advance
Ⓘ Nô1 Column Ⓘⓥ Nô4 Column
Ⓘⓘ Nô2 Column Ⓥ Nô5 Column
Ⓘⓘⓘ Nô3 Column
━━▶ Zulu Advance

15 *The Course of the War*

Sir Bartle Frere, the High Commissioner, was convinced that the Zulu nation should be restrained. He therefore demanded unacceptable conditions from Cetewayo, the Zulu Chief. When these were not answered in early 1879, Great Britain declared war on the Zulu nation. Before this, preparations for the forthcoming war had been taking place in the Colony of Natal and a large force was gathered together under the command of Lieutenant-General Lord Chelmsford. It consisted of 7 regiments of British regular infantry; 2 squadrons of mounted infantry; 1 naval brigade; 2 companies of Royal Engineers; 800 Colonial volunteers and police; 300 native horsemen, and a native infantry contingent about 9,000 strong, totalling 6,639 imperial and colonial troops; there were 9,035 natives with 802 conductors and drivers in charge of the 700 wagons that formed the transport train.

The force was to enter Zululand in five columns at different points, concentrating on Ulundi, the capital. Lord Chelmsford attached himself and his staff to the strongest and most important third column, made up of the 1st and 2nd Battalions 24th Regiment: 1 Squadron of mounted infantry; about 200 Natal volunteers; 150 Natal Police; 2 Battalions of the native contingent; some native Pioneers and 6 Royal Artillery guns. Crossing the Buffalo River on 11 January the column moved slowly forward, constructing roads for the guns and transport over swamps and heavy ground. It was not until 20 January that camp was pitched at the foot of the Isandhlwana Hill; the tents and long lines of picketed horses were in regular order, but the wagons that should have been ranged end-to-end around the camp to form a laager were drawn up uselessly in line in the rear.

Receiving information that large numbers of the enemy were on a range of hills about twelve miles away, Chelmsford marched out at daylight on 22 January with the 2nd Battalion 24th Regiment, the mounted infantry and four guns. Lieutenant-Colonel Pulleine was left in command of the camp with 6 companies of the 24th, 2 guns of the Royal Artillery, and about 80 mounted men and 4 companies of the native contingent reinforced during the morning when Colonel Durnford rode in with some of the second column and the rocket-battery. Reports began to come in of large numbers of the enemy approaching from all directions, and so Durnford took to the front of the position two troops of Natal native horsemen and the rocket-battery, escorted by a company of the native contingent. Coming upon large bodies of rapidly moving Zulus about five miles from the camp, he extended his men and opened a steady fire but was forced into a steady retreat by overwhelming numbers, while the rocket-battery, deserted by its escort, was overrun and slain to a man. Sorely pressed, Durnford's men disputed every inch of ground until they made a desperate last stand in a dried-up river bed near the camp.

The Zulus attacked the camp in a half-circle, with another force pushing round the English left to cut the wagon road and line of retreat to Rorke's Drift. The defenders were firing steadily and to good effect while the guns, which had been firing shell, now poured in case-shot at close quarters. At this the Zulus wavered and the wide-swept horns of

The defence of Rorke's Drift, 22 January 1879.

their army worked their way round the flanks to show themselves in the rear of the English position just at the moment when the native contingent broke and fled in disorder, laying open the right and rear of the 24th. The firing began to slacken, because reserve ammunition boxes were screwed down and could not be opened. The Zulus poured through the fatal gap in the line and the English soldiers were lost in the middle of a fierce hand-to-hand conflict as horse and foot, English and Zulu, struggled slowly in confused groups through the camp towards the road to Rorke's Drift. Surrounded by bodies, the 24th stood their ground and fought to the last man, while fleet-footed Zulus chased fugitives trying to reach the river. More than 1,300 Europeans and natives were lost in this action, but at least 2,000 Zulus were killed and hundreds wounded.

Shortly after 3 pm on 22 January, mounted fugitives from Isandhlwana

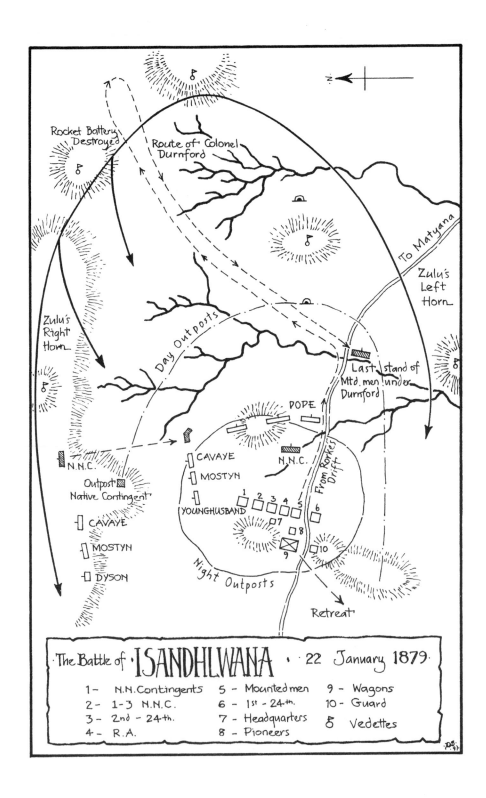

The Battle of ISANDHLWANA · 22 January 1879 ·

1 – N.N.Contingents	5 – Mounted men	9 – Wagons
2 – 1-3 N.N.C.	6 – 1st - 24th.	10 - Guard
3 – 2nd - 24th.	7 – Headquarters	8 Vedettes
4 – R.A.	8 - Pioneers	

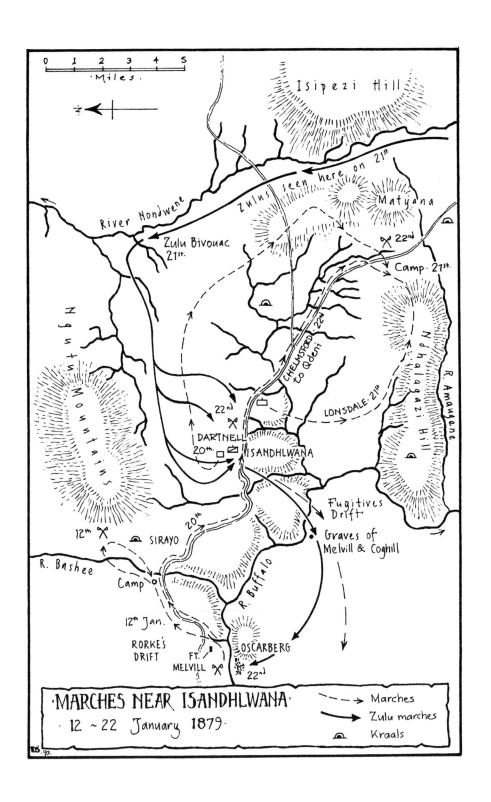

MARCHES NEAR ISANDHLWANA
12 ~ 22 January 1879

– – →	Marches
→	Zulu marches
⌂	Kraals

Isipezi Hill

Zulus seen here on 21st

Matyana

River Nondwene

Zulu Bivouac 21st.

✕ 22nd

Camp. 21st.

Ngutu Mountains

CHELMSFORD 22nd to Qdeni

LONSDALE · 21st

Ndhalagazi Hill

R. Amauene

22nd ✕

DARTNELL

20th.

ISANDHLWANA

Fugitives Drift

Graves of Melvill & Coghill

12th ✕

⌂ SIRAYO

20th

R. Bashee

Camp

R. Buffalo

OSCARBERG

12th Jan.

RORKE'S DRIFT

FT. MELVILL ✕

22nd

galloped into Rorke's Drift to tell the story of the disaster and to report that a large force of Zulus was now advancing on the post. A mission station of two stone buildings with thatched roofs at a crossing point of the Buffalo River, Rorke's Drift was in direct line of communication with Natal. It was garrisoned by a company of the 2nd Battalion 24th Regiment under Lieutenant Bromhead and Lieutenant Chard of the Royal Engineers. In the small hospital were some sick and wounded men.

Chard hastily ordered the place to be put in a state of defence; the walls were to be loop-holed and barricaded, and parapets were to be built up from bags of mealies around overturned ox-wagons. A company of native infantry, part of the garrison of the Drift, fled on hearing of the approach of the Zulus so that the strength of the force was 128, of whom thirty-five were sick or wounded men in hospital. About 4,000 Zulus appeared at 4.30 pm and from then until after midnight the post was continuously attacked. During the course of the conflict, repeated attacks drove back the desperately fighting defenders until they were confined to one building and an enclosure with a redoubt of mealie bags. The hospital, defended to the last by its patients, was set on fire and provided the light by which the fighting took place until the small hours of the morning, when the Zulus retired, carrying away their wounded and leaving about 400 dead around the post. The garrison lost seventeen killed and twelve wounded. Lieutenants Chard and Bromhead, together with nine other soldiers, received the Victoria Cross for their gallantry.

Alarmed by the sound of firing, Chelmsford's force had returned to Isandhlwana to spend an anxious night amid the ruins of the camp. Next morning the men marched towards Rorke's Drift expecting to find the post burned to the ground and its garrison slain, but they discovered that its defence had secured the Colony of Natal from invasion. Chelmsford's despatches reached London in February and accelerated the sending of powerful reinforcements. In South Africa, colonial troops undertook duties at Capetown and set free the regular garrison; the warship *Shah* embarked the St Helena garrison and sailed for Durban, providing an immediate force of 650 men including 300 bluejackets, while the movement orders of the 57th Regiment were cancelled and the troops were sent to Natal.

At the end of January three fortified posts guarded the frontier of Natal: Colonel Wood had a well-entrenched camp at Kambula Hill and the remains of the third column held Rorke's Drift, now heavily fortified, while Colonel Pearson, at Etshowe with about 1,200 European soldiers, was right in the middle of occupied territory and had either to be reinforced or relieved. Deciding on the latter, on 27 March Chelmsford sent out a column formed of the 57th and 91st Regiments; 6 companies of the 60th; 5 companies of the 99th and 2 companies of the 3rd Regiment; a naval brigade; a squadron of mounted infantry; 2 field-guns; 4 rocket tubes and 2 Gatling guns, making 3,390 Europeans and 2,230 natives, with 122 wagons. Over a comparatively open route, the column marched cautiously in the closest possible order, surrounded by a screen of mounted troops and bivouacking at night in a laager of wagons. On the third day, 31 March, large bodies of Zulus were seen and an attack was anticipated at the Gingihlovo stream where the British laagered for the night. At daybreak, two dense columns of Zulus came rapidly in sight on the further side of the river crossing at different points and deploying into a wide and loose order, while at the same time another force came in to attack the southern and western faces of the defences. The Gatling guns opened fire at 1,000 yards and, although frequently jamming, knocked over numbers of Zulus but failed to stop their advance. When the leading lines of Zulus got within 300 yards, a sudden sheet of flame burst from the English position and lines of natives fell as though swept down by a scythe. From the cover afforded by the long grass, the Zulus kept up a heavy but erratic rifle fire with the weapons they had captured at Isandhlwana; attack after attack was made with despairing courage. None got to close quarters; the Zulus were blasted by withering and steady volleys until they were scattered in confusion all over the plain. Chelmsford now launched the cavalry at the Zulu flank and the little band of horsemen put the enemy groups to hasty and disordered flight. British losses were eleven killed and fifty-two wounded in this action, which made it possible for Pearson's garrison at Etshowe to be relieved and withdrawn to Tugela.

Colonel Evelyn Wood at Kambula made a diversion in the north in order to draw away forces who might have opposed the march to Etshowe, planning an audacious operation calculated to draw a large Zulu force in reprisal. He attacked the Inhloblane mountain some twenty miles from Kambula; this was a table-top eminence about three miles long with precipitous sides, with the only access to the summit being a few difficult paths winding through rocks; it was commanded at every point by strong positions of defence in caves and overhanging heights. It was occupied by a powerful Zulu tribe whose kraals were perched on an almost inaccessible terrace. The attack was entrusted to the mounted troops, divided into two parties: 400 white men and 277 natives under Lieutenant-Colonel Redvers Buller went against the eastern end and formed the main attacking force, while 200 white men and 440 natives under Lieutenant-Colonel Russell created a diversion at the other end of the mountain.

The two forces left Kambula and on 28 March, under cover of a morning mist, Buller's party made a successful surprise assault up a narrow and very steep path, and the Zulus were routed in disorder on all sides, but just as Buller was about to withdraw from the heights a Zulu army was seen moving swiftly towards the Kambula camp. Colonel Wood ordered Russell's force to a point where it could cover Buller's

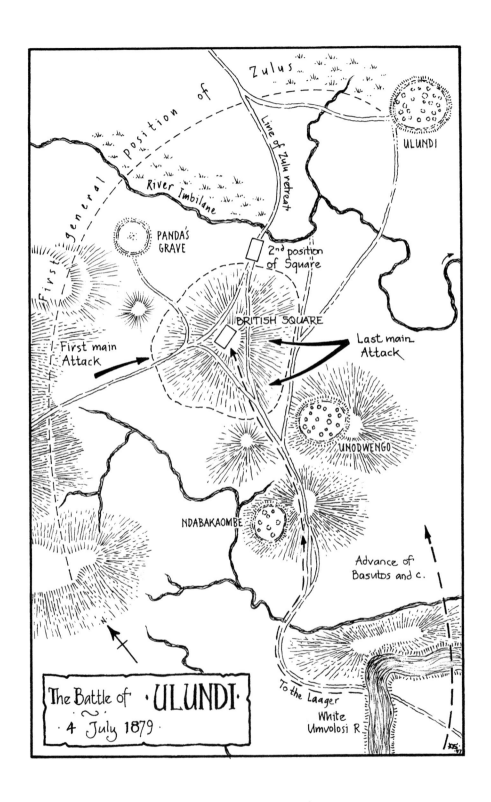

Zulus

ULUNDI

First general position of

Line of Zulu retreat

River Imbilane

PANDA'S GRAVE

2nd position of Square

BRITISH SQUARE

First main Attack

Last main Attack

UNODWENGO

NDABAKAOMBE

Advance of Basutos and c.

To the Laager
White Umvolosi R.

The Battle of · ULUNDI ·
· 4 July 1879 ·

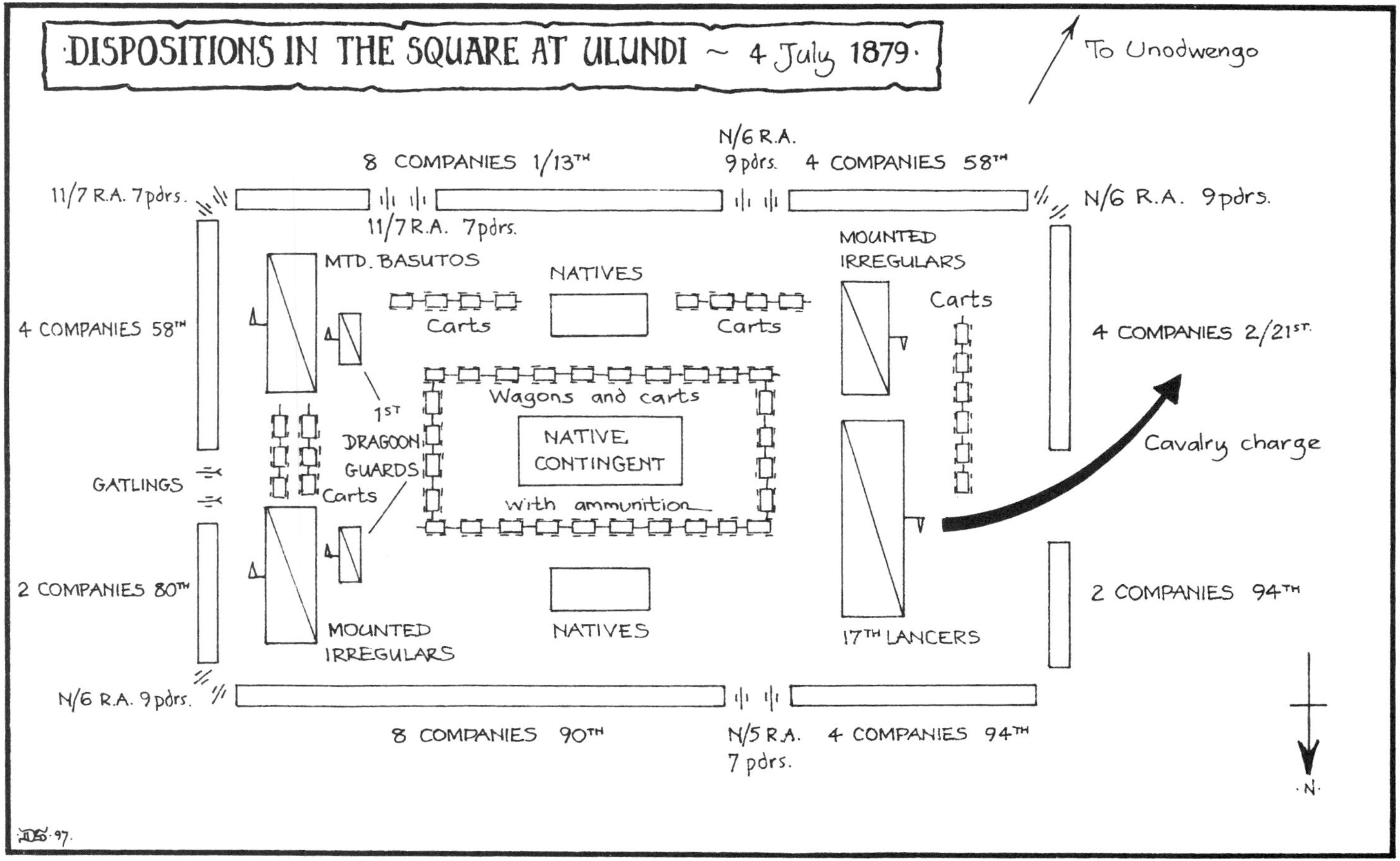

DISPOSITIONS IN THE SQUARE AT ULUNDI ~ 4 July 1879.

To Unodwengo

N

N/6 R.A. 9 pdrs.

4 COMPANIES 2/21ST.

Cavalry charge

2 COMPANIES 94TH

N/6 R.A. 9 pdrs.

4 COMPANIES 58TH

MOUNTED IRREGULARS

Carts

17TH LANCERS

N/6 R.A. 9 pdrs.

N/5 R.A. 7 pdrs.

4 COMPANIES 94TH

8 COMPANIES 1/13TH

11/7 R.A. 7 pdrs.

MTD. BASUTOS

NATIVES

Carts

Carts

1ST DRAGOON GUARDS

Carts

MOUNTED IRREGULARS

Wagons and carts

NATIVE CONTINGENT

with ammunition

NATIVES

8 COMPANIES 90TH

11/7 R.A. 7 pdrs.

4 COMPANIES 58TH

GATLINGS

2 COMPANIES 80TH

N/6 R.A. 9 pdrs.

DGS '97.

retreat, but it went to the wrong place and took no further part in the operations. On the upper plateau, the heartened natives began to press very heavily upon the small party, leaving them as their only line of retreat a precipitous path at the western end of the plateau, down which many of the horses, although African bred and therefore surefooted, fell headlong from top to bottom. Buller was encumbered with wounded men and many of his horses had been killed, but he conducted the retreat with steadiness and heroism. With his Frontier Light Horse and a Boer contingent, he led the rearguard that held the enemy in check until the party reached level ground and were able to make their way back to Kambula.

On 29 March, the Zulu army attacked the Kambula position defended by just over 2,000 men of all arms, including natives and sick. It consisted of a large wagon laager surrounding a hospital and stores, with a strong redoubt holding three companies of the men on a small knoll about 150 yards to the west. The Zulu army attacked with its right wing circling round the camp to the north and centre; the left wing kept to the south, out of artillery range. To prevent the whole Zulu army from delivering a simultaneous combined attack, Wood sent Buller and Russell out with the mounted men to tempt the Zulu right wing to a premature engagement. Pursued by the fleet-footed Zulus, the small party retreated to the camp until they drew the enemy within range, when the artillery opened fire. Committed to the attack, the Zulus pressed on and, in spite of inflicting heavy losses, did not get closer than 200 yards to the laager and redoubt. The Zulu centre and left assaulted the west and south of the camp, taking advantage of the broken ground that sheltered them from rifle fire, but Wood threw in a counter-attack of two companies of the 80th Regiment, whose massed musketry forced the Zulus back. Throughout the day they made attack after attack, each being beaten back by sheer weight of fire until in the late afternoon they began to retire, hotly pursued by Buller and his mounted men who kept pace with the running Zulus whilst maintaining a ceaseless and galling fire from the saddle in a pursuit that lasted more than seven miles. The British force lost twenty-eight killed and fifty-five wounded in this operation.

By the end of June, Lord Chelmsford had been strongly reinforced by four generals, two regiments of cavalry, two batteries of artillery, five battalions of infantry, and strong detachments of the Engineers and the Service Corps. Slowly and in the face of little opposition the force marched towards the Zulu king's kraal at Ulundi. On 3 July, Chelmsford crossed the Umvolosi River into open country with his force of 4,166 Europeans and 958 natives with twelve guns and two Gatlings, marching in a hollow square with the native contingent, ammunition and tool-carts in the centre; the force was screened by the cavalry, scouting wide on either side. When they were within a mile and a half of Ulundi, the Zulus began to mass and move towards the huge square, which halted with every man facing outwards, the cavalry falling back and entering its protection.

Erratically firing their captured rifles, the Zulus advanced in a great converging circle. The artillery opened fire and shells were soon exploding with great effect amongst the masses of Zulus advancing over the open ground. When the natives came within rifle range, steady and well-aimed infantry volleys began to take their toll and the Gatlings, though impeded by frequent jamming, rattled out showers of bullets. Prevented from making contact by sheer weight of fire, the Zulus began to waver and fall back. Chelmsford sent out the 17th Lancers to sweep down upon the now fleeing Zulus in a well-timed charge that turned the defeat into a hopeless rout. Buller and his mounted riflemen followed and the small knots of Zulus were scattered and overthrown. It was estimated that more than 20,000 Zulus were in the field at Ulundi and that their losses exceeded 1,500. The English lost thirteen men killed and seventy-eight wounded.

Sir Garnet Wolseley had been sent out to supersede Lord Chelmsford, but to all intents and purposes the war was over when he arrived, although Cetewayo himself was not captured until 29 August.

16 *The Battle at Rorke's Drift 22/23 January 1879*

It is a relief to turn from the contemplation of this disastrous field (Isandhlwana) – a field which might verily be called the Field of Blood – to consider the noble heroism of those who, behind their extempore entrench-ments at Rorke's Drift, repeated, with greater success, something of the glories of Thermopylae. They knew perfectly well what would follow upon any failure on their part, and they were prepared, if need were, to sacrifice their lives to the last man in order to gain time for some temporary rep-aration of the previous days' disaster. Unless the gap had been stopped by their heroic resistance the whole northern portion of the Colony would probably by this time have been laid waste. They have done a deed which will live for ever in the military history of their country, and which may be placed side by side with any of those achievements of which Englishmen are rightly proud.

(*The Natal Witness*, 28 January 1879)

On 22/23 January 1879, a puny force of 128 British soldiers defending a hastily fortified mission station in South Africa, held out for twelve hours against almost continuous onslaughts by some 4,000 Zulu warriors. The name of the remote outpost was Rorke's Drift, and it has since been hallowed as symbolising one of the most heroic stands in the annals of military history. Individual acts of gallantry resulted in the award of eleven Victoria Crosses – the highest number ever conferred in a single action. Seven of these went to the 2nd Battalion of the 24th Regiment, whose 'B' Company formed the main garrison.

The post at Rorke's Drift was a Swedish Mission Station which had been taken over by the military and used as a Base Hospital and magazine for stores. It was situated on the Natal side of the Buffalo River from which it was approximately 800 yards. About 400 yards behind it was a rocky hill – the Oskarberg – which overlooked the station.

On the extreme left (west) stood the hospital, a single-storey building about seventy-five feet long, under a thatched roof with a verandah running the entire length of its 'front', which faced the river. The interior rooms formed several wards. About thirty yards to the right (east) of the hospital was the Mission House which had been converted into a magazine. Still further to the right was a stoutly constructed stone kraal

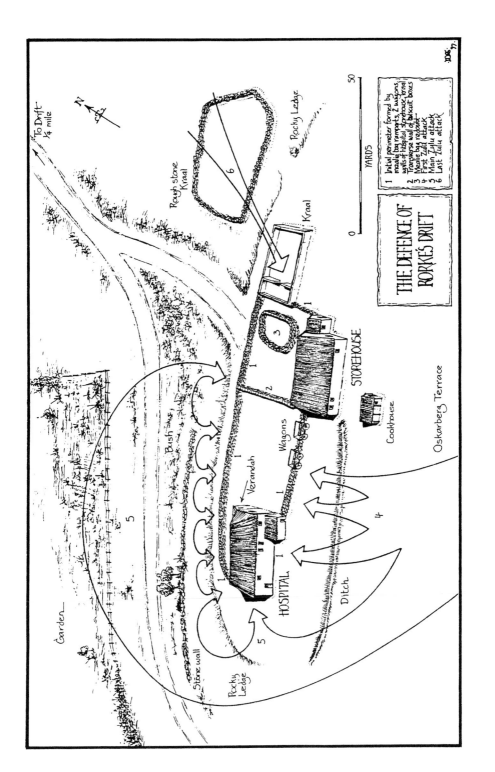

THE DEFENCE OF
RORKE'S DRIFT

YARDS

0   50

1   Initial perimeter formed by mealie bag ramparts, 2 wagons, walls of hospital, storehouse, kraal
2   Transverse wall of biscuit boxes
3   Mealie bag redoubt
4   First Zulu attack
5   Main Zulu attack
6   Last Zulu attack

To Drift
¼ mile

N

Rough stone Kraal

Rocky Ledge

Kraal

STOREHOUSE

Cookhouse

Oskarberg Terrace

Wagons

Verandah

HOSPITAL

Ditch

Store wall

Rocky Ledge

Garden

Bush

divided by a wall into two pens, while further east from this was another larger cattle kraal. Behind the hospital and about twelve yards from it ran a ditch with a two-foot bank along its entire length, and behind the magazine was a small cookhouse.

When, on the morning of 22 January, Colonel Durnford had been summoned by Lord Chelmsford to leave Rorke's Drift and take command at Isandhlwana when the bulk of the force marched out, Lieutenant Chard (5th Company, Royal Engineers) had been left in command of the post at Rorke's Drift. His force consisted of about 128 men, chiefly of 2/24th Regiment, many of whom were sick patients in the Mission Station Hospital. It was never considered that this site would ever need to be defended, for which it was quite unsuited.

The soldiers at the post had heard the firing coming from the direction of Isandhlwana with intense curiosity, but only found out what it signified at about 3.15 pm, when Lieutenant Adendorff of Lonsdale's Native Contingent and a Natal Carbineer Lieutenant Sibthorpe, galloped up. Adendorff stopped at the river to warn Lieutenant Chard of the impending arrival of a Zulu force and told him of the disaster at Isandhlwana; Sibthorpe raced on to Helpmekkar to warn the base camp. Chard and his fellow subaltern, Lieutenant G Bromhead, commander B Company, 2nd Battalion, 24th Regiment, immediately set to work fortifying the mission station, constructing a defensive perimeter; the windows

The Battle of Rorke's Drift, 22 January 1879
Painting by Alfonse de Neuville

of the hospital and magazine were barricaded and the walls pierced with loopholes. A breastwork about four feet high, running between the two buildings, was constructed from mealie bags, and biscuit boxes made a wall extending from the western corner of the magazine to the northern mealie-bag breastwork.

As the Zulu regiments of Dabulamanzi, Cetewayo's brother, advanced swiftly on the post, linking arms to cross the river like a monstrous black water snake in their eagerness to wash their spears, the little garrison worked furiously. At 4.30 pm, Private Wall, on lookout duty on top of the Oskarberg behind the post, warned of the enemy's arrival with a memorable cry: 'Here they come . . . black as hell and thick as grass!' The attack, expected from the front, was even more threatening as the Zulus, by crossing the river higher up, were able to encircle the post.

At this point, a company of the Natal Native Contingent, stationed at the river with orders to withdraw to the defences when the enemy approached, fled the scene and were immediately followed by the rest of their comrades from within the post. This lessening of numbers was tackled by building a low barricade across the enclosure. Almost at once, the Zulus came flooding round the foot of the Oskarberg to attack the south of the post.

In the heat of an action, his attention fixed on what is happening to his front, it is rare for any soldier to be able to give an accurate account of the battle in which he is fighting. But this was no normal battle, being a closely confined struggle with every man within sight of his surrounding comrades. Perhaps one of the most authentic accounts of the Defence of Rorke's Drift was that of Private Henry Hook, of B Company, 2/24th whose gallantry and strength in saving wounded in the burning hospital earned him the Victoria Cross. The following account by Private Hook was published in *The Royal Magazine* of February 1905 under the title 'How they held Rorke's Drift'.

> Everything was perfectly quiet at Rorke's Drift after the column (Durnford's force) had left, and every officer and man was going about his business as usual. Not a soul suspected that only a dozen miles away the very men that we had said 'Goodbye', and 'Good luck' to were either dead or standing back-to-back in a last fierce fight with the Zulus. Our garrison consisted of B Company of the 2/24th under Lieutenant Bromhead, and details which brought the total number of us up to 139. Besides these, we had about 300 men of the Natal Contingent; but they didn't count, as they bolted in a body when the fight began. We were all knocking about, and I was making tea for the sick, as I was Hospital Cook at the time.
>
> Suddenly, there was a commotion in the camp, and we saw two men galloping towards us from the other side of the river, which was Zululand. Lieutenant Chard of the Engineers was protecting the ponts over the river

and, as senior officer, was in command at the drift. The ponts were very simple affairs, one of them being supported on big barrels, and the other on boats. Lieutenant Bromhead was in the camp itself. The horsemen shouted and were brought across the river, and then we knew what had happened to our comrades. They had been butchered to a man. That was awful enough news, but worse was to follow, for we were told that the Zulus were coming straight on from Isandhlwana to attack us. At the same time a note was received by Lieutenant Bromhead from the Column to say that the enemy was coming on, and that the post was to be held at all costs.

For some little time we were all stunned, then everything changed from perfect quietness to intense excitement and energy. There was a general feeling that the only safe thing was to retire and try to join the troops at Helpmakaar. The horsemen had said that the Zulus would be up in two or three minutes; but luckily for us they did not show themselves for more than an hour. Lieutenant Chard rushed up from the river, about a quarter of a mile away, and saw Lieutenant Bromhead. Orders were given to strike the camp and make ready to go, and we actually loaded up two waggons. Then Mr Dalton, of the Commissariat Department, came up and said that if we left the drift every man was certain to be killed. He had formerly been a sergeant-major in a line regiment and was one of the bravest men that ever lived. Lieutenants Chard and Bromhead held a consultation, short and earnest, and orders were given that we were to get the hospital and store-house ready for defence, and that we were never to say die or surrender.

Not a minute was lost. Lieutenant Bromhead superintended the loopholing and barricading of the hospital and storehouse, and the making of a connection of the defences between the two buildings with walls of mealie-bags and waggons. The mealie bags were good big heavy things, weighing about 200 pounds each, and during the fight many of them were burst open by assegais and bullets, and the mealies (Indian corn) were thickly spread about the ground.

The biscuit boxes contained ordinary biscuit. They were big, square, wooden boxes, weighing about a hundredweight each. The meat boxes, too, were very heavy, as they contained tinned meat. They were smaller than the biscuit boxes. While these preparations were being made, Lieutenant Chard went down to the river and brought in the pont guard of a sergeant and half-a-dozen men, with the waggons and gear. The two officers saw that every soldier was at his post then we were ready for the Zulus when they cared to come.

They were not long. Just before half past four we heard firing behind the conical hill at the back of the drift, called Oskarberg Hill, and suddenly about five or six hundred Zulus swept round, coming for us at a run. Instantly the natives – Kaffirs who had been very useful in making the barricade of waggons, mealie bags and biscuit boxes around the camp – bolted towards Helpmekaar, and what was worse their officer and a

European sergeant went with them. To see them deserting like that was too much for some of us, and we fired after them. The sergeant was struck and killed. Half-a-dozen of us were stationed in the hospital, with orders to hold it and guard the sick. The ends of the building were of stone, the side walls of ordinary bricks, and the inside walls or partitions of sun-dried bricks of mud. These shoddy inside bricks proved our salvation, as you will see. It was a queer little one-storeyed building, which it is almost impossible to describe; but we were pinned like rats in a hole, because all the doorways except one had been barricaded with mealie bags and we had done the same with the windows. The interior was divided by means of partition walls into which were fitted some very slight doors. The patients' beds were simple rough affairs of boards, raised only about half a foot above the floor. To talk of hospital and beds gives the idea of a big building, but as a matter of fact this hospital was a mere little shed or bungalow, divided up into rooms so small that you could hardly swing a bayonet in them. There were about nine men who could not move, but altogether there were about thirty. Most of these, however, could not help to defend themselves.

As soon as our Kaffirs bolted, it was seen that the fort as we had first made was too big to be held, so Lieutenant Chard instantly reduced the space by having a row of biscuit boxes drawn across the middle, about four feet high. This was our inner entrenchment, and proved very valuable. The Zulus came on at a wild rush, and although many of them were shot down they got to within about fifty yards of our south wall of mealie bags and biscuit boxes and waggons. They were caught between two fires, that from the hospital and that from the storehouse, and were checked; but they gained the shelter of the cookhouse and ovens, and gave us many heavy volleys. During the fight they took advantage of every bit of cover there was, anthills, a tract of bush that we had not had time to clear away, a garden or sort of orchard which was near us, and a ledge of rock and some caves (on the Oskarberg) which were only about a hundred yards away. They neglected nothing, and while they went on firing, large bodies kept hurling themselves against our slender breastworks.

But it was the hospital they assaulted most fiercely. I had charge with a man that we called Old King Cole of a small room with only one patient in it. Cole kept with me for some time after the fight began, then he said he was not going to stay. He went outside and was instantly killed by the Zulus, so that I was left alone with the patient, a native whose leg was broken and who kept crying out, 'Take my bandage off, so that I can come'. But it was impossible to do anything except fight, and I blazed away as hard as I could. By this time I was the only defender of my room. Poor Old King Cole was lying dead outside and the helpless patient was crying and groaning near me. The Zulus were swarming around us, and there was an extraordinary rattle as the bullets struck the biscuit boxes, and queer thuds as they plumped into the bags of mealies. Then there was the whizz and rip of the assegais, of which I had experience during the Kaffir Campaign of 1877–8. We had plenty of ammunition, but we were told to save it and so we took careful aim at every shot, and hardly a cartridge was wasted. [Private Dunbar shot no fewer than nine Zulus, one of them being a Chief.]

From the very first the enemy tried to rush the hospital, and at last they managed to set fire to the thick grass which formed the roof. This put us in a terrible plight, because it meant that we were either to be massacred or burned alive, or get out of the building. To get out seemed impossible; for if we left the hospital by the only door which had been left open, we should instantly fall into the midst of the Zulus. Besides, there were the helpless sick and wounded, and we could not leave them. My own little room communicated with another by means of a frail door like a bedroom door. Fire and dense choking smoke forced me to get out and go into the room. It was impossible to take the native patient with me, and I had to leave him to an awful fate. But his death was, at any rate, a merciful one – I heard the Zulus asking him questions, and he tried to tear off his bandages and escape.

In the room where I now was, there were nine sick men, and I was alone to look after them for some time, still firing away, with the hospital burning. Suddenly in the thick smoke I saw John Williams, and above the din of battle and the cries of the wounded I heard him shout, 'The Zulus are swarming all over the place. They've dragged Joseph Williams out and killed him.' John Williams had held the other room with Private William Horrigan for more than an hour, until they had not a cartridge left. The Zulus then burst in and dragged out Joseph Williams and two of the patients, and assegaied them. It was only because they were so busy with this slaughtering that John Williams and two of the patients were able to knock a hole in the partition and get into the room where I was posted. Horrigan was killed. What were we to do? We were pinned like rats in a hole. Already the Zulus were fiercely trying to burst in through the doorway. The only way of escape was the wall itself, by making a hole big enough for a man to crawl through into an adjoining room, and so on until we got to our innermost entrenchment outside. Williams worked desperately at the wall with the navvy's pick, which I had been using to make some of the loop-holes with.

All this time the Zulus were trying to get into the room. Their assegais kept whizzing towards us, and one struck me in front of the helmet. We were wearing the white tropical helmets then. But the helmet tilted back under the blow and made the spear lose its power, so that I escaped with a scalp wound which did not trouble me much then, although it has often caused me illness since. Only one man at a time could get in at the door. A big Zulu sprang forward and seized my rifle, but I tore it free and, slipping a cartridge in, I shot him point-blank. Time after time the Zulus gripped the muzzle and tried to tear the rifle from my grasp, and time after time I wrenched it back, because I had a better grip than they had. All this time Williams was getting the sick through the hole into the next room, all except one, a soldier of the 24th named Conley, who could not move because of a broken leg. Watching for my chance I dashed from the doorway, and grabbing Conley I pulled him after me through the hole. His leg got broken again, but there was no help for it. As soon as we left the room the Zulus burst in with furious cries of disappointment and rage.

Now there was a repetition of the work of holding the doorway, except that I had to stand by a hole instead of a door, while Williams picked away at the far wall to make an opening for escape into the next room. There was more desperate and almost hopeless fighting, as it seemed, but most of the poor fellows were got through the hole. Again I had to drag Conley through, a terrific task because he was a very heavy man. We were now all

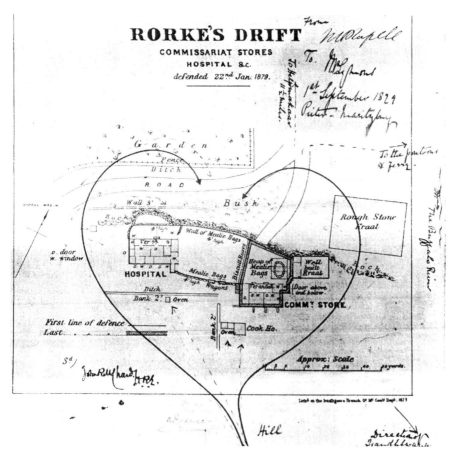

A sketch-map of Rorke's Drift, drawn by Lieutenant Chard, who was decorated with the Victoria Cross for his gallant conduct as one of the two commanders at the Drift.

The Zulu War: The entrenched position at Rorke's Drift.

Graves of Royal Engineers in the cemetery at Rorke's Drift. A wreath was laid and a
service held while our party was there.

in a little room that gave upon the inner line of defence which had been
made. We (Williams and Robert Jones and William Jones and myself) were
the last men to leave the hospital, after most of the sick and wounded had
been carried through the small window and away from the burning
building: but it was impossible to save a few of them, and they were
butchered. Privates William Jones and Robert Jones during all this time
were doing magnificent work in another ward which faced the hill. They
kept at it with bullet and bayonet until six of the seven patients had been
removed. They would have got the seventh, Sergeant Maxfield out safely,
but he was delirious with fever and, although they managed to dress him,
he refused to move. Robert Jones made a last rush to try and get him away
like the rest, but when he got back into the room he saw that Maxfield was
being stabbed by the Zulus as he lay on his bed. Corporal Allen and Private
Hitch helped greatly in keeping up communication with the hospital. They
were both badly wounded, but when they could not fight any longer they
served out ammunition to their comrades throughout the night. As we got
the sick and wounded out they were taken to a verandah in front of the
storehouse, and Dr Reynolds under a heavy fire and clouds of assegais, did

everything he could for them. All this time, of course, the storehouse was being valiantly defended by the rest of the garrison. When we got into the inner fort, I took my post at a place where two men had been shot. While I was there another man was shot in the neck, I think by a bullet which came through the space between two biscuit boxes that were not quite close together. This was at about six o'clock in the evening, nearly two hours after the opening shot of the battle had been fired. Every now and then the Zulus would make a rush for it and get in. We had to charge them out. By this time it was dark, and the hospital was all in flames, but this gave us a splendid light to fight by. I believe it was this light that saved us. We could see them coming, and they could not rush us and take us by surprise from any point. They could not get at us, and so they went away and had ten or fifteen minutes of a war-dance. This roused them up again, and their excitement was so intense that the ground fairly seemed to shake. Then, when they were goaded to the highest pitch, they would hurl themselves at us again.

Hook goes on to tell how the cartridge-chambers of the hot Martinis jammed repeatedly, how the cries of the thirsty casualties drove some of the defenders to venture outside to the water cart, how the Zulu attacks

The Oskarberg Hill over which Zulus initially attacked, and from where they sniped during the siege.

gradually died away, and, with dawn, Hook was able to scout the vicinity of the fort to collect Zulu weapons and despatch their wounded. At last, at about six o'clock Colonel Russell rode up with some mounted infantry from Chelmsford's approaching column, and the siege was finally ended. Hook still found plenty to do:

> There was no time to sit down and mope, and there were the sick and wounded as well as the rest to look after. So when the Commander-in-Chief arrived I was back at my cooking in my shirt-sleeves, making tea for the sick. A sergeant ran up and said, 'Lieutenant Bromhead wants you'. 'Wait till I put my coat on,' I said. 'Come as you are, straight away,' he ordered, and with my braces hanging about me, I went into the midst of the officers. Lord Chelmsford asked me all about the defence of the hospital, as I was the last to leave the building. An officer took our names, and wrote down what we had done. When the relief had come up, the men of the column were sent out to bury the Zulus. There were 351 dead blacks counted, and these were put into two big holes in front of the hospital. The column made the Kaffirs who were with them dig the trenches, but although they dug the

Rorke's Drift. Taken towards the redoubt and stone kraal, in front of the storehouse.

Memorial to Zulu dead at Rorke's Drift.

holes they positively refused to bury the bodies. There were only a few badly wounded left, as the Zulus had carried off their wounded as they retired. A great many dead were found in a mealie field not far from the hospital.

As for our own comrades, we buried them. This was done the day after the fight, not far from the place where they fell, and at the foot of the hill.

Writing in March 1879, in a contemporary journal *MAGA*, Alexander Allardyce penned a fulsome tribute to the defenders of Rorke's Drift:

If we can hold the Zulus so well at bay with so small a force and such insufficient protection as Rorke's Drift affords, there is good hope that we shall find ourselves more than a match for them when Lord Chelmsford's columns again take the field.

17 *Rorke's Drift Today*

Despite all the heroism displayed in a confined area, there does not seem to be as much of an evocative atmosphere at Rorke's Drift as can be detected at Isandhlwana, probably because the extensive reconstruction has changed its appearance. It is still possible to detect the position of the stores and the redoubt, as they are marked with stones, and the natural defence features are still apparent. On the day after the battle, wrecked buildings were pulled down and the material used to build a loopholed fortification some ten feet high, and incorporating the commissariat store. Later, Fort Melvill was built, an extensive system of fortifications overlooking the Drift and the pont moorings; its remains can still be seen. When Swedish missionaries returned after the war, they demolished the fortifications near the store and built a house that was very similar to the original building but it is difficult to discover if it stands on the same site. Today a stone dwelling stands where once stood the burned-out church, and on the site of the storehouse is a chapel built in 1882. The mealie-bag redoubt and the cattle kraal are marked out by lines of red bricks.

Rorke's Drift is now the property of the Evangelical Lutheran Church of South Africa, and the site has a museum which provides comprehensive details of the battle, with pictures and numerous artefacts. Conspicuous in the centre of the clearly defined perimeter is a stone obelisk, bearing the names of those killed, with a cross and the numeral XXIV. In that connection it is worth remembering when viewing the Regimental Museum's Rorke's Drift relics at Brecon, that at the time of the Zulu War, the 24th of Foot's title was '2nd Warwickshire' and it was not until three years later, in 1881, that the 24th became officially designated South Wales Borderers

At the time of visiting the Drift on the 100th Anniversary of the battle, a party of representatives from the Royal Regiment of Wales was with us. The Regiment was formed in 1969 when the South Wales Borderers were merged with the Welch Regiment. Appropriately, they held a service and laid a wreath in the cemetery at Rorke's Drift.

In 1996 – 117 years after the battle – the British Army were back at Rorke's Drift when Brigadier David Bromhead, Colonel of the Welch Regiment and great-great-nephew of that Bromhead who won a Victoria Cross defending the Drift, with representatives of the Royal Engineers, plus a party of thirty-six cadets from the Southampton and Portsmouth

Officer Training Corps, came to build a new community centre for the impoverished local community.

Climbing to the top of the Oskarberg Hill – now called 'Shiyane' (the Eyebrow) – overlooking the Mission Station, it is possible to take the imagination back as one views Isandhlwana and the Saddle in the distance, and glasses enable the trail of white cairns drifting away towards the Buffalo River, bending and sweeping round towards the Mission Station, to reveal that same crossing where arms and shields were linked as the Zulus crossed *en route* to the Drift. When looking down at today's buildings, narrow your eyes and see the red-coated defenders taking up position, as Private Wall calls out from your very spot, 'Here they come . . . black as hell and thick as grass'!

As at Ulundi, there is a sadly small and insignificant memorial, behind the native craft shop, to the Zulu dead, of whom 351 lay around the little post when they withdrew on the second day, reputedly so impressed by the heroic action of their British foe that they allowed them to survive as an act of mercy, beginning a mutual respect which survives today.

Rorke's Drift is situated some thirty-six miles west of the Natal town of Dundee, twenty miles from the nearest asphalt road, the last dozen miles being over a dirt track.

18 *Mini Memories of Walking the Battlefields of the Zulu War*

Maps Required:
A Guide Map for the Tourist for the Republic of South Africa
(South African Tourist Corporation, London)
Touring Atlas of the Republic of South Africa
(Map Studio Production (Pty) Ltd, Johannesburg)

The Battlefield of Isandhlwana, fought 22 January 1879, must surely rank with any other scene of conflict known as one of the most easily comprehended and evocative of all fields. Perhaps the most crushing defeat suffered by Britain in her long history of Colonial wars, losing fifty-

Isandhlwana. Cairn marking spot where Younghusband was killed, high above the camp area of 1879.

Isandhlwana. The donga defended by Durnford and his men in 1879.

two officers and 1,277 other ranks at a cost to the victorious Zulus of about 3,000 dead which caused Cetewayo, the Zulu King, to say 'An assegai has been thrust into the belly of the nation.'

Isandhlwana is a chill and awe-inspiring place, its natural features unchanged from the day of the battle, the sphinx-shaped mountain rearing up to tower over surrounding countryside, to its right a rocky incline dotted with acacia bushes, to the left a great plain stretching forty-five miles east to the old Zulu capital, Ulundi. Apart from man-made constructions, the only physical change would seem to be the enlarging of Durnford's donga due to rampant soil erosion. From paintings made at the time, it would seem that the actual ground is much as it was 117 years ago, with virtually no cover except scattered boulders and shallow dongas.

The most spectacular view is obtained by climbing the 300 feet or so to the top of the 'crouching-lion-like' mountain; a steep and breathless journey, there is a route that does not require much rock climbing. From here the whole terrain can be seen and assessed, and it is not impossible to imagine what the camp looked like, with rows of tents, a mass of wagons, and innumerable draught oxen. There is the plateau with its hidden ravine from which the Zulu hordes poured when discovered by Shepstone's Horse, the valley up which they attacked, then carpeted with grass three feet high but now cropped close by cattle and goats; the donga where Colonel Durnford's men held up the attack temporarily; the site of Captain Younghusband's final stand and, away to the south, a straggling line of cairns that form the resting place of those fugitives who lost their race to the Buffalo River and supposed safety of the Natal bank. Quite the most eye-catching feature, however, are the dotted monuments to the various regiments and the innumerable white-washed stone cairns, mass graves of those remains gathered together and buried four months later when Chelmsford's men re-visited the battlefield. By then, there were only skeletons to bury, the sun and animal scavengers had left little by which the dead could be identified, save a scattered and pathetic assortment of tattered uniforms, letters, photographs and all the personal impedimenta carried by soldiers on active service.

In a sense, perhaps there was a certain merciful aspect to this, in that it concealed from the shocked and saddened burial parties the fact that all the bodies had been ritually disembowelled by the stabbing, slashing Zulus, in the belief that it released the victim's spirit, which otherwise would return to haunt the slayer.

During 1958 official efforts were made to 'tidy-up' the weatherbeaten cairns, rebuilding them and renewing their white-painted covering. This inevitably revealed remains, bones, boots, buttons and the like, so that, in time, a battlefield trade sprang up with native children selling Martini-Henry cartridge cases, flattened leaden bullets, badges and buckles. But, in the early 1990s it was discovered that systematic vandalisation of the cairns had been taking place, as native diggers sought relics for which Western collectors of Victorian memorabilia would pay handsomely. This grave looting had become such a routine and planned operation that the South African Police began investigations, made raids and eventually arrests leading to prosecutions, with applications for extradition from Britain, the main conduit for distribution of the loot.

On the saddle between Isandhlwana Mountain and Black's Kopje is a small museum, displaying the usual assortment of artefacts, relics and the like, picked up on the field, with the crowning feature a massive diorama showing the various stages of the battle. There was also a dilapidated school and a trading store, both badly sited and visually intrusive; a road passed through the area where the British camp once stood.

Having said all that, it is quite possible that by now considerable changes and improvements have taken place in the area because at the time of writing the Kwa-Zulu Heritage Foundation are planning to 'restore the battle site to a condition worthy of the memory of those who fell, at the same time making it a source of employment and income for the local clansmen who live in one of the most economically depressed parts of KwaZulu (Zululand)'. In addition to the worthwhile social aims, it is promised that: 'Visitors (who will be able to spend the night in rustic accommodation near the battlefield) will have the benefit of a museum and interpretation centre which will fully explain the significance of the features around them' plus available literature. A new school will be built, there will be a shop selling food and refreshments, the road will be rebuilt to skirt the battlefield, with buildings in nineteenth-century style and built with stone from ruins in the area.

It all sounds good and looks good in the glossy coloured brochure – but it might not be to the Battlefield Walker's benefit in the long run!

Isandhlwana is not a difficult battlefield to understand but, being a fairly spread-out field so far as the British positions are concerned (which greatly contributed to the eventual disaster), requires a fair amount of walking to adequately cover. Thus, when first engaged, Durnford was some 5,000 yards from the camp, and it is about 1,500 yards from the donga, where he made his stand, to the wagon park; from the donga, taking a route along what was roughly the British line, to Young-husband's company position is more than 2,000 yards; while Cavaye's

At Isandhlwana May 1979. Guests and dignitaries at the 100th Anniversary Commemoration, May 1979.

Overshadowed by the huge Mountain at Isandhlwana, battlefield marker and graves, in
May 1979, 100th Anniversary.

position on the spur was about 1,200 yards north of the camp. Things are
made easier by the fact that the 'firing-line', where the last stands took
place, is clearly marked by the white cairns of the defenders' burial places.
When Chelmsford's force returned to the area on 21 May 1879 and set
about the grim task of burying the bodies, rather than transport these
skeletal remains elsewhere, they would have dug mass gravepits in the
areas where they lay thickest. This means that by far the most cairns are
in and behind the camp area, and on the rocky plateau where
Younghusband made his last stand; and on the saddle between the
Mountain and Blacks/Stony Kopje.

These peregrinations might once have caused a problem which by now perhaps no longer applies, in that at the time of our party's visit it was possible to freely visit the areas in and around the existing road, but to visit far-flung parts of the field, where important sites were indicated by markers, it was necessary to obtain a permit from the Magistrate at Nqutu, the nearest town!

In May 1979, our party from Southampton in Hampshire sat on a rocky outcrop beneath the shadow of that extraordinary hill, whose name means 'little hand' or 'the place of the stomach of the ox', listening to Frank Chadwick of the South African Museum's Service describe the battlefield to us. Here we also made the acquaintance of Ian Player, noted South African historian (and brother of Gary Player, the famous golfer!) who, during the course of our visit, opened many doors for us and introduced us to innumerable people, not the least among them being Prince Buthelazi, the Zulu statesman and politician. We sat among the ululating wives of the King of Zululand at the lively ceremony on the battlefield, watched the parades, marching and Zulu dancing, spoilt only by the gyrating warriors' leopard skins, monkey tails, shields and assegais being underpinned by feet encased in white 'trainers'. Perhaps all this tended to lessen our reverence on this hallowed field, but that emotion was quickly rekindled by a long and dusty trudge to Fugitives Drift.

The only escape route from the massacre was west, across hills and gullies to the flooded Buffalo River, over a rocky bluff which today's walkers can avoid; the road back to Rorke's Drift was denied by the right-horn of the Zulu army. It is five to seven miles from the fighting area at Isandhlwana to the river, and only the lucky ones managed to find horses (among them was Horace Smith-Dorrien, who lived to command a British army at the World War One battle of Le Cateau in 1914). It is horrifying, even today, to visualise the many men who had just fought a fierce battle and were now being harassed by nimble and triumphant warriors, leaping from boulder to boulder in their eagerness to 'wash their spears'. The ground is rough, stony and boulder-strewn, with thorn-bushes and aloes, intercepted by marsh, dongas and ravines. Lieutenants Melville and Coghill attempting to save the colours, lost in the fierce current of the flooded Buffalo River, who struggled up the steep far bank of the Natal side, within thirty feet of possible safety were killed by their pursuers. The white stone monument and their graves, studied by all of us with reverence, were incredibly vandalised a few years after our visit. The river was in spate on the fateful day, so not a single man on foot survived, even many mounted fugitives were caught or perished in the river.

By now, the battlefield walker will have acquired a very fair impression of the sheer intensity and the ferocity of this colonial war where no prisoners were taken, and there was no Colditz or any Red Cross food parcels, which makes every field a spine-chilling venue. After Isandhlwana, perhaps the mind boggles most on top of Hlobane Mountain where, on 28 March 1879, that archetypal Victorian soldier, Redvers Buller, whose mounted force climbed the steep and rocky inclines in darkness, mist and rain, won his Victoria Cross. Trapped by a Zulu impi, the horsemen set their mounts at a sheer precipitous drop and escaped with difficulty. One hundred years later, even standing at the top of the cliff and looking downwards made one feel giddy!

Immediately following the Hlobane combat and arising directly from it, was the Battle of Kambula on 29 March 1879, with Redvers Buller and his cavalry force again taking a prominent part both in attacking the advancing Zulus' right flank and then in the pursuit after the natives had been driven back. Wood's position at Kambula was strong, on a high

The memorial marker at Ulundi, beyond which is the area where Cetewayo's kraal lay.

Monument to British dead at Ulundi, Zululand.

ridge, with a fort at its rear, with wagon laagers encircling the camp and entrenchments on three sides, still clearly visible. An unchanged desolate area save for grazing herds, tended by native boys, all of whom seemed to have bullets, cartridge cases and other relics for sale.

On 12 March 1879 a company of the 80th Regiment, escorting a wagon convoy, were forced by the rapid rising of the Intombi River to bivouac on both sides of the river, where an attack by a large force of Zulus, coming out of the morning mist, overwhelmed and massacred most of them. We made a pilgrimage to the site at Mayer's Drift where there is a small cemetery and a memorial and piles of stones over graves of the British dead. Two names emerge from this fight: Lieutenant Harwood, who was court-martialled for deserting his men, and Sergeant Booth who was awarded the Victoria Cross for leading them to safety.

Another court-martial to emerge from the Zulu War and become well known in its day was that of Lieutenant Jahleel Brenton Carey, in command of the escort when the Prince Imperial of France (serving with the British Army) was killed in a Zulu ambush at a kraal near the Ityotyozi River in Natal. The fateful donga with its memorial and graves of two other members of the party now seems a sad, familiar place.

The Centenary Commemoration included a large gathering at Ulundi, the old Zulu capital, where, on 4 July 1879, the whole British force formed into one huge square, beat off all Zulu attacks, and then pursued them with cavalry. Every Zulu dignitary, including the King and Prince Buthelazi, was present, making speeches in Zulu, Afrikaans and English, with translators working at full stretch! It was quite impossible to achieve any idea whatsoever as to how the area looked a century earlier, except that on the area where the British square stood is what has been called 'a rather tasteless' domed monument, in the south passageway of which is a plaque bearing the inscription: 'In memory of the Brave Warriors who fell here in 1879 in Defence of the Old Zulu Order'. Along with the small memorial plaque at Rorke's Drift, this is the only known memorial commemorating the Zulu dead of the War.

Based on the town of Vryheid, for the Zulu War part of the Tour, our host Alf Wade, who had lived in the area all his life and was an enthusiastic military historian, escorted our party to many places of interest including the local fort and Raadsal (Council Chamber). Among these places was Dingaan's Kraal, where on 6 February 1838 the Zulu King Dingaan signed an agreement with Piet Retief, the Voortrekker leader, then had the Voortrekker party murdered on the same day on Matiwane Hill. Later that year, on 16 December, the Boer leader Andries Pretorius defeated a Zulu impi at Blood River, and subsequently discovered the remains of Piet Retief's party at the foot of Matiwane Hill, where a monument was subsequently erected and duly photographed by our party, being acknowledged as a battlefield bonus.

Back to the War, two more fields were visited – Inyezane and Gingindhlovu, both in the heart of the Natal sugar-belt and much of both have been ploughed under. They are very easy to locate and are within 6/7 miles of each other. The battle at Inyezane was fought on 22 January 1879, when a Zulu impi was repulsed; there is a small cemetery there. Gingindhlovu has little to show today for its battle fought on 2 March 1879, when a British wagon laager repulsed a large Zulu force, except a little military cemetery and a small granite cross at the road turn-off to the Farm Kia Ora, where the burned-out Zulu military kraal was situated. A few miles east of the cemetery, on a slight rise near the south bank of the Inyezane River, is the site of Chelmsford's laager, almost bisected by the present road from Gingindhlovu to Eshowe.

Eshowe is the oldest town in Zululand, situated on a hilltop surrounded by attractive afforested countryside. Originally a Norwegian Mission Station, Eshowe was garrisoned by Pearson's Column from late January until early April 1879, where they built fortifications and remained in a state of siege. Engineers built an angular oblong fort, 200 yards long and 50 yards wide, walls 6 feet high, and a moat 7 feet deep and 20 feet wide; a drawbridge led to the main gate and a loopholed palisade of stout logs surmounted the parapet. When Pearson marched out on Chelmsford's orders, the Zulus fired the camp, but do not seem to have done a very good job, because parapet and trenchlines are in a remarkably good condition, with gun positions easily discernible. In later years the fort became overgrown with luxuriant vegetation which preserved it from disintegration, although the south wall and trench have been destroyed to make way for a Norwegian Cemetery and a road. Today it houses the Zululand Historical Museum – an interesting place.

Part Six

South Africa – The First Boer (Transvaal) War 1881

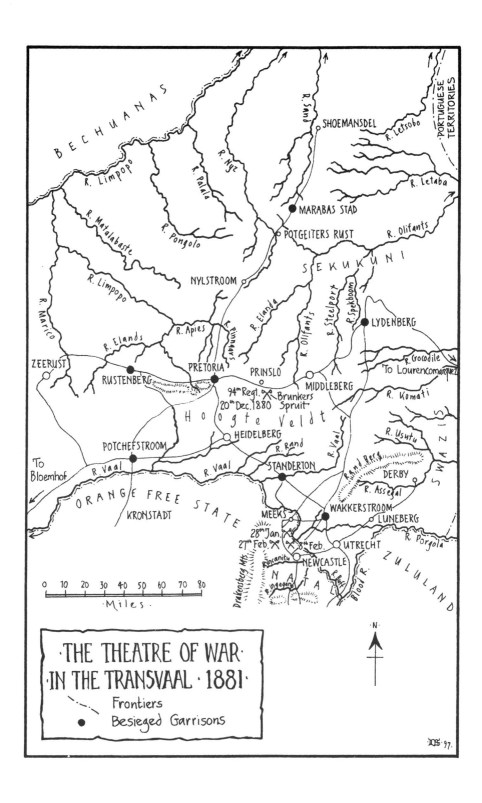

THE THEATRE OF WAR
IN THE TRANSVAAL · 1881

Frontiers
Besieged Garrisons

19 *The Course of the War*

The Transvaal was formally annexed to Great Britain in April 1877, but three years later, on 16 December, the Boers proclaimed a Republic. On 20 December a detachment of the 94th Regiment marching from Lydenburg to Pretoria was intercepted by a strong party of mounted Boers who, when the column-commander refused to turn back, opened fire with deadly effect. In ten minutes 155 officers and men out of a total of 259 became casualties before the wounded British commander surrendered. Losing only two men killed and five wounded, the Boers were friendly towards their captives and helped to treat the wounded.

Sir George Pomeroy Colley, High Commissioner for South-Eastern Africa, hurried forward towards the frontier with a few companies of infantry stationed in Natal: a naval brigade, a squadron of Dragoons and mounted infantry, together with the Natal Mounted Police. Colley despised the Boers and was eager to distinguish himself before he was superseded by an officer of higher rank. Leading a relief column to raise the siege of the Transvaal towns, on 28 January 1881 he moved out to attack the Boers on Laing's Nek, a ridge about twenty-three miles north of Newcastle. The British force totalled about 1,160 men and consisted of five companies of the 58th, five companies of the 3rd Battalion of the 60th Regiment, seventy-five men of the Naval Brigade, 150 mounted men under Major Brownlow and four guns. At 9 am the British force formed up with the mounted squadron on the left. After the guns had shelled parts of the enemy's position and the naval brigade had sent rockets into the Boer reserves in the rear of the Nek, the 58th advanced, covered by the mounted squadron on their right. In the face of heavy fire from a strong Boer force holding the hilltop, the mounted men swept up the hill, although the ground was completely unsuitable for cavalry and the horsemen should have been used as mounted infantry. The leading troop took heavy casualties and soon all their commanders were down. Fatigued and broken by the efforts of their uphill charge and unable to make any headway, the whole squadron gave way and retreated down the hill. Meanwhile the 58th was slowly progressing through the long entangling grass of the steep ascent in the face of a deadly accurate fire from the invisible Boers on the ridge above. When the cavalry was repulsed, the Boers moved down and opened fire on the now-exposed right flank and rear of the 58th. Soon every mounted officer was down, and with men falling fast on all sides, the order to retire was given. As befitted the last occasion on which the colours were carried into action by a British

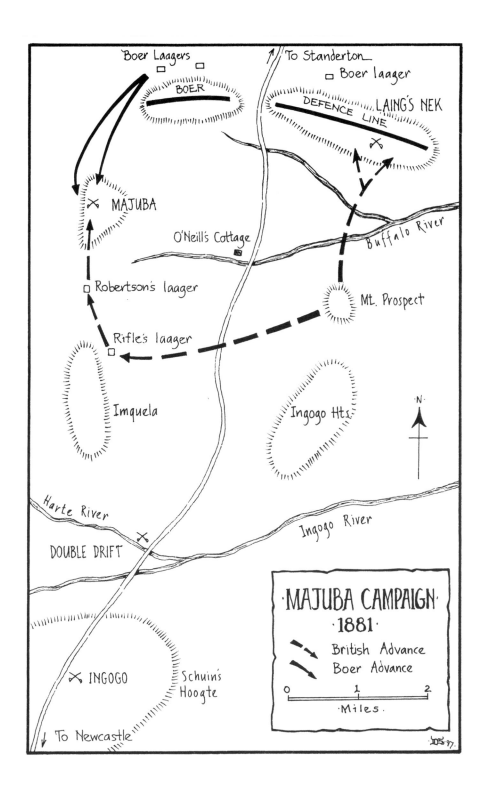

Boer Laagers

BOER

To Standerton
Boer laager

LAING'S NEK

DEFENCE LINE

✕

Y

MAJUBA

O'Neill's Cottage

Buffalo River

Robertson's laager

Mt. Prospect

Rifle's laager

Imquela

Ingogo Hts.

·N·

Harte River

Ingogo River

DOUBLE DRIFT

✕ INGOGO

Schuin's Hoogte

↓ To Newcastle

·MAJUBA CAMPAIGN·
·1881·

British Advance
Boer Advance

0   1   2

·Miles·

JOS 97.

battalion, the men fell back without haste or confusion 'in good order and with an erect and soldierly bearing' to re-form at the foot of the slope.

In spite of considerable British bravery, the battle of Laing's Nek was an unquestionable and severe defeat with 198 casualties – the 58th had to bury seventy-five officers and men out of a total strength of 494. The Boers lost fourteen killed and twenty-seven wounded. At the cease-fire, they behaved with great humanity and freely allowed the wounded lying in front of their position to be cared for, bringing water to them and helping to bandage their wounds.

General Colley, commander British force on Majuba, who was killed.
Illustrated London News, March 1881

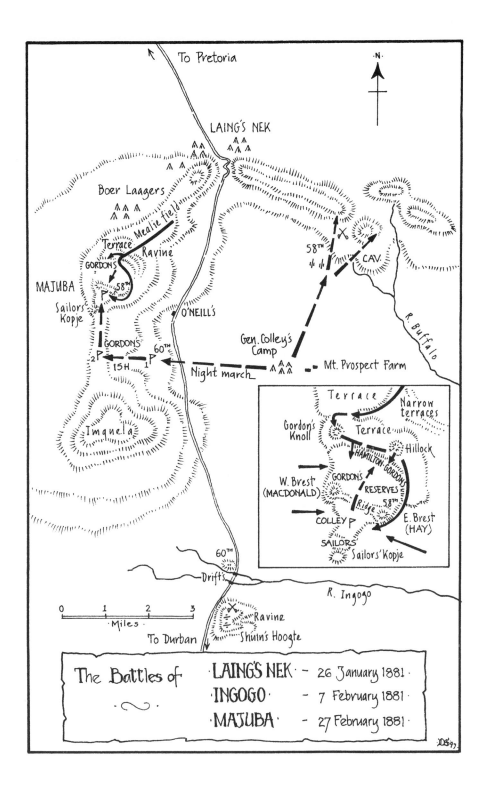

To Pretoria

N

LAING'S NEK

Boer Laagers

Terrace Mealie field

Ravine

Terrace

GORDONS

58ᵀᴴ

MAJUBA

58ᵀᴴ

Sailors' Kopje

P

O'NEILL'S

CAV.

R. Buffalo

Gen. Colley's Camp

GORDONS

P 2

60ᵀᴴ

P 1

15H

Night march

Mt. Prospect Farm

Imquela

Terrace

Narrow terraces

Gordon's Knoll

Terrace

Hillock

HAMILTON-GORDONS

W. Brest (MACDONALD)

GORDON'S

RESERVES

Ridge

58ᵀᴴ

COLLEY P

E. Brest (HAY)

SAILORS

Sailors' Kopje

60ᵀᴴ

Drifts

R. Ingogo

0   1   2   3
·Miles·

Ravine

To Durban

Shuin's Hoogte

The Battles of

LAING'S NEK   – 26 January 1881 ·

·INGOGO·   – 7 February 1881 ·

·MAJUBA·   – 27 February 1881 ·

DS 97

The confident Boers now began to intercept the British line of communications and to cut off convoys, so that the British camp was isolated. Determined to clear the Boers from the road, Colley marched out on the morning of 8 February with five companies of the 60th Rifles, two field- and two mountain-guns and a small detachment of mounted men. Leaving the mountain-guns and a company of infantry on a commanding crest north of the River Ingogo, about five miles south of his camp, he crossed with the main body and formed up on the south bank, where a gentle slope rose to the foot of a flat-topped ridge strewn with rocks and boulders and irregularly cut by rocky depressions. As the troops ascended the rise to the ridge, the Boers galloped forward and, taking advantage of the cover afforded by the intersecting valleys, directed a heavy and active fire on the guns and the skirmishers. The mountain-guns came into action and the engagement became heavy until at noon companies of the 60th were pushed forward in the face of a deadly fire from behind cover.

The guns were in action with case shot at a range of less than 500 yards, and the gunners, who were freely exposed, suffered heavily until the withdrawal of the guns, which fired only occasionally for the rest of the action. A company of the 60th who had advanced to cover the guns in the face of close-range Boer fire had many casualties. Realising that the enemy was being reinforced, Colley sent back to the camp for three companies of the 58th, who were ordered to move out and occupy the ridges north of the river and to cross it in support of the troops already deeply engaged and reduced by heavy losses. Convinced that the enemy intended to attack him next morning in overwhelming strength, Colley decided to withdraw under cover of darkness. It was a very cold, black night with the rain falling in torrents and, after the wounded had been searched for in the darkness and the horses from the abandoned ammunition wagons had been hitched to the guns, the force moved back in hollow square with the guns in the centre and the infantry in skirmishing order on four sides. The swollen and rapidly running river had to be crossed by the detachment in a body with locked arms, but even so many men were swept away. At four o'clock in the morning the force reached Colley's camp, although companies of the 58th Regiment spent the night on the northern ridges and were not withdrawn until the following day. The British losses amounted to 139 officers and men against the Boers' eight killed and six wounded.

On 17 February Brigadier-General Sir Evelyn Wood VC arrived in Newcastle with the reinforcements from India: the 15th Hussars, the 2nd Battalion 60th Rifles and the 92nd Highlanders. Wood told Colley to attempt no further advance until he was stronger, and then he himself returned to Pietermaritzburg while Colley marched the new arrivals to his old camp. Sir George Colley was rated one of the most brilliant officers ever to have passed through the Staff College, although his experience of actual warfare was slender and he was unfamiliar with the character and temperament of the Boers. Thoroughly incensed by his two bloody defeats and regardless of his instructions not to advance further, he decided on a reconnaissance-in-force to the summit of the Majuba mountain, east of Laing's Nek – the highest point in the area. Knowing that a Boer force occasionally held the hilltop in daytime, Colley resolved to climb it by night, and at 10 pm on 26 February he marched out with a force of 22 officers and 627 men.

It was not until 5 am that the exhausted force, hopelessly confused during their upward scramble, gained the summit. Now only about 400 strong, the weary soldiers dropped where they stood to wait for daybreak. No entrenching tools had been brought, and some of the men tried to obtain cover by throwing up barriers of turf and stones. At dawn the Boers in the lower camp saw the British occupation of the mountain and considered a withdrawal but, seeing the troops on the summit to be in no great strength and without artillery, they began to climb the mountainside under cover of boulders and shrubs. The older men, who were picked shots, supported the storming party, firing at every soldier who exposed himself over the edge of the plateau.

As the morning passed, the attacking Boers hemmed in the British position on the north, the east and the south-west, climbing slowly and steadily upwards and moving quickly from cover to cover, protected by the steady and accurate fire of their comrades. As they were not in sufficient strength to hold the whole edge of the plateau, the defenders had to move from point to point in order to repulse the enemy advance. At noon the Boers reached the crest and opened a deadly short-range fire. Unnerved by the accurate shooting, the morale of the British soldiers began to waver and the reserve, lying in the centre dip of the plateau out of reach of the enemy fire so that they had not suffered any losses, huddled for cover behind rocks and, when ordered up in support of the firing line, refused to move in spite of the threats and pleas of their officers. Sir George Colley was shot through the head and killed just before the remaining British soldiers suddenly decided that they had had enough and fled. Standing on the edge of the plateau, the Boers directed an accurate and persistent fire on the fugitives, picking the men off as if they were shooting game. Only the entrenchment made by the company of the 92nd prevented the slaughter from being much greater, although heavy fire soon made even this untenable and the survivors retreated under a murderous fire from the Boers, who then occupied the position. The surviving fugitives from the Majuba and the entrenchment reached camp under cover of artillery fire without any Boer attempts at pursuit.

On 23 March peace terms were signed by Sir Evelyn Wood and the Boer leaders, giving the Transvaal people the right to complete self-government subject to the suzerainty of the Queen.

The total British force in South Africa or on the way there at the close of hostilities was made up of 13 infantry regiments, 5 cavalry regiments, 22 guns and 3 naval brigades – a total of nearly 20,000 men, exclusive of the British garrisons besieged in the Transvaal. If every Boer capable of bearing arms had been in the field, their forces would not have totalled more than 8,000 men. Throughout the short war the Boers lost 43 killed and 58 wounded, whilst the British had more than 800 casualties.

20 *The Fight on Majuba Hill*
27 *February 1881*

This action was vividly described by Mr Cameron, War Correspondent
of the *Standard*, in the *Illustrated London News* of 25 April 1881:

> The correspondent states that General Sir George Colley, who observed
> that the high peak which overlooked the right of the enemy's position,
> although held during the day by a Boer picket, was left unoccupied at night,
> had determined to seize and hold the point at once, fearing that if he
> delayed any longer the enemy might also discover its value, and intrench it
> as they had done with Laing's Neck. Boer working parties had been seen
> in close proximity to the top during the day, on Saturday, Feb. 26; so, to
> make possession a certainty, the order was given for 180 Highlanders of the
> 92nd Regiment, 148 men of the 58th, 150 Rifles, and 70 Bluejackets to
> assemble at half-past nine in the evening. They marched off in silence,
> reached Majuba Hill, three miles and a half from the British camp, and had
> a long and toilsome climb of three hours to the top. They got up there
> between four and five in the morning, before daylight. 'We found
> ourselves,' he says, 'on a spacious plateau some thousand yards round,
> sloping gently downwards from the summit, where was an oblong hollow
> basin, about two hundred yards long by sixty wide, the rocky ridges of
> which, as it seemed to us, constituted a natural citadel that we fancied
> would prove impregnable.' It was distant not more than two thousand
> yards from the nearest Boer intrenchments on Laing's Neck, and at an
> elevation of two thousand feet above them.
>
> The British soldiers were posted all round, at intervals of ten paces, leav-
> ing the Naval Brigade and fifty men of the 58th Regiment as a reserve in
> the central hollow. When daylight came, they looked down on the Boers'
> encampment, laagers formed of waggons with tents inside. It was about
> seven o'clock when the Boers perceived that the British were on the top of
> the hill above them. This discovery at first seemed to excite great alarm
> and confusion among the Boers, who began to drive in their horses and
> cattle, and even prepared to remove the waggons. But their panic was
> apparently stopped by the authority of the commander, and some parties
> of them now came up the hill. Firing commenced at nine o'clock, on a part
> of the summit held by Lieutenant Hamilton, with only twenty men of the
> 92nd Highlanders. Commander Romilly, R.N., of the Naval Brigade, was
> killed by a chance shot early in the morning; but during the whole

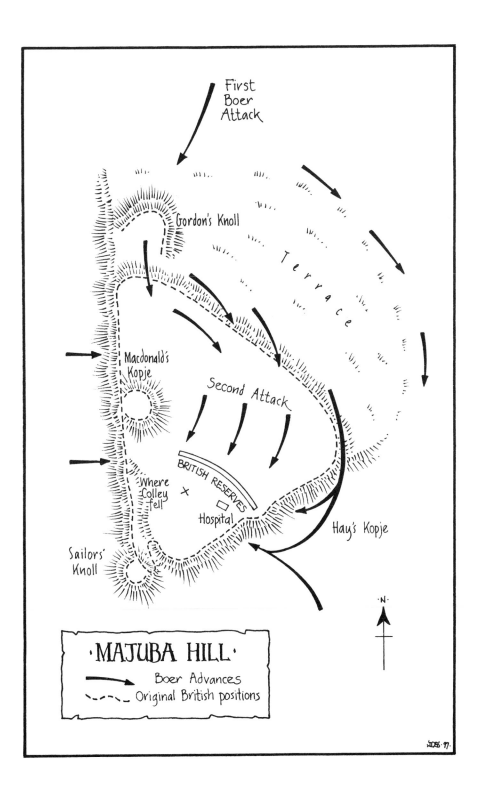

First
Boer
Attack

Gordon's Knoll

T e r r a c e

Macdonald's
Kopje

Second Attack

BRITISH RESERVES

Where
Colley
fell

×

Hospital

Hay's Kopje

Sailors'
Knoll

·N·

·MAJUBA HILL·

⟶ Boer Advances
- - - - ⟶ Original British positions

JOS · 77·

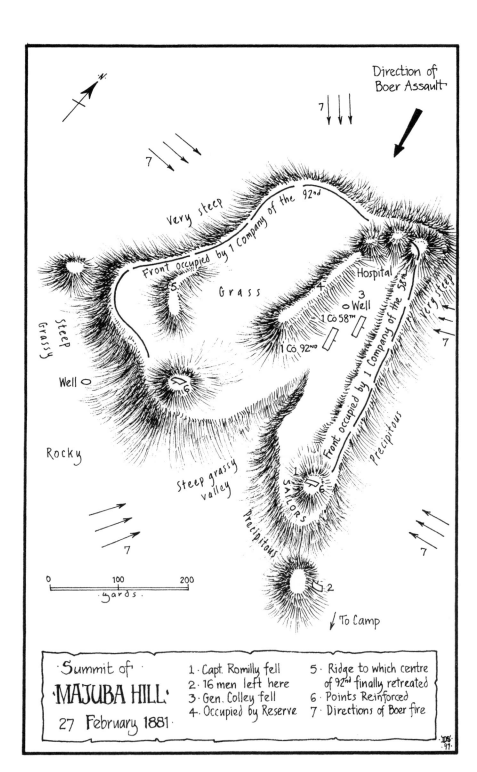

Direction of Boer Assault

N.

7

7

Very steep

Front occupied by 1 Company of the 92nd

Grass

5

Hospital

4

3
o Well

1 Co 58th

1 Co 92nd

Very steep

7

Steep grassy

Well o

6

Front occupied by 1 Company of the 58th

Precipitous

Rocky

Steep grassy valley

1

SAILORS

6

Precipitous

7

7

0   100   200

yards.

2

To Camp

Summit of
·MAJUBA HILL·
27 February 1881·

1 · Capt. Romilly fell
2 · 16 men left here
3 · Gen. Colley fell
4 · Occupied by Reserve

5 · Ridge to which centre of 92nd finally retreated
6 · Points Reinforced
7 · Directions of Boer fire

forenoon the casualties were not very numerous. The correspondent now goes on to say:

'We had been exposed to five hours of unceasing fire, and had become accustomed to the constant humming of bullets, which at noon almost ceased, when the General, wearied with the exertions of the previous night, lay down to sleep. Communication by heliograph had been established with the camp, and confidence in our ability to hold our own had increased, rather than abated. Lieutenant Hamilton, however, who, with his few men, had been opposing the enemy alone throughout the morning, did not share in the general assurance. A little after twelve he came back from his position for a few minutes to tell us that, having seen large numbers of the

The Transvaal War: All that we saw of the Boers at Majuba Hill.

enemy pass to the hollow underneath him, he feared that they were up to some devilment. Reinforcements were promised him and he returned to his post, but these did not reach him until it was almost too late.

'Shortly afterwards, Major Hay, of the 92nd, Colonel Stewart, Major Fraser, and myself were discussing the situation, when we were startled by a loud and sustained rattle of musketry, the bullets of which shrieked over our heads in a perfect hail. Lieutenant Wright, of the 92nd, rushed back, shouting out for immediate reinforcements. The General, assisted by his Staff, set about getting these forward, and then for the first time it dawned upon us that we might lose the hill, for the soldiers moved forward but slowly and hesitatingly. It was only too evident they did not like the work before them. By dint of some hard shouting and even pushing they were most of them got over the ridge, where they lay down, some distance behind Hamilton and his thin line of Highlanders, who, although opposed to about five hundred men at 120 yards, never budged an inch.

'It seems that the advance of the enemy had been thoroughly checked, when one of our people – an officer, I believe – noticing the Boers for the first time, ejaculated, "Oh, there they are, quite close," and the words were hardly out of his lips ere every man of the newly arrived reinforcements bolted back panic-stricken. This was more than flesh and blood could stand, and the skirmishing line under Hamilton gave way also, the retreating troops being exposed, of course, to the Boer fire with disastrous effect.

'I was on the left of the ridge when the men came back on us, and was a witness of the wild confusion which then prevailed. I saw McDonald, of the 92nd, revolver in hand, threaten to shoot any man who passed him; and, indeed, everybody was hard at work rallying the broken troops. Many, of course, got away and disappeared over the side of the hill next to the camp; but some hundred and fifty good men, mostly Highlanders, bluejackets, and old soldiers of the 58th, remained to man the ridge for a final stand.

'Some of the Boers appeared, and the fire that was interchanged was something awful. Three times they showed themselves, and three times they as quickly withdrew, our men, when that occurred, at once stopping their fire. I could hear the soldiers ejaculate, "We'll not budge from this. We'll give them the bayonet if they come closer," and so on, but all the time drop-ping fast, for Boer marksmen had apparently got to work in secure positions, and every shot told, the men falling back hit, mostly through the head.

'It was a hot five minutes, but nevertheless I thought at the time we should hold our own. I expected every minute to hear the order given for a bayonet charge. That order unfortunately never came, although I am sure the men would have responded to it. But our flanks were exposed, and the enemy, checked in front, were stealing round them; across the hollow on the side of the hill facing the camp we had no one, and as the men were evidently anxious about that point, frequently looking over their shoulders, Colonel Stewart sent me over to see how matters were going on. There I reported all clear, and, indeed, if the enemy had attempted to storm the hill on that face he would have been decimated by the fire of his own people aimed from the other side.

'We were most anxious about our right flank. It was evident that the enemy were stealing round it, so men were taken to prolong the position there. They were chiefly bluejackets, led by a brave young officer, and, as I watched them follow him up, for the third time that day, the conviction

British troops retreating from Majuba Hill
(from a contemporary print)

flashed across me that we should lose the hill. There was a knoll on the threatened point, up which the reinforcements hesitated to climb. Some of them went back over the top of the plateau to the further ridge, others went round.

'By-and-by there was confusion on the knoll itself. Some of the men on it stood up, and were at once shot down; and at last the whole of those who were holding it gave way. Helter skelter they were at once followed by the Boers, who were able then to pour a volley into our flank in the main line, from which instant the hill of Majuba was theirs. It was *sauve qui peut*. Major Hay, Captain Singleton, of the 92nd, and some other officers, were the last to leave, and these were immediately shot down and taken prisoners.

'The General had turned round the last of all to walk after his retreating troops, when he also was shot dead, through the head. A minute or two previously Lieutenant Hamilton, requesting the General to excuse his presumption, had asked for a charge, as the men would not stand the fire much longer. Sir George Colley replied, "Wait until they come on, we will give them a volley and then charge," but before that moment arrived it was too late.

'To move over about one hundred yards of ground under the fire of some five hundred rifles at close range is not a pleasant experience, but it is what all who remained of us on the hill that day had to go through. On every side, men were throwing up their arms, and with sharp cries of agony were pitching forward on the ground. At last we went over the side of the hill.

'The Boers were instantly on the ridge above, and for about ten minutes kept up their terrible fire on our soldiers, who plunged down every path. Many, exhausted with the night's marching and the day's fighting, unable to go further, lay down behind rocks and bushes, and were afterwards taken prisoners: but of those who remained on the hill to the very last probably not one in six got clear away. The Boers were everywhere assisting our disabled men. Dr Landon, who, when the hill was abandoned by our panic-stricken troops, had steadily remained by his wounded, was lying on the ground with a shot through his chest. The Boers, as they rushed on the plateau, not seeing or not caring for the Geneva Cross, had fired into and knocked over both him and his hospital assistant; so there was only one, Dr Mahon, left to look after a great number of very bad cases.'

21 *Majuba Today*

Majuba remains today just as it was at the time of Colley's disastrous attack in 1881; still towering, a huge tabletop mountain dominating the surrounding landscape, rising from a broad base in precipitous folds 6,500 feet above sea-level. Apart from a memorial marker set below the summit at the first crest, there is little to denote its local significance – the stone bears two metal plates with inscriptions in Afrikaans and English:

> The Battle of Majuba Amajuba 27th February 1881 in the 1st War of Independence. British Commander Lieut. General Sir George Pomeroy Colley left his camp at Mount Prospect with about 400 men and occupied this mountain before dawn. The Boers, with a force of about 375 men, led by Commander N.J. Smith, Field-Cornet C.R. De Wet and Field-Cornet J. Loos, attacked the hill on three sides and by skilful use of natural cover, drove the British back without themselves suffering heavy losses.

A memorial stone in a roadside carpark at Laings Nek. The cavalry attacked up the hill on the right, the infantry on the left hill.

Majuba Hill, from the side from which the British climbed the hill. Taken from the battlefield of Laings Nek.

Comments arising from using a recording device at the time of climbing this hill indicate the severity of the feat, and explain quite a lot about the subsequent events. For instance, it is revealed that the climb, in broad daylight, took forty minutes to reach the first crest, the ascent being extremely steep, and a weary voice comes from the machine 'this climb was one of the most tiring things I can ever recall doing in my entire life, made worse by the high altitude'.

Our party climbed the mountain up one of the routes followed by the Boers, consisting of a deep cleft rising to the summit. It is clear that the configuration of the summit had a vital role in what transpired. Almost the entire summit is taken up by a shallow depression ranging in places from ten to forty feet deep, with a rocky rim measuring about 900 yards in circumference, being an integral part of the summit on the south and west sides. However, the northern side (which would have been facing the Boer camps) features 100 yards of rolling grassy slope from the rim to the actual brow of the mountain. To cover that aspect, the defensive perimeter required to be extended to nearly 1,500 yards, which still allowed considerable areas of dead ground for the defenders, because of the varying degrees of slope in the ascent.

It is an eerie and evocative area, dotted with memorials and monuments, the largest being the cemetery surrounded by a crumbling rock
wall. Within it are two crosses, a monument and a separate smaller white
cross. The first two crosses bear the inscriptions to Henry Rates and his
comrades of HMS *Boadicea*'s Naval Brigade, the other in memory of an
NCO and twenty Privates of the 92nd Gordon Highlanders; the monument bears the names of officers and men of the 58th Regiment killed on
the mountain, and the other cross is in memory of Captain Mause of that
Regiment. The knolls were later given relevant names, thus MacDonald's
Kopje, Sailors' Knoll, Hay's Kopje and Gordon's Knoll. There is a separate memorial on the spot where Colley fell. Captured by the Boers early
in the action and a key to it, is Gordon's Knoll, on the Boer side of the
hill; Hector MacDonald fought stoutly on the kopje bearing his name,
and had the Gordon Highlanders on the knoll known – in the dark – they
could have fired down on the Boers and repulsed them; in the inner area
fronting it most British casualties occurred. The land dropping away from
Sailors' Knoll is very steep and is where the British climbed during the
night; the Boers came up beyond Hay's Kopje and it drops away behind

In the 'basin' or bowl on top of Majuba Hill, with the cross marking where General
Colley fell. In the background is MacDonald's Kopje.

The little cemetery with memorials on top of Majuba Hill. There are two memorials in the enclosure: one is to Henry Rates and his comrades of the HMS *Boadicea*'s Naval Brigade; the other is to an NCO and 20 Privates of the 92nd Gordon Highlanders. The monument bears the names of Officers and Men of the 52nd Regiment killed here; the white cross is in memory of Captain Maude of that regiment.

a very steep slope down to Laing's Nek and the area of the British approach march.

Within such a limited area it is easy to visualise what took place and, with imagination, to cast oneself in the role of the British soldiers and sailors involved in a battle that was completely beyond any of their expectations. There is a well-known woodcut in *Illustrated London News* depicting fleeing Highlanders hurtling down the steep slopes, and standing at the top of that identical drop brings it very clearly to life. Without doubt, Majuba – like Isandhlwana – is a highly emotive name, bringing to mind a rare and ignoble defeat in the otherwise triumphant pageant of Victorian colonialism.

22 *Mini Memories of Walking the Battlefields of the First Boer War*

Maps Required:
A Guide Map for the Tourist for the Republic of South Africa
(South African Tourist Corporation, London)
Touring Atlas of the Republic of South Africa
(Map Studio Productions (Pty) Ltd, Johannesburg)

These fields of the First Boer War were visited by a party of battlefield walkers in 1979 when in South Africa for the Centenary of the Zulu War. As befits dyed-in-the-wool battlefield walkers, the party endeavoured to cram in not only the fields of 1879, where official ceremonies were taking place, but also some of the scenes of conflict of the South African War 1899–1902, as well as the earlier Boer War. They were the first fields of war encountered by the party on entering the country and were visited *en route* from Johannesburg to the residences of hosts in Ladysmith and Vryheid, among other places. Such a crowded itinerary inevitably meant a certain blurring of details and memories which, with the passing of the years, have to be revived by notes dictated and written at the time of taking photographs, etc.

With the exception of perhaps the opening encounter at Bronkhorst Spruit on 20 December 1880, when the 94th Regiment were ambushed as they marched from Middleburgh to Pretoria, the fields of this short war are relatively unchanged. It may well be that that opening encounter site can be readily recognised today, and it is known that our party visited the area, but lacking notes or photographs (for some reason!) nothing can be said about it.

However, Laing's Nek, a wide pass in the Drakensberg foothills some twenty-five miles from Newcastle in Natal on the direct north road to Standerton in the Transvaal, is relatively unchanged today; the Ingogo River field lays south of that area. The pass over Laing's Nek is about the centre of a rough semicircle of hills, some six miles in length, culminating towards the west in the lofty square-topped Majuba Mountain; the road skirts the foot of Majuba till it rises to the Laing's Nek Ridge in the re-entering bend of this semicircle. To the east, the ground is an undulating grassy plateau rising steeply to a tablehill about 1,000 yards across, the key to the position, and it was against its outer or eastern end that Colley directed his attack. Approaching Laing's Nek there is a sign by the roadside, a small wooden board on a post which says 'Laing's Nek 1480m'; beyond it, on the rising ground to the left, is the ground over which the British attacked and, on the right, the towering height of Majuba. There is a roadside carpark in which stands a memorial stone, with the battlefield behind it – the cavalry attacked up the hill on the right of the stone, the infantry on the left.

For some reason the party did not find Laing's Nek an easy battlefield to 'read'; under the hot sun the bare slopes stretched away on all sides, giving little help to the ardent efforts of the mind's eye to 'people' them with red-coated infantry and white-helmeted cavalry. We felt particularly aggrieved by this because we knew that it was the very last occasion when a British regiment carried its colours into action, when the 58th Regiment (2nd Battalion The Northamptonshire Regiment) advanced, headed by the Regimental Colours. Those same colours can be seen today in the National Army Museum in London, having been carried on parade until handed over on 17 July 1962.

Then came a roadside sign, pointing to Colley's grave. Like hounds after a fox, we bumped down a very rough track, both cars following each other in gigantic clouds of dust, and after a mile or so, came upon deserted ruined native dwellings. Halting, field-glasses were employed to discover on the far horizon, some three ridges away, a white monument set amid trees, which we assumed was the grave we sought – but the track was too rough to risk hired cars any further!

Part Seven

South Africa – The South African (Boer) War 1899–1902

23 *The Course of the War*

Take a community of Dutchmen of the type of those who defended themselves for fifty years against all the power of Spain at a time when Spain was the greatest power in the world. Intermix with them a strain of those inflexible French Huguenots who gave up home and fortune and left their country for ever at the time of the revocation of the Edict of Nantes. The product must obviously be one of the most rugged, virile, unconquerable races ever seen upon earth. Take this formidable people and train them for seven generations in constant warfare against savage men and ferocious beasts, in circumstances under which no weakling could survive, place them so that they acquire exceptional skills with weapons and in horsemanship, give them a country which is eminently suited to the tactics of the huntsman, the marksman, and the rider. Then, finally, put a finer temper upon their military qualities by a dour fatalistic Old Testament religion and an ardent and consuming patriotism. Combine all these qualities and all these impulses in one individual and you have the modern Boer – the most formidable antagonist who ever crossed the path of Imperial Britain. Our military history has largely consisted of our conflicts with France, but Napoleon and all his veterans have never treated us so roughly as these hard-bitten farmers with their ancient theology and their inconveniently modern rifles. (*The Great Boer War*, A Conan Doyle (1900))

Beginning in 1891, the discovery of gold and diamonds in the Dutch Republics of South Africa had attracted such large numbers of foreigners that they outnumbered the native Boers; they furnished most of the wealth on which the republics flourished, yet were denied any voice in government. Negotiations to amend this policy produced no results, and the Jameson Raid of 1895 provided a pretext for further stubbornness. The resulting situation became increasingly serious, causing reinforcements to be sent to existing British garrisons, and in October 1899, renouncing Imperial rule, the Boer Republics of the Transvaal and the Orange Free State firmly rejected being a part of a huge dominion of South Africa united under the British Crown, and declared war. Denys Reitz, serving with the Pretoria Commando, described how he, a teenager, saw it begin:

> At dawn on the morning of the 12th [of October] the assembled Commandos moved off. As far as the eye could see, the plain was alive with horsemen, guns and cattle, all steadily going forward to the frontier. The

scene was a stirring one, and I shall never forget riding to war with that great host.
(*Commando*, Denys Reitz (1967))

The campaign that was to follow was the most inglorious and yet the most difficult since the American War of Independence some 125 years before. No one in authority, with the exception of a disdained handful of officers, envisaged anything different from the constant succession of small wars that had been waged over the past fifty years of the Victorian era. None realised that hostilities would last for three years, with some 40,000 Boer farmers inflicting numerous defeats upon the most experienced Regular Army of the day. It was a war that asked too much of both generals and troops, some of whose ideas were still hidebound in Crimean, even Peninsular War, days. The Boers, all exceptional marksmen and horsemen, fighting on familiar terrain, could only be beaten by a display of military skill and individual resourcefulness far in advance of the hidebound methods of the barrack square.

The war began badly as, fearing to be branded the aggressors, the British government presented every opening advantage to the enemy – they sent out a force far too small, so that it suffered serious initial reverses of the type that peppered the conflict from beginning to end. It took only a few weeks of hostilities to make it evident that the enterprise was far beyond the strength of the army maintained for the security of the Empire, and far greater demands were imposed upon the Queen's Army than it could ever hope to satisfy. Before the war ended, nearly half a million soldiers from all parts of the British Empire had been brought to South Africa to win a war that sadly damaged Britain's reputation. The last of the 'Gentleman's Wars', and the first of the modern conflicts, by its ruthless revelation of the precision of twentieth-century weapons, the Boer War ushered the British soldier – long accustomed to fighting savages and tribesmen armed with muzzleloaders and spears – into the era of modern warfare.

Eventually, after strenuous efforts, all difficulties were overcome, but the various mishaps that occurred during the course of the three-year struggle were blown up into disasters producing unparalleled outbreaks of public hysteria. Although the military events in South Africa strained Britain's military strength to the utmost, the British Army learned the lesson well and the inestimable experience gained probably turned the tide for the British Expeditionary Force in France in the early days of World War I.

Thus, in October 1899 fast-moving Boer columns advanced both east and west: General Piet Cronje and his Transvaalers invested Mafeking; Free State forces besieged Kimberley; and the main Boer effort, under Transvaal General Joubert, moved into Natal towards Ladysmith,

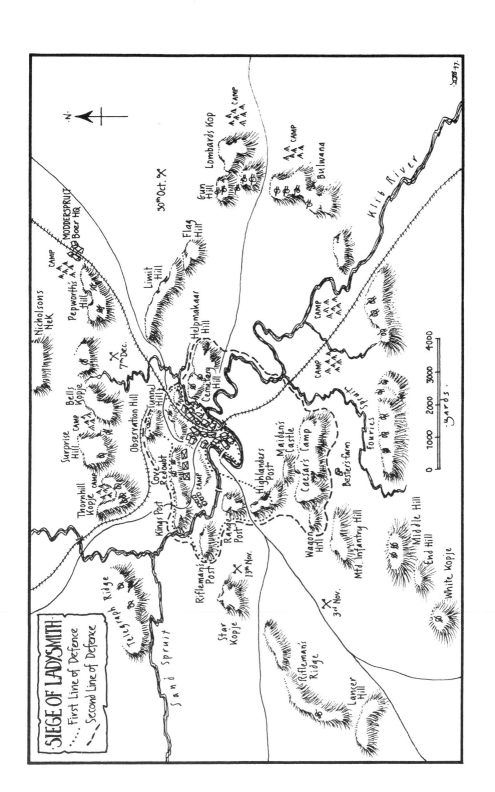

SIEGE OF LADYSMITH

.... First Line of Defence

— — — Second Line of Defence

N

Telegraph Ridge

Sand Spruit

Thornhill Kopje

Surprise Hill

CAMP

Nicholsons Nek

Bells Kopje

CAMP

Observation Hill

Cove Redoubt

Kings Post

Star Kopje

Riflemans Post

13th Nov.

3rd Nov.

Riflemans Ridge

Lancer Hill

White Kopje

End Hill

Middle Hill

Mtd. Infantry Hill

Wagon Hill

Caesar's Camp

Maiden's Castle

Highlanders Post

Range Post

GOD CAMP

Tunnel Hill

Cemetery Hill

7th Dec.

Helpmakaar Hill

Bester's Farm

Fouries Spruit

Limit Hill

Flag Hill

Pepworth's Hill

CAMP

MODDERSPRUIT Boer HQ

30th Oct.

Gun Hill

Lombards Kop

CAMP

Bulwana

CAMP

Klip River

CAMP

CAMP

CAMP

0   1000   2000   3000   4000

Yards.

opening the ball with a fierce action at Talana Hill on 20 October where the British commander General Penn Symons was killed. In quick succession followed Elandslaagte on 21 October, then Lombard's Kop and Nicholson's Nek on 30 October, before the tenacity of the highly mobile Boers persuaded General White to withdraw into Ladysmith, where Joubert put him under leisurely but effective siege. At Elandslaagte retreating burghers were repeatedly charged by British cavalry.

Now came a strange lull in the war – Ladysmith, Kimberley and Mafeking being besieged in a casual manner by the inexperienced Boers. General Ben Viljoen, Assistant Commandant-General to the Transvaal Burgher Forces, held decided views on the events of the time:

> The whole siege of Ladysmith and the manner in which the besieged garrison was ineffectually pounded at with our big guns for several months,

The Town Hall, Ladysmith 1899. Damaged by Boer shelling.

seem to me an unfathomable mystery which, owing to Joubert's untimely death, will never be satisfactorily explained.
(Contemporary statement)

Mr Easton, the *New York Journal* correspondent with the Boers, reported to his newspaper:

New commandos of Boers arrived every few days and these newcomers were eager for immediate assault, but General Joubert quietly persisted in carrying out his own plan. Suddenly it was announced to the surprise of nine out of ten Boers surrounding the town, that it was not his intention to make an assault, but to lay siege to the place. He then took 2,000 men as a flying-column and proceeded to Colenso and then to Escourt.
(*New York Journal*, Easten (1901))

It was a fatal error with Natal and Cape Colony virtually defenceless and at their mercy, allowing a large force to be assembled in Britain and hastily shipped to South Africa; reservists and volunteers rushed to the Colours, many formations marching through the streets of London *en route* to the docks.

In South Africa the force was under command of General Sir Redvers Buller, an archetypal Victorian commander considerably experienced in Colonial wars, with a reputation for bravery endorsed by a Victoria Cross from the Zulu War. Buller divided his army: he would lead a force into Natal to relieve Ladysmith, while General Lord Methuen took a relief column to Kimberley. Methuen's first action was at Belmont on 23 November, where a steep escarpment barred the way. It was a neat but costly action resulting in a British victory.

Then they came to the Modder River where Methuen, unaware of de la Rey's formidable entrenchments giving an excellent field of fire for his men's Mauser rifles, decided upon a frontal attack, confirming Cronje's assumption. When asked his reason for the belief, Cronje had a ready answer: 'The English do not make turning movements. They never leave the railway because they cannot march.'

Eventually a flanking development on the left turned the action into a British victory at a casualty cost of 7 per cent of Methuen's force; next morning the Boer trenches were empty of everything except spent cartridge cases and empty gin bottles.

Britain's 'Black Week' began with Gatacre's defeat at Stormberg in Cape Colony on 10 December when, in the words of Lord Roberts, Gatacre displayed 'a want of care, judgement, and even of ordinary military precautions' in attempting a night attack without competent guides to lead him to the Boers. 'Plodding aimlessly on in its dense formation and if there were any attempt at scouting ahead and on the flanks the result showed how ineffectively it was carried out.' (*The Great Boer War*,

A Conan Doyle (1900)). Stumbling into a smaller enemy force, the column was routed at considerable cost, compounded when it was later discovered that some 600 men had been left behind on a mountain to be taken prisoner. On the same day, further north at Magersfontein, Methuen, reinforced by the Highland Brigade, decided upon a night approach march to frontally attack Boer positions on a low range of hills, the last between the relief force and besieged Kimberley. As at Modder River, de la Rey had skilfully placed his defensives to give the best field of fire and, as daylight came at 4 am, the four regiments of the Highland Brigade, who set out in pouring rain at 9.30 pm in a mass quarter-column formed of ninety lines each of forty men, kept in formation by ropes carried by flanking officers, began to deploy about 300 yards from the nearest Boer trenches.

> In an instant there crashed out of the darkness into their faces and ears a roar of point-blank fire, and the night was slashed across with the throbbing flame of the rifles. At the moment before this outflame some doubt as to their whereabouts seems to have flashed across the mind of their leaders. The order to extend had just been given, but the men had not had time to act upon it. The storm of lead burst upon the head and right flank of the column, which broke to pieces under the murderous volley. Wauchope [General commanding the Brigade] struggled up, and fell once more, for ever. Men went down in swathes . . . by the hundred they dropped – some dead, some wounded, others knocked down by the rush and sway of the broken ranks. At such a range and in such formation a single Mauser bullet may well pass through many men . . . the first necessity was to gain shelter from the deadly fire which had stretched six hundred of their number upon the ground. (*The Great Boer War*, A Conan Doyle (1900))

The clear light of day revealed the broken Highland formation strewn over the veldt before the Boer positions; as the sun rose and the day grew hotter, the backs of legs revealed by thrown-up kilts became flayed and blistered. Now and then sporadic attacks were made and thrown back; in early afternoon a spontaneous and orderly retreat began, but soon turned into a rout: 'Next morning, the whole force with bitter and humiliated hearts were back at the camp at Modder River.' (*The Great Boer War*, A Conan Doyle (1900))

At daybreak on Friday 15 December, Buller began the misconceived assault that was to complete the triumvirate of British military disasters within the week. Lack of intelligence and bad reconnaissance at Colenso brought defeat as once again British formations were to walk into a fire-trap of unseen Boers in unknown numbers: the Guards at Modder River, the Highland Brigade at Magersfontein, and now the Royal Artillery at Colenso plus, for good measure, General Hart's Irish Brigade in an attempted river crossing. Colonel Charles Long, in command of twelve field guns and six naval guns, subscribed to the theory that guns should be pushed right forward into the face of the enemy and destroy him at close range or, as he put it: 'The only way to smash these beggars is to rush in at 'em.' Moving ahead of the infantry, guns, caissons and limbers went jingling forward, to unlimber solitarily 700 yards from the river and more than a mile in front of the infantry. Long later admitted: 'the light was a bit deceptive and I got a bit closer than I intended.' Coming under heavy fire, the twelve guns, in a neat line on the open, unprotected plain, were soon in difficulties:

> The teams fell in heaps . . . almost every gun had its litter of dead around it . . . from a most deadly rifle fire and the automatic quick-firers [had] found the range to a nicety and the little shells were crackling and banging continually over the batteries. The guns could not be worked, and yet they could not be removed, for every effort to bring up teams ended in the death of the horses. The survivors took refuge in a small hollow . . . for two hours the little knot of heart-sick humiliated officers and men . . . looked out at the bullet-swept plain and the line of silent guns. (*The Great Boer War*, A Conan Doyle (1900))

Volunteers went out to save the guns, among them young Lieutenant Roberts, only son of Lord Roberts, said to have been laughing and twirling his stick like a jockey, but before he had gone thirty yards he was shot from his saddle; later he was awarded a posthumous Victoria Cross.

The attempts were abandoned and later in the day the Boers came out and carried the guns away. The Boer commander General Botha was much affected by events:

> I was on the hill above the bridge there and with the field glasses could see it all. All our people were watching: it was a terrible thing to see, like looking down at a play from the gallery. When the teams and the men were shot down, just swept away by our fire . . . and when we saw another lot of men and more teams dash to work to save the guns we held our breath; it was madness; nothing could live there. Then came another lot, and another, and another . . . I was sick with horror that such bravery should be so useless. God, I turned away and could not look; and yet I had to look again. It was too wonderful. (*The Boer War*, Eversley Belfield (1975))

On the British left flank, Hart's Irish Brigade advanced into an unexpected loop of the River Tugela to come under very heavy cross-fire upon their right flank and shrapnel from the front.

> Incredible as it may appear after the recent experiences of Magersfontein and Stormberg, the men in the two rear regiments appear to have been advanced in quarter column, and not to have deployed until after the enemy's fire had opened. (*The Great Boer War*, A Conan Doyle (1900))

Shouting angrily, the Irishmen pushed on to reach the bank of the river, only to discover that no ford existed:

> and they lay down, as had been done in so many previous actions, unwilling to retreat and unable to advance, with the same merciless pounding from front and flank. In every fold and behind every anthill the Irishmen lay thick and waited for better times . . . for five hours, under the tropical sun, the grimly parched men held on. (*The Great Boer War*, A Conan Doyle (1900))

The British commander Buller, remarked: 'Hart has got himself into a devil of a mess down there.' He ordered the retreat, which was carried out reluctantly by the Irish.

In despair, Buller heliographed White in besieged Ladysmith, saying: 'The enemy is too strong for my force . . . I cannot break in . . . fire away as much ammunition as you have and make the best terms you can'. Finding it hard to credit the suggestion as being genuine, White spurned it.

In gloomy, mist-enshrouded, mid-winter Britain, few thoughts occupied any minds other than the Black Week 10 to 17 December 1899.

In mid-December Field Marshal Lord Roberts, aged 67, was appointed commander of all British forces in South Africa, with General Herbert Kitchener, aged 49, his Chief-of-Staff – they landed in Cape Town on 10 January 1900 and immediately began planning a surprise eastward flank march to relieve Kimberley. Meanwhile, in Natal, Buller was about to embark upon the most costly battle of his abortive campaign to relieve Ladysmith by attacking Spion Kop, the most formidable hill in the whole line of the Tugela Heights separating them from the besieged city. With most of the army looking on, a small number of men scrambled courageously to the top of the hill during the night, only to find that its rocky surface prevented the digging of any shelter more than eighteen inches deep. When day came, some 3,000 men lay exposed on the rocky plateau, crowded into an area of a little over three acres, and coming under furious fire from Boers in commanding positions around them.

Leaving 1,500 killed, wounded and missing on Spion Kop, the British came down, and Buller moved his army back across the Tugela: 'while Ladysmith, sick with hope deferred, waited gloomily upon half rations of horse-flesh for the next movement from the south' (*The Great Boer War*, A Conan Doyle (1900)).

In contrast to Buller's blunderings, Roberts put the finishing touches to his meticulously planned offensive, an outflanking operation led by French's cavalry avoiding a head-on collision with the Boers' strong defensive positions. Pushing aside opposition at the two rivers, Riet and Modder:

all day they rode, hussars, dragoons and lancers over the withered veldt, until men and horses dropped with heat and exhaustion. A front of nearly two miles was kept, the regiments moving two abreast in open order; and the sight of this magnificent cloud of horsemen sweeping over the great barren plain was a glorious one. (*The Great Boer War*, A Conan Doyle (1900))

In three days they reached their goal, and Kimberley was relieved on 15 February, thousands lining the streets to cheer General French's squat figure as he led his men in.

Outflanked and in danger of being cut off from his capital at Bloemfontein, Cronje pulled out of Magersfontein and moved east along the Modder River, burdened by large numbers of women and children with some 400 wagons; many of his men had become 'voetgangers' – horseless ones. Pursued by French's cavalry and quickly surrounded by force-marched British infantry, Cronje was trapped in the steep banks of Paardeberg Drift, where he held off costly and reckless attacks by Kitchener. Returning after illness, Roberts set about shelling the entrapped Boers into surrender.

On 27 February – Majuba Day – after a nine-day siege, Cronje reluctantly surrendered 2,700 Transvaalers and 1,400 Free Staters, having lost 117 killed – it was nearly 10 per cent of the entire Boer Field Force.

The Relief of Ladysmith Main Street, 28 February 1900.

President Paul Kruger, his cause suddenly and dramatically stricken, cried: 'The English have taken our Majuba Day away from us!' Perhaps this first decisive victory was some consolation for Colley's defeat nineteen years earlier.

On that same day, Buller finally bestirred himself and made another attempt to relieve Ladysmith, against a Boer force depleted in numbers and dispirited; after six hours of heavy fighting the way to the town was cleared.

Events now began to move swiftly, as the heavily reinforced British began to advance on all fronts; Roberts took Bloemfontein, the capital of the Orange Free State, on 13 March and reached Kroonstad on May 12, while Buller in Natal swept Boer resistance away at Glencoe and Dundee on 15 May. Roberts sent 1,700 cavalry and a posse of newspapermen to relieve Mafeking on 17 May, unleashing in Britain an unbridled rejoicing that has never been equalled, bringing a new word into the English language – to 'maffick' or exult riotously. Next came an invasion of the Transvaal: Johannesburg fell on 31 May and the capital, Pretoria, on 5 June; Roberts and Buller joined forces at Vlakfontein on 4 July and ended all formal resistance. Roberts went home, leaving Kitchener in command, but things were far from over as de Wet, de la Rey, Botha and others conducted active guerrilla warfare, forcing Kitchener to build blockhouses to protect communication. In an action at Tweebosch on 7 March 1901, de la Rey defeated a British force and actually captured General Methuen, causing Kitchener to 'go all to pieces' and retire to bed for thirty-six hours. But his policy of containment began to work at last and in April 1902 he met with the Boer leaders, and on 31 May a peace treaty was signed at Vereeniging. In 1906 the Transvaal became a self-governing colony, followed by the Orange Free State in 1907, and in 1910 the two Boer colonies joined Cape Province and Natal to become the Union of South Africa.

A Chronology of the War

Phase I: The Boer offensive, the British besieged
   1899
   Oct   13   Boers invaded Natal
          14   Sieges of Kimberley and Mafeking started
          20   Battle of Talana
          21   Battle of Elandslaagte
          30   Battle of Lombard's Kop
          30   Siege of Ladysmith started
          31   Buller arrived at Cape Town

Phase II: British attempts to relieve Kimberley and Ladysmith

Nov	23	Battle of Belmont
	25	Battle of Graspan
	28	Battle of Modder River
Dec	10	Battle of Stormberg
	11	Battle of Magersfontein } Black Week
	15	Battle of Colenso
	17	Roberts appointed Commander-in-Chief

1900

Jan	6	Boer attack on Ladysmith
	10	Roberts arrived in Cape Town
	23/4	Battle of Spion Kop
Feb	5	Battle of Vaal Krantz

Phase III: British offensives and collapse of organised Boer resistance

Feb	15	Relief of Kimberley
	27	Surrender of Cronje at Paardeberg
	28	Ladysmith relieved
Mar	7	Battle of Poplar Grove
	13	Bloemfontein captured
	31	de Wet's successful ambush at Sannah's Post
May	3	Roberts began the march from Bloemfontein to Pretoria
	31	Roberts entered Johannesburg
June	5	Roberts entered Pretoria
	11	Battle of Diamond Hill
July	30	Prinsloo surrendered at Brandwater Basin
July/Aug		Burning of farms used by guerrilla fighters authorised
July/Aug		First de Wet hunt
Sept	11	Kruger fled to Europe
	25	British reached Koomati Poort, the end of Delagoa Bay railway line

Phase IV: The guerrilla war

Nov 29	Roberts finally handed over to Kitchener
Nov/Dec	Second de Wet hunt
Dec	Hertzog and Kritzinger entered Cape Colony

1901

Jan/Feb	Third de Wet hunt
Mar/Apr	French's Transvaal drive
Mar	Middleburg Peace Conference between Kitchener and Botha
July	Smuts entered Cape Colony
Sept	Botha's attempted invasion of Natal
Oct 30	Benson killed

1902

Jan/Feb		Large drives against de Wet in Orange Free State
Jan	25	Ben Viljoen captured
Mar	7	de la Rey captured Methuen at Tweebosch
Mar	23	Peace negotiations started
Apr	11	Kemp's defeat at Roodewall
May	30	Peace of Vereeniging signed. War cost Britain £220m.

24 The Battle of Spion Kop
23/24 January 1900

It would be difficult to improve upon the following account of the dramatic disaster suffered by Redvers Buller's British force, as published at the time in a contemporary journal:

The term 'Spion Kop', often applied to the range from which it stands up as a remarkably shaped hill, about 1,400 feet high, is about two miles in extent from east to west in its higher features. At its eastern extremity there are two points, called by us the 'Twin Peaks', which are 200 feet lower than the main hill, and from these peaks the ridge bends to the north-east, then descending gradually. There is another chain of hills standing back to the eastward at some distance, called Brakfontein, 14 miles to the north-east of which lies Ladysmith.

The highest features of Spion Kop are peculiar, and its occupation in a fog so dense as to prevent its configuration being appreciated led to disastrous results. The top contour has the shape of a triangle with a flattened nose towards north-north-east, and its base running 300 yards east and west; but to the eastward of this top contour, and 75 feet lower, there is a saddle-back projecting north-east, terminated by a rocky knoll covered by aloe trees. Until late in the fight the British troops made no effort to occupy this knoll, and from it on January 24th many of our soldiers were shot lying in a trench, which was so completely enfiladed that 70 men who were firing in a north-westerly direction were shot in the right side of the head by Boers concealed in the aloes.

On the west end of the main hill there is a flat, narrow plateau jutting out 1,200 yards in a north-westerly direction.

The main hill descends on its southern side by a gradual slope for two miles to Wright's Farm, which is half a mile north of Trichardt's Drift.

Most of the casualties our troops suffered on the hill were due, as we stated above, to the faulty position taken up when the Boers fled from the summit in a dense fog. There was a balloon available, but without it a sketch might have been easily made, for a well-trained cavalry brigade was at hand.

Many disadvantages to the public service accrued from the Commander-in-Chief having deputed to Sir Charles Warren the command of the striking force of the army, but the first and very unfortunate instance was the

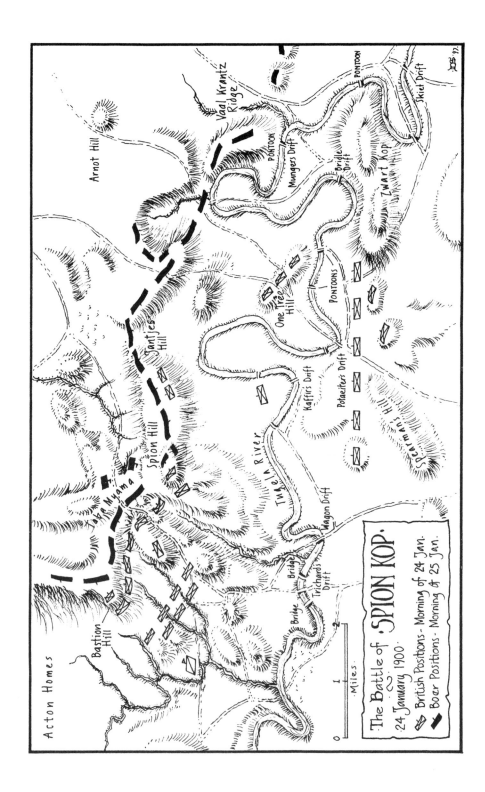

The Battle of 'SPION KOP.'
24 January 1900.

⟋ British Positions - Morning of 24 Jan.
▬ Boar Positions - Morning of 25 Jan.

Miles

0   1   2

Acton Homes

Bastion Hill

Tabanyama

Spion Hill

Tjantjes Hill

Arnot Hill

Vaal Krantz Ridge

PONTOON

Mungers Drift

Bridle Drift

Zwart Kop

PONTOON

Skiet Drift

One Tree Hill

PONTOONS

Spearman's Hill

Kaffirs Drift

Potgeiteri Drift

Tugela River

Wagon Drift

Bridge

Trichards Drift

Bridge

fettering by the General of his cavalry Brigadier. Spion Kop might have been easily accurately sketched, for Lord Dundonald could have occupied it January 18th or 19th with little or no loss; but Sir Charles Warren preferred to keep his cavalry close to the infantry.

The Commander-in-Chief rode over early on January 22nd to Three Tree Hill, and told Sir Charles Warren that he disapproved of his scheme for a prolonged cannonade of the Boer position, and favoured an attack on their right flank; but he left the decision to Sir Charles Warren intimating, however, that unless some attack on the Boers was carried out, he

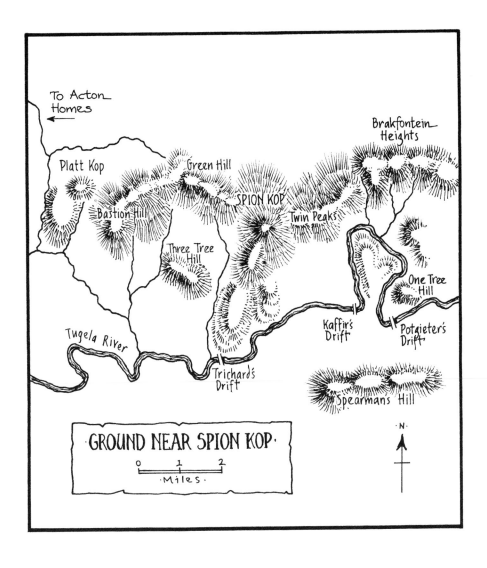

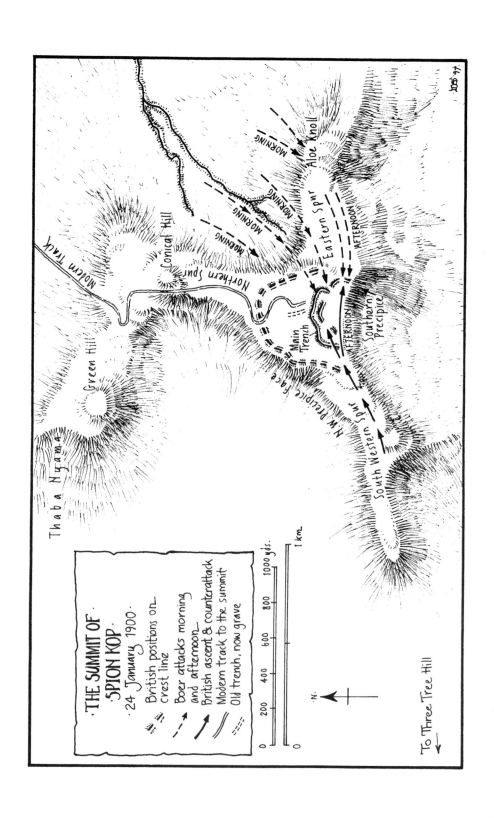

THE SUMMIT OF
· SPION KOP ·
· 24 January 1900 ·

British positions on
crest line

Boer attacks morning
and afternoon

British ascent & counterattack

Modern track to the summit

Old trench, now grave

0   200   400   600   800   1000 yds.

0   1 km.

N

To Three Tree Hill

Thaba Nyama

Green Hill

Modern Track

Conical Hill

Northern Spur

Main Trench

N.W. Precipice Face

Eastern Spur

Aloe Knoll

MORNING

MORNING

MORNING

MORNING

AFTERNOON

AFTERNOON

AFTERNOON

Southern Precipice

South Western Spur

DS '97

intended to withdraw all the troops to the south of the Tugela River. Sir Charles Warren then elected to attack Spion Kop.

He marched with 1,700 men of his own brigade at 8.30 pm, January 23rd, beginning the climb of the mountain at 11 pm, guided by Colonel Thorneycroft. The progress was painfully slow, for the night was very dark, and light rain fell throughout the march; but at 3.30 am, when the troops reached the summit, the Boer picket on it fled, after firing one volley, leaving one man bayoneted.

The Boers in their flight carried the news to their line of outposts; many

wagons were packed, the oxen inspanned, and were moved off northwards and eastwards, accompanied by their owners. Commandant Schalk Burger, in command of the Boers east of Spion Kop, sent for reinforcements. Louis Botha, galloping to Acton Holmes, moved the big Krupp guns farther to the east, and removed one heavy Krupp piece, which was then in the valley immediately north of Spion Kop, to a position on the Tabanyama range, 3,000 yards from the hill which Woodgate had occupied.

At 6 am, January 24th, 250 Carolina burghers ascended the Aloe Knoll of the Spion Kop unseen, while Botha brought up men on the north and north-west sides of the hill.

When General Woodgate reached the summit without opposition the mist was so dense that he could not appreciate the configuration of its top contours; but 200 yards of trench were dug, the left flank facing northwards, and the right and shorter face slightly drawn back and facing north-north-east. The work was not well executed, for the ground was very hard, and the men were worn out from incessant marching and counter-marching, with broken rest at night. Moreover, the sandbags which had been collected at the bivouacs had been left behind when the ascent was commenced.

At 8 am, when the mist, which had been lifting, fell again, it was still impossible to note the configuration of the ground, and when the morning finally cleared at 8.30 the Boers opened fire from Aloe Knoll, from which spot throughout the day, at from 300 to 400 yards, easy targets were found on the soldiers as they lay in the trenches, firing to the north-west, 70 of them being shot through the right side of the head.

The Boer heavy guns north of Spion Kop, and on Twin Peaks, soon got the range, assisted by the directions given by a heliograph party stationed on Aloe Knoll.

General Woodgate walked along the trenches in which the men were lying down answering fire at close range. He was mortally wounded about 9 am, after dispatching a message which was received at Sir Redvers Buller's head-quarters at Spearman's Hill, stating the situation. Captain Vertue, his Brigade-Major, who had shown a disregard of danger similar to that of his heroic General, was killed soon afterwards.

General Sir Charles Warren, who had been moving from point to point of his command since 3 am, ordered General Coke at 9 am to reinforce the troops on the summit. He sent up the Imperial Light Infantry, but the officer commanding did not realise where his men were most wanted, and soon afterwards Coke ordered up the Middlesex Regiment, under Colonel Hill.

At 11 am General Coke, at his repeated request, was allowed to go up the hill, taking the 2nd Dorset Regiment, and at this time the greater part of his command was on the hill-top, or in reserve immediately below it.

There were still two other generals available, and about 10,000 men, but no attempts were made to molest the Boers, who were seen moving men and heavy guns from west to east on the northern part of the Tabanyama range, in order to assail the troops on Spion Kop.

At 10 am January 24th, General Sir Charles Warren learnt by signal from the summit that General Woodgate was dying and that reinforcements were required, but he still failed to appreciate the danger of the situation, nor did he realise till the end of the fight that Aloe Knoll was not held by our troops.

At 11.45 am Sir Charles Warren, acting on a suggestion (heliographed) from the Commander-in-Chief, who was on the hill overlooking Potgieter's Drift, signalled to Spion Kop that Colonel Thorneycroft was appointed a Brigadier, and was to command all troops on the summit, but he omitted to inform General Coke, who was then ascending the hill, of his supersession.

After General Woodgate fell, Colonel Crofton on the left and Thorneycroft on the right had striven nobly to induce the front sections, which were extended along the crest from 50 to 150 yards in front of the trench, to maintain their position under a heavy fire of artillery and well-aimed rifles; but by 10.30 am Colonel Bloomfield (Lancashire Fusiliers), who had given a fine example to his men, was wounded, and those on the right flank were driven back into the trench. The danger of the pressure on the men in front became more severe, and at 11 am Colonel Thorneycroft led an heroic charge with 40 men towards the crest; many were shot, the rest lay down.

Thorneycroft, who, when he was running forward, had twisted his ankle badly in a fall, from behind a rock fired on the nearest Boers with his pistol. In spite of all his efforts, the enemy by noon had gained the crest, and the British trench then became the front line, but was choked with dead, wounded, and dying men, and there were but few effective soldiers in it who were still using their rifles.

Colonel Crofton, who was working vigorously to maintain the defence on the left of the summit, passed on a message to Colonel Thorneycroft on the opposite flank that he, Thorneycroft, had been appointed to command the troops on the hill. This was the result of the suggestion of the Commander-in-Chief. The officer as he was himself carrying it across to Thorneycroft, passed a group of soldiers opposite to a threatened point of the attack. He led them forward, and in doing so dropped the message, and, then, becoming involved in the firing line, which under the circumstances he could not leave, he never saw Colonel Thorneycroft for several hours.

Thorneycroft had, however, been told by another officer, but before he had grasped the significance of the message, he sent the officer who brought it away to guide reinforcements, then ascending the hill, to a point where they were most required.

At 1 pm some of the troops in the right face of the trench, all their officers having been killed or wounded, surrendered, in spite of Colonel Thorneycroft's efforts, who, followed by a few resolute men, limped over to avert the shameful disaster. Thorneycroft and the Boers met for a few minutes at speaking distance, and 167 British soldiers followed the Boers over the crest. When Thorneycroft and his few followers were hurrying back to some cover behind rocks, fire was reopened.

At that moment one company of the 2nd Middlesex had reached the left of the trench, and when Thorneycroft was limping out on the right, Major Savile led forward a section with fixed bayonets to stop the surrender.

He was too late, however. The section was driven back, and Major Savile was wounded, but at the same moment another company of the Middlesex coming up near Thorneycroft, he led a cheering string of men across the fire-swept plateau, charging the Boers, who fled down the hill with their demoralised prisoners.

Now the Boer guns, which had ceased fire to allow, as it was thought, of the taking over of the position, reopened on Thorneycroft's triumphant little band as they stood on the crest firing on the retreating Boers, and the accurately placed shells forced Thorneycroft and his men back to cover of some rocks.

Then, the Boers, collecting some men under the northern crest of the summit, charged the centre of the trench, in which the men had been hither-to steady, and they, panic-stricken, ran back from it. Colonel Crofton, with Bugler Russell, ran forward sounding the 'Advance', and the men, stop-ping in their flight, were about to return, when Captain Dyer (2nd Middlesex) with his company, broke through the panic-stricken crowd of soldiers, and re-occupied the trench, where Colonel Thorneycroft remained until 2 pm, being the driving power of the men in the firing line at that portion of the defence.

At 2.30 pm he wrote to Sir Charles Warren, describing the situation, and urging the necessity of an attack being made on the enemy's guns if the British position on the hill was to be maintained. No steps were taken to carry this recommendation into effect.

General Coke, when he was slowly climbing the hill from the lowest of three plateaux which occur in the sharp ascent, ordered the reinforcements then going up to halt on the second plateau until further orders, as he believed that there were more men on the summit than could be usefully employed.

In complete ignorance of the fight which was being waged under Crofton and Thorneycroft, he signalled to Sir Charles Warren at the moment when the men were surrendering in the front trench, the words, 'Holding on well'. A quarter of an hour later he received a report from Colonel Hill of the surrender, while he himself was still slowly climbing up the spur, and he now sent up nine companies.

When General Coke at 3 pm received a message asking for reinforcements, he had not realised the fact of his supersession, and sent on the Cameronians (2nd Scottish Rifles), who, under Colonel Cooke, of Lyttelton's brigade, had been within call since 2 pm. Colonel Cooke led in front of the first company, in perfect order, across the plateau at the double to the front trench, the succeeding companies as they came up going to the right and left of the position alternately.

Some of the men in the trench immediately to the left of where the men had surrendered – and it should in fairness be stated that the slaughter in that part of the trench had been very severe – were now demoralised, and this induced the Boers to mount the crest again and come forward. They were charged by a company of the Cameronians, and driven back, and two companies of the battalion henceforth held successfully the left or north-west corner of the summit.

There were continuous charges on the slope and the summit, but gradually the Boers gained ground, and eventually held nearly all the second contour of the hill. At 3.30 pm about forty Boers, creeping forward under the east edge of the crest, got nearly behind Colonel Thorneycroft, but were then checked.

It is remarkable that though General Coke and Colonel Thorneycroft now signalled to the same effect to General Warren regarding the situation, neither of these officers appreciated the necessity of retaking the Aloe Knoll on the east and driving the Boers from the north-west crest.

At 7 pm Commandant Oberman led a few determined men up the east slope, when he opened fire on the Scottish Rifles at 20 yards' distance, but was hotly received and driven back.

Neither Colonel Hill nor General Coke knew that they had been superseded by Thorneycroft, nor did he know that General Coke had been giving orders for some hours.

At 6.30 pm Thorneycroft wrote to Sir Charles Warren a brief statement of the position on the summit, ending with the words, 'The situation is critical'.

Throughout a long day's fighting Colonel Thorneycroft had received no communication from the General in Command. When the Colonel looked down the hill he had seen 10,000 men under Generals Clery and Hildyard lying inactive. He and his men had been shelled with remarkable accuracy, while the British guns, for some reason unknown to him, had ceased to fire. He was ignorant that Sir Charles Warren had spent the day in collecting supplies and entrenching tools at the foot of the hill, with the intention of holding it; and that he was preparing to bring up guns; and that Thorneycroft now decided to evacuate the position. He had fought with unsurpassed resolution for eleven hours, but at 8 pm, after a few minutes' consultation with the only two senior officers he had seen throughout the fight, defined his views, and expressed his determination to retire in the pithy sentence: 'Better six battalions off the hill than a mop-up in the morning.'

The Scottish Rifles were ordered to form a rear-guard. They carried all the wounded men they could from the summit.

At 2 am General Coke reached Sir Charles Warren, who then telegraphed to the Commander-in-Chief, begging him to come over; and he, arriving at dawn, carried out the retirement across the Tugela.

The total British casualties from January 19th to January 24th were 87 officers and 1,860 other ranks, killed, wounded, or taken prisoners. The Boers lost about 400 men.

At nightfall Louis Botha, who had realised the loss which had been inflicted on the British troops on the summit of Spion Kop, hoped that they might abandon the hill, and if they did so intended to reoccupy it. A messenger sent to Schalk Burger, on the Boer left flank, returned with a report that he and his men had fled towards Ladysmith when Colonel Buchanan-Riddell, with the 3rd King's Royal Rifle Corps, had captured Twin Peaks. Shortly afterwards Botha learnt that most of his men had left their positions, and that, moreover, in passing, they had frightened away the burgher ox-wagons, which had been massed to the north-east of Spion Kop in a place of safety.

Botha collected men from Brakfontein and a few from Acton Holmes who had not been affected by the panic felt by those who had been engaged at Spion Kop and Twin Peaks, and he was personally determined that he would not retire. At 3.30 am he learnt from burghers who had gone up to Spion Kop to look for the body of a dead comrade that the British troops had retired from the summit, which he reoccupied at 4.30 am with a few men. He fully deserved the success, for his men for many hours had fought with determined courage, the Carolina detachment on Aloe Knoll losing 62 per cent of its number.

Some mistakes

General Sir Charles Warren had worked strenuously all day in amassing stores and entrenching tools, and in making other arrangements for the prolonged occupation of the hill, in the defence of which, however, he exercised no beneficial influence. If he had gone up himself his presence for half an hour on the summit would have prevented all the confusion which ensued as to the command of the troops. Great delay and inconvenience and consequent loss of life was caused by the fact that when his camp and head-quarters were shifted no intimation was given to those who wished to refer to him for instructions.

Much as all soldiers must admire Colonel Thorneycroft's indomitable personal courage, sustained for eleven hours, there are few who will attempt to justify his action in withdrawing the troops from a position for the maintenance of which he was responsible, and for which many brave men had given their lives.

This was the boldest and most successful offensive tactical operation undertaken by the Boers.

25 *Spion Kop Today*

There can be no natural reason whatsoever for the topography of the top of Spion Kop to have changed in the seventy-nine years that had passed between the bloody conflict on the summit and the breathless arrival of our party. And, indeed it has not, except for those man-made and installed artefacts commemorating the sacrifices made by British and Boers in January 1900, when coincidentally heralding the arrival of a new century. In the same way as does the summit of Majuba Hill, that other British Valhalla in South Africa, Spion Kop lays broodingly desolate in the bright sunlight, sharing with Majuba a pervasive aura that can leave no modern intruder unaffected. The battle arena now forms part of the Spion Kop Nature Reserve and is visited by more sightseers than in the past; nevertheless it remains an eerie and mystical place.

From the wooded heights of Mount Alice, overlooking Potgieter's

The memorial on top of Spion Kop. Stretching away from it is the trench-line held by Thorneycroft's Mounted Infantry, who were buried *en masse* in the trench where they fell.

The massed grave of the Lancashire Fusiliers in the trench where they were killed, on top of Spion Kop. A single cross, of iron, lies on the whitewashed stones.

Drift and standing 1,000 feet above the Tugela River, an inspiring panorama is spread out – a semicircle of heights falling away to a low undulating ridge named Brakfontein, over which passes the road to Ladysmith, about eighteen miles away. Looking down at the Tugela, it appears to be 'a silver serpent on a shield of green'. The semicircle of heights is marked by two massive buttresses, Spion Kop on the left, Val Krantz to the right.

As seen from the south-west, Spion Kop is a conical-shaped mountain, rising 1,470 feet above the level of the Tugela. It has a narrow saddle 1,200 yards long, running roughly north; from its pommel, off towards the east, there is a ridge which, at about 450 yards, throws up a small bump – Alice Knoll – and then, at about 2,000 and 2,250 yards respectively, lies Twin Peaks, then it falls away to merge into the Brakfontein Heights. At the other end of the saddle, where Conical Hill towers up to end only 90 feet or so below the highest point of Spion Kop, there is a gully separating Spion Kop from Green Hill, the loftiest feature on the Tabanyama heights; like Twin Peaks, Green Hill is about 200 feet lower than the summit of Spion Kop. To the east, south-east and west the sides of Spion Kop are steep, often nearly perpendicular; only to the south is the formidable mountain approachable.

The trench on top of Spion Kop in which are buried men of the Lancashire Fusiliers and the South Lancs, under Colonel Crofton.

Spion Kop. The memorial to fallen Boers on the edge of the summit where they ascended to the attack. It bears the names of 66 dead with their commanders.

On the day of the battle, the summit was closed-in with dense cloud, and only when it dispersed did the British troops realise that they had not reached the top, and from commanding positions above them, the Boers were able to pick them off, the Lancashire Fusiliers being particularly exposed to a deadly enfilading fire from Aloe Knoll.

On arriving on the mist-enshrouded summit, the soldiers attempted to dig trenches with their small regulation tools, but were halted at eighteen inches by solid rock, thus the resulting shallow ditch, nowhere more than two and a half to three feet deep, ran roughly east and west, with a slight curve in its centre causing it to be a boomerang shape. The Lancashire Fusiliers lined the trench on the right, the Mounted Infantry in the centre, and the Royal Lancaster Regiment on the left, in what was to be their graves. When the fighting ended, their bodies were left where they had slumped forward, in a mass grave covered with piles of rocks and stones, later painted white and enclosed with a wire fence. All the stones and memorials on top of Spion Kop are regularly re-painted by the Natal Historical Society.

There is an impressive monument to the Boer Commandos who fought on the summit on that memorable day; and numerous other memorials, such as the marble cross on a pedestal to the memory of Lieutenant T K Flowers-Ellis of Johannesburg; there are also many tablets bearing lettered plaques.

However, perhaps the most evocative of all that is up there is not a designated memorial at all, yet the imagination brings to life the tragic events happening on and around the large flat 'billiard-table' rock with another slab arising to its front, like the headstone of a grave. During our tour of these South African battlefields our party was 'taken in hand' by Ladysmith attorney Pitch Christopher, who had served with British infantry in World War II, and whose luxurious house in the town was that same one used by General Sir George White as his HQ during the 1899 siege. Escorting us to the summit of the Kop, he stood by this rocky configuration and pointed out the long white stone-covered trench stretching from the rocks across the plateau, beginning some twenty yards from the rocks, the grave of Lancashire Fusiliers, left where they had fallen.

He told us how, in 1905, his grandfather had taken his father to where we were standing, and around those rocks they had picked-up thirty-six Mauser cartridge cases from bullets fired by a Boer who had lain on the flat rock, his rifle barrel steadied in the cleft in the upright slab. From that perfect position, he had calmly and systematically shot through the head man after man in succession along the line of lying soldiers at point-blank range.

Nearly twenty years later there arose an odd sequel to this cameo, when I was reading in a novel by fiction writer Joanna Trolloppe her account of a Boer father carefully placing his teenage son on that horizontal slab, to carry out sniping activity – as part of the fictional narrative of the story. From the acknowledgement given at the front of the book to Pitch Christopher, it is evident that he took her up there, just as he did us.

Our party laboriously climbed to the top of Spion Kop, despite being informed that it was possible to drive a Jeep up there, although it was a rough ride requiring a skilful driver. But we walked for, as one of our party said: 'If walking was good enough for my grandfather, it is good enough for me!'

26 *Mini Memories of Walking the Battlefields of the South African (Boer) War*

Maps Required:

A Guide Map for the Tourist for the Republic of South Africa
(South African Tourist Corporation, London)
Touring Atlas of the Republic of South Africa
(Map Studio Production (Pty) Ltd, Johannesburg)

In early October 1899 a force of about 14,000 Transvaalers invaded Natal with Ladysmith as their main objective. Here General Sir George White had a garrison of about 8,000 troops; Major-General Sir Penn Symons had a force of 4,000 at Dundee, forty miles away. It was against them, at Talana Hill near Dundee, that the first shots of the war were fired on 20 October, when 3,500 Boers occupied the hill during the night. The short battle that followed was a technical British victory, the British losing their commander General Penn Symons, whose grave can be seen in the English churchyard at Talana.

On the day before Talana, the Boers had occupied Elandslaagte, which lay on the line of the British retreat from Dundee to Ladysmith; General French, a newly arrived British cavalry leader, took a force to deal with them, and the Boers were defeated in a costly battle when Colonel Ian Hamilton dashingly led a British force against them. The fleeing Boers were charged by British cavalry and, being quite unused to such tactics, were completely routed and thereafter held a deep hatred for the cavalry. Our party was taken round the battlefield by a local historian and saw unnamed Boer graves alongside the railway line and under the conical hill; others can be seen in Ladysmith cemetery, but we were told that, for many years, crosses littered the fields.

By the beginning of November the Boers were besieging the town of Ladysmith, held by some 14,000 soldiers, with many refugees, under command of General Sir George White. During the 118 days' investment until 26 February 1900, shelling killed 1,800 soldiers and civilians, with as many more lost by disease. The little siege museum, next to the town hall, is very good and well laid out with a host of contemporary photographs of the starving days when the town was said to be a

The grave at Dundee of the British Commander General Penn-Symons, mortally
wounded at Talana, the first battle of the South African War 1898–1902.

'manure-pit'. Sunk in the pavement outside the Royal Hotel is a brass
plaque marking where a shell from the Boers' 'Long Tom' field guns killed
Dr Stark by blowing off his legs. It was this same Royal Hotel where
a battlefield walker's bonus found all seven of our party invited to a
Rotary luncheon at which our spokesman addressed the members.

   Living in the house used by General White as his headquarters during
the siege, at the time of our visit, was Pitch Christopher, an attorney who
had served as company commander in a Scottish infantry regiment during
World War II; it was he who took us to the summit of Spion Kop and,
together with Sheila Henderson, to many of the battlefields surrounding
the town.

One such site was Tchrengular, where a personal touch was added by being taken over the area by the late George Tatham, who owned Hydewood Farm on which the battlefield lay. A noted local historian, Mr Tatham showed us, among other things, the remains of earthworks occupied by the Dublin Fusiliers in an action at the end of October when, realising that the Boers were on higher ground at one end of the Tchrengular Ridge and taking heavy losses from their fire, they were surrendered by Colonel Carleton, their commander.

On 15 December 1899, in an ill-informed attempt to relieve Ladysmith,

At Manchester Fort at Caesar's Camp outside Ladysmith, the Naval Brigade had their galley, suitably marked by the cooks.

Buller led 21,000 men of all arms in an attempt to turn the 6,000 entrenched Boers' left flank; but, hindered by difficult terrain, they were decimated by accurate rifle fire. British artillery batteries under Colonel Long moved forward on their own and unlimbered eighteen guns on the completely open veldt; within a few minutes guncrews and horses took heavy losses and they ceased fire, and were soon abandoned; Colonel Long was mortally wounded. Today it is possible to find the gully where the team horses sheltered and where Long died; there are six small cairns in the long grass, marking the position of the six righthand guns. In a gallant effort to save the guns, Field Marshal Lord Roberts's son, a lieutenant in the 60th Rifles and ADC to Buller, died winning a Victoria Cross; he is commemorated by a monument near Colenso station. Buller himself was wounded by a shell burst and ordered a withdrawal, after suffering more than 1,000 casualties and losing ten guns; the Boer losses were six dead and twenty-one wounded. Many British dead were buried in a beautiful Garden of Remembrance, 3 km from Colenso on the Winterton Road. In Colenso itself there is the R E Stevenson Museum, near the old bridge and the police station.

Lieutenant Frederick Roberts, killed whilst winning the Victoria Cross at Colenso, is buried in the small war cemetery just beyond Chieveley station. His memorial stands out from others commemorating those who died in the hospital there from wounds or enteric fever, and stands serene beneath large trees in a rarely visited but very peaceful place.

Chieveley has other claims to fame because it was there that an armoured train, carrying a 7-pounder muzzle-loading gun and over 100 men, was derailed by Boers on 15 November 1899. There were some casualties and prisoners were taken, among them the young Winston Churchill, war correspondent for the *Morning Post*, who later spectacularly escaped.

A very personal battlefield bonus was a pilgrimage to the grave of the Prince Imperial of France, killed in a Zulu ambush on 1 June 1879, near a native kraal seven miles from Itelezi Hill overlooking the Ityotozi River. As author of the book *Captain Carey's Blunder* (Leo Cooper Ltd, 1973) which tells the story of this tragic encounter, the site bore a definite familiarity: there was the native kraal where the patrol was resting when attacked by Zulus, there the donga in which the Prince was killed when his horse ran away. Today it is marked by a marble cross donated by Queen Victoria in 1880, and small memorials mark the resting place of Troopers Abel and Rogers, who were also killed.

Battlefield walking is not solely stretching the imagination to transform peaceful places into scenes of conflict, nor to seek crumbling earthworks or hypothetical boundaries. Part of its fascination lays in visiting adjacent historical sites relevant to the battlefield under review. Sometimes these offshoots provide a real bonus, as in the case of Pretoria,

Monument to commemorate the Battle of Blood River, Pretoria.

a most attractive and interesting city, offering a host of historical and relaxing features. Unique among them is the Voortrekker Monument, built as a national shrine to commemorate the heroes of the Great Trek, which started in 1836. The monument is built on the summit of a hill called Skanskop and is a striking landmark visible for miles around Pretoria; massive figures of the Great Trek leaders guard the four corners of the monument, which is set inside a symbolic laager, in imitation granite, of sixty-four life-size ox-wagons. This is the number of wagons behind which Andries Pretorius fought at the Battle of Blood River on 16 December 1838. Inside the huge building is the Hall of Heroes, containing a marble frieze of twenty-seven panels dedicated to the Great Trek; through a large circular opening in the floor of the Hall can be seen below a pink marble cenotaph, designated as a memorial to Trek leader Piet Retief and his men. There is a museum at the Monument largely devoted to the Great Trek.

South of the town, on the Maria van Riebeeck Road, is Fort Klapperkop, built in 1895 by the old South African Republic; it holds a good military museum depicting the military history of the South African Republic from 1852 until the end of the South African War in 1902.

There is much to see in Pretoria beyond items of military interest in

Bronze replica of a Boer trek wagon, at the Blood River Commemorative
Monument, Pretoria.

what is claimed to be a city of gardens and fine architecture. Among its
sites of interest are the following:

- Heroes' Acre, the old cemetery containing the graves of many South
  African heroes and statesmen.
- Paul Kruger's House, restored to its original 1900 condition when the
  President lived there.
- The National Zoological Gardens, where wild animals can be seen in
  their natural habitat, via an overhead cable railway.
- Church Square, in the heart of Pretoria, surrounded by interesting
  buildings, and with a huge statue of Paul Kruger in its centre.
- The Union Buildings, from which a commanding view of the city can
  be obtained; here is the Delville Wood Memorial to South African
  soldiers in World War I, and a Garden of Remembrance leading down
  to a huge equestrian statue of General Louis Botha.

Among the many museums in Pretoria are the National Cultural
History and Open Air Museum, the Police Museum, the South African
Museum of Science and Technology, the Transvaal Museum and the
Pretoria Art Museum.

The other large city encountered in our tour was Johannesburg, where we arrived and left at the Jan Smuts Airport. Not as appealing as Pretoria, nevertheless it contains a real bonus that MUST be visited – the South African National Museum of Military History, situated in the Herman Eckstein Park. This large and very comprehensive museum is divided into departments concerned with such major aspects of military history as aircraft, ammunition, armoured vehicles, artillery, naval exhibits, etc., plus related topics ranging from medals, buttons and badges to medical matters and prisoners-of-war. A surprise personal bonus was the sight of an original Churchill tank *Sweet Sue* T172204 of World War II, bearing 25th Tank Brigade signs – in which the author served!

The public library in Johannesburg houses the African Museum on its top floor, with three galleries dealing with the Black Races, history of Europeans in South Africa, and the growth of Johannesburg.

Part Eight

USA – The American War of Independence 1775–83

27 *The Course of the War*

This protracted conflict, fought more than 200 years ago, was one of the most far-reaching events of modern history, and it is almost impossible to conceive how world events would have been shaped had this relatively small war not caused the loss of British colonies in America and the birth of the United States of America.

Long-standing disagreements between Britain and the thirteen colonies flamed into open rebellion at Lexington in April 1775 when 700 soldiers from the British garrison at Boston opened fire on a gathering of colonists. Then, after destroying supplies at Concord, the British had their first taste of colonial guerrilla warfare as they marched back to Boston harassed by swarms of militiamen, hidden behind trees and stone walls who poured musket fire into their packed ranks. Two months later on Bunker Hill overlooking Boston Harbour 2,200 British regular troops lost practically half their number when repeatedly assaulting earthworks manned by American militiamen. Throughout the war the Americans made greater use of entrenchments than most armies of the period. Tactically a British victory, Bunker Hill gave the Americans tremendous pyschological encouragement, turning their superstitious awe of the regulars into a characteristic undisciplined and brash over-confidence.

In July 1775 George Washington became commander of the continental forces and began his monumental task of transforming an armed rabble into an army. Among other handicaps, he was plagued by a shortage of trained officers, as the best American leaders were in the northern campaigns. The remainder of that year and the first half of 1776 saw an inadvisable and ill-equipped attempt to invade Canada by small forces under Benedict Arnold and General Montgomery who, after capturing Montreal, were repulsed at Quebec and eventually withdrew from Canadian soil.

In July 1776 General Howe sailed from Halifax and landed in New York harbour with 32,000 men including 9,000 Hessian infantry. (During the American Revolution, the British hired about 32,000 mercenaries from Hesse-Cassell, Hesse-Hanau, Brunswick/Luneburg, Waldock, Ansbach-Bayreuth, Anhalt-Zeroso and Hanover. These troops were not particularly good and desertion was common; at no time were there more than 20,000 of them in the Western Hemisphere.) Out-manoeuvred in the Battle of Long Island, Washington saved his army by a brilliant withdrawal when Glover's amphibious regiment of Massachusetts fishermen ferried every single man to safety. Later, they acquired a reputation fighting as gunners or infantrymen, when the army did not require their special skill in inland water operations.

With his little army growing smaller as enlistments expired, Washington retreated through New Jersey, pausing to lead a force of 2,400 men across the River Delaware on Christmas night 1776 and completely destroying the Hessian garrison at Trenton. Most armies went into winter quarters during hard weather so that any general or army that was willing or able to fight during the winter gained surprise successes. Lord Cornwallis rushed up 5,000 regulars to trap Washington's 1,600 regulars and 3,600 militia, who escaped by leaving camp fires burning and slipping away into the night. Washington next defeated British reinforcements advancing from Princetown, to conclude a brilliant ten-day campaign that 'fanned the dying embers of the Revolution into a lively flame'.

In early 1777, General Burgoyne, General Howe and Colonel St Leger, aided by Brant's Indians and Johnson's Tories, embarked on a three-pronged offensive which demanded close co-ordination and timing, difficult to achieve over the rough trails and in the trackless forests of North America. Burgoyne captured Fort Ticonderoga in July, as Howe in New Jersey moved out against Washington, who refused battle, while Morgan's riflemen harassed Howe's flanks. Frontiersmen, such as those led by Morgan, operated independently in groups. Their long rifle, proven in many Indian wars, was a vastly superior weapon to the smoothbore musket which could only fire with 40 per cent accuracy at 100 yards against the rifle's 50 per cent accuracy at 300 yards. By using a greased patch around the ball, the rifle's range, accuracy and penetration were improved. However, it took twice as long to load and, unable to carry a bayonet, was useless against a bayonet attack and could not stand ground when rapid fire was required.

By drawing Howe southwards, Washington did much to prevent Howe linking up with Burgoyne, although he was defeated at Brandywine and Germanstown, where it was shown that short-term American volunteers were not yet ready to meet the regulars in formal combat, falling easy victims to bayonets that were on them before they could re-load. The musket had a 20 per cent hit probability at 150 yards, but infantry could charge 100 yards in a minute so that troops close enough to suffer casualties from musketry were also within charge range. The psychological effect of the bayonet brought the British many victories during the American Revolution.

Burgoyne's force consisted of 7,200 troops including 3,000 German mercenaries and 138 guns in the biggest artillery train seen in America, plus an Indian and Canadian scouting arm that tactically blinded Gates's army. The American militiaman, knowing nothing of frontier fighting methods, was terrified of the Indians but the arrival of Morgan's riflemen in early September reinforced Gates's outnumbered, demoralised and badly led army and they turned the tables by outwitting Burgoyne's scouts, causing his army to grope.

St Leger on the Mohawk with 875 British, Tory and Hessian troops and 1,000 Iroquois Indians under Brant, besieged Fort Schuyler and at Oriskany ambushed Herkimer's relieving force, but later the fort was relieved by Benedict Arnold, when St Leger retreated. On 16 August, a force of 2,000 militia plus 400 Green Mountain Boys wiped out two forces of Brunswickers at Bennington, killing 207 and taking 700 prisoners out of a total of 1,350 men.

By September, Burgoyne knew that Howe was not going to join him as planned so decided to strike out for Albany, hoping to meet St Leger. Crossing the Hudson, Burgoyne attacked the Americans at Freeman Farm – a tactical landmark because riflemen bore the brunt of the battle. Morgan's men in brown linen hunting shirts and buckskin breeches, almost invisible amid the autumn colouring of the woods, took heavy toll of the scarlet-clad British infantry advancing in close order across forest clearings. The battle swayed backwards and forwards in the forest before ending at dusk in a tactical draw.

Burgoyne entrenched his army on Bemis Heights, hoping for help from Clinton's force in New York, but this commander did little except create a minor diversion up the Hudson before retiring back to New York. So, on 7 October, Burgoyne made a desperate attempt to break out, only to be driven back, with 600 casualties, by a counter-attack led by Arnold, with Morgan's riflemen playing a conspicuous part. Withdrawing to Saratoga, Burgoyne's 5,700 men were surrounded by a force three times their strength, and constantly harassed by riflemen. On 17 October 1777 came the turning point of the Revolution when Burgoyne surrendered on the promise of his army being paroled back to Britain, but this was not honoured.

Under conditions of great hardship Washington and his army spent the winter of 1777/8 at Valley Forge, where Baron von Steuben painstakingly taught the starved and cold little continental army discipline and tactical skill. At the same time, Legions of Light Horse were raised by Harry Lee and William Washington to aid the militiamen who up to now had been at the mercy of the British dragoons. They were organised as four units of fifty men each, usually combining as a corps.

In June 1778, Sir Henry Clinton took over command from Howe and, evacuating Philadelphia, led his army of 10,000 redcoats (the baggage train was ten miles long) back to New York, followed by Washington's army on a parallel route. Clinton turned to give battle at Monmouth, which ended in an empty American victory although the continental troops proved themselves equal to the British regulars and, in a fair fight with musket and bayonet, Wayne's men shattered a Guards Regiment.

Throughout 1779 and the following year, Washington blockaded the British in New York during a dreary period when, with his army slowly disintegrating from expired enlistments, only the personality of their leader kept the American cause alight. There were no major operations but some hard-fought minor actions and guerrilla warfare such as Wayne's recapture of Stony Point in July 1779.

For nearly two years there had been continuous guerrilla warfare between Tories and patriots in the southern colonies but no large-scale fighting until Clinton moved to conquer the Carolinas. In December 1778, the British captured Savannah, and its garrison under General Prevost successfully withstood siege in September/October 1779 when a large French force, with continentals and militia, invested the town; the final French assault on 8 October was thrown back after hand-to-hand fighting in the most severe conflict of its type since Bunker Hill. The French Commander d'Estaing embarked his troops and sailed away, leaving Savannah in British hands. Leaving New York under the command of the German General von Knyphausen in December 1779, Clinton sailed with 8,000 men to attack Charleston, which was besieged from February until May 1780. The surrender of 5,400 men and great quantities of arms and equipment was considered the worst American disaster of the war. Clinton returned to New York, leaving Cornwallis with 8,000 men to pacify South Carolina, where guerrilla warfare involving Banastre Tarleton's Tory Cavalry Legion went on throughout the summer. In August 1780 General Gates's army of 3,000 militia and 900 continentals were overwhelmed at Camden by Cornwallis with 2,400 British and Tory regulars; Tarleton's cavalry crushed the continentals in a rear attack to begin the American rout. Considering that militia were a disorganised, ill-trained and ill-disciplined group and were usually deployed in skirmisher lines or purely used for defensive purposes, it is not surprising that they were defeated by a smaller regular force.

Washington sent General Greene with a force of his best continentals to check Cornwallis, and a victory was gained at Kings Mountain in October 1780 when British Colonel Patrick Ferguson's Corps of Tory riflemen were shot to pieces by a slightly larger force of mountainmen sharpshooters in a fight that was remarkable because both forces were composed entirely of Americans. By mid-December 1780, Greene's army had grown to 3,000, including 1,400 continentals, while Cornwallis led a force of 4,000 well-equipped and trained regulars. In January 1781, Greene split his forces and sent General Morgan with 1,000 men on a wide western sweep, chased by Tarleton who was decisively defeated at Cowpens in what was perhaps the most brilliant tactical operation ever fought on American soil. Morgan placed his unreliable militiamen in front, with permission to retire after they had fired two rounds; behind them were his continentals with eighty dragoons. Tarleton's regulars, taking casualties from the two volleys fired by the militia before they fled to the cover of a low hill in the rear, came to grips with the continentals, who made a desperate stand with musket and bayonet. Meanwhile Morgan had rallied his militia and led them entirely round the field, under cover of the ridge, to hit the British in their left rear. Simultaneously, the American dragoons struck their right and eventually only Tarleton and a few scattered riders escaped. The Americans had about 70 killed and wounded; the British 110 killed and 830 captured out of their original 1,100.

Greene retreated into Southern Virginia closely pursued by Cornwallis, who had destroyed his baggage in order to increase his mobility. In March 1781 at Guilford Courthouse Greene's army of 4,400 men, two-thirds inexperienced militia, turned to face Cornwallis's 1,900 regulars. In wooded country, Greene positioned his troops in three lines; in turn each was driven back by the outnumbered British who, in spite of heavy losses, fought with great gallantry. Greene broke off the action and retreated after inflicting such casualties on Cornwallis that he had to abandon the campaign and withdrew into Virginia. Greene attacked several isolated British garrisons in the Carolinas at Hobkirk's Hill, Fort Ninety-six and Eutaw Springs, suffering a series of tactical defeats which nevertheless led to a strategic victory. Although his strength seldom exceeded 3,000 men, Greene had forced the invaders out of the South mainly because of the 1,600 continentals who formed the backbone of his army. Unpaid, ill-equipped and always hungry, these men marched hundreds of miles and fought at least four major actions and innumerable lesser affairs in proving themselves the equal of the British regular.

In July 1780, Rochambeau with 5,000 French troops landed at Newport but a British naval blockade prevented operations against New York, where Washington maintained his blockade despite four mutinies in his army during 1780/1. General Benedict Arnold defected to the British in September 1780.

In April 1781, Washington sent Lafayette with 3,500 men (including 1,200 veteran continentals) and Wayne with 1,000 continentals to Virginia, where for several months the pair skilfully manoeuvred against the superior numbers of Cornwallis, who had been reinforced. In July at Jamestown Ford, Wayne, caught by surprise, rallied and repulsed the British, although he took heavy losses. The French force under Rochambeau moved from Newport and joined Washington outside New York as Cornwallis marched with 7,000 troops to Yorktown in August, watched by Lafayette with 4,500 at nearby West Point, Virginia, where he was reinforced with 3,000 French troops brought by the fleet of Admiral de Grasse. French battalions were organised into nine companies: eight companies were fusiliers and one grenadier company, with a 'paper' strength of about 740, although French regiments were usually nearer to their establishments than British, Americans or Hessians. British Admiral Graves, badly handling his nineteen ships against de Grasse's twenty-four at the Battle of the Capes, withdrew to New York, so giving command of the sea to the French and sealing Cornwallis's fate.

Leaving a mere 2,000 men to contain Clinton's 17,000 in New York, Washington force-marched his army and the French force under Rochambeau, embarking them at the head of the Chesapeake in French ships to reach Yorktown on 28 September. The Allied French and American army was formed of some 9,500 Americans and 7,800 French regular soldiers with a good artillery train of field and siege-guns.

Hoping for aid from Clinton, Cornwallis withdrew his 8,000 men into the inner fortifications at Yorktown, so allowing the Allies to bring their siege artillery within range of his entire position. After a four-day bombardment, the Allies stormed two important redoubts, established new batteries and repulsed a British counter-attack. His position impossible, Cornwallis surrendered on 19 October 1781, to virtually end the American Revolution. In November 1782, the Treaty of Paris was signed concluding the war and recognising the independence of the United States. The last British troops left New York in November 1783.

28 *The Battles at Saratoga 19 September and 7 October 1777*

Freeman Farm (19 September)

Deserted by his Indian scouts, General Burgoyne, the British Commander, lacked information of the enemy, who were well-entrenched on Bemis Heights, so that he advanced through the broken wooded terrain in three unco-ordinated columns: Burgoyne himself with Hamilton commanded in the centre, General Fraser was on the right and General von Riedesel on the left. By noon the centre column had reached the clearing in which stood Freeman Farm, with Riedesel's column about a mile and a half to the east on the River road, and Fraser in the woods to the west.

Suddenly, to turkey-call signals, Morgan's riflemen crept within range and picked off every officer of the advance guard around the farm, causing such panic that the remainder of the guard rushed back to their main body without firing a shot. The riflemen chased after them but were dispersed by volleys from the British infantry. Burgoyne advanced his

At Concord in Massachusetts in April 1775 rebellious American farmers fire the shots that echoed around the world.

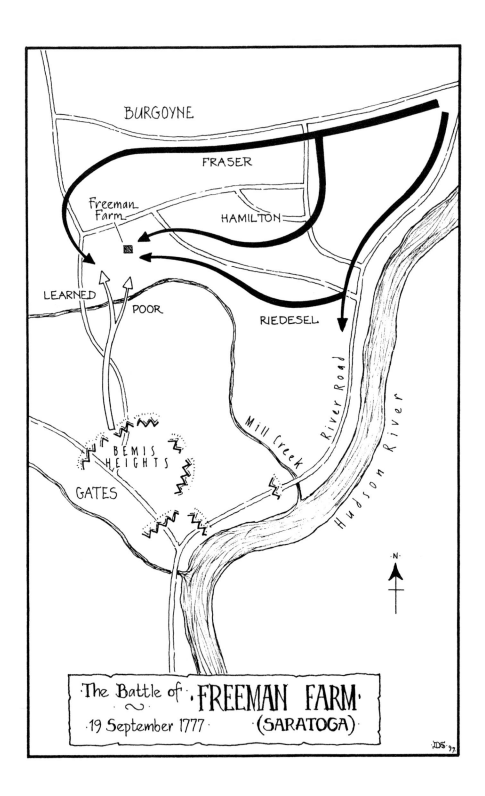

BURGOYNE

FRASER

Freeman Farm

HAMILTON

LEARNED

POOR

RIEDESEL

River Road

Mill Creek

Hudson River

BEMIS HEIGHTS

GATES

N

The Battle of ·FREEMAN FARM·
·19 September 1777· (SARATOGA)

DS 97.

Battle of Saratoga – Freeman Farm. The clearing at the farm.

column to form along the northern edge of the clearing of Freeman Farm with the 20th, 62nd and 21st Regiments arranged from left to right and the 9th Regiment in reserve (only the battalion companies of these four regiments were involved as their light and grenadier flank companies were with Fraser). Morgan's riflemen and Dearborn's light infantry took up firing positions along the southern edge of the clearing, supported by seven other American regiments of continental line brought down from Bemis Heights by General Benedict Arnold.

On the British right, Fraser's force (grenadier and light companies, a battalion of loyalists, a regular battalion, some guns and a few Indians) turned back Arnold's attempt at out-flanking the centre column. Then they remained relatively inactive on the heights for the rest of the day.

For three to four hours the three British regiments stood shoulder-to-shoulder in the European manner under a constant heavy fire which repeatedly sent them back to the shelter of the woods. When the superior number of Americans charged into the clearing in pursuit they were driven back by British discipline, bayonets and the four light guns, two on each flank. American reinforcements allowed them to extend their line and force the three British regiments to thin out to prevent being over-lapped on their right; nevertheless they repeatedly went forward in bayonet attacks. Suffering heavy losses, the centre column became exhausted and were in a desperate situation when the Germans came to their aid.

Hearing the fire-fight, Riedesel had sent four guns to support the centre column and, receiving orders from Burgoyne at 5 pm, left some 800 men to protect the baggage along the River road and moved out with 500 infantry and two guns. Cheering and beating their drums, the small force advanced on the American right flank, where there were no patrols covering the regiments attacking the centre column. Arnold was back at Bemis Heights trying to persuade the lethargic General Gates to send reinforcements. Lacking leadership the Americans began to fall back and, as darkness was falling, Burgoyne with Riedesel's reinforcements launched a counter-attack which caused the Americans to withdraw. Burgoyne camped on the battlefield and, had he continued his attack on the following day, he would probably have defeated Gates.

Burgoyne lost 600; out of the 800 men in three British regiments 44 per cent were casualties. American losses were 319.

Bemis Heights (7 October)

After the Battle of Freeman Farm, Burgoyne dug-in, building the Balcarres Redoubt in the Freeman Farm area, the Breymann Redoubt 500 yards north and erected stockades, and three great redoubts were started on high ground overlooking the area. Seeking information of the American positions on Bemis Heights, Burgoyne planned a reconnaissance-in-force by 1,500 of his remaining 5,000 regulars plus 600 auxiliaries under Captain Fraser. At about 10.30 am Burgoyne's force moved forward in three columns whilst Fraser's auxiliaries vanished into the wooded hills on their right flank. When two-thirds of a mile on, Burgoyne's 1,500 men took up a good position in a wheat field on a gentle rise north of Mill Creek which gave an excellent frontal field of fire for their ten guns. The right flank of the line was held by Balcarres with his light infantry; Riedesel was in the centre with a composite group of Brunswickers and the 24th Regiment; and Major John Acland with the British Grenadiers held the left of the line. Both flanks rested against thick woods.

But American soldiers did not play the game of war in the European manner, possessing a rooted dislike of charges across open ground into the mouths of waiting cannon and formed ranks of disciplined regulars. They were much better fighters in the woods and there were plenty of trees and cover on the approaches to both flanks of Burgoyne's line.

Subsequently, Morgan's riflemen were sent to work around the high ground to turn Burgoyne's right whilst Poor took his brigade of 800 veterans of the New Hampshire Continental Regiments of Cilley, Hale and Scammell, von Cortlandt's and Livingston's New York Militia and the Connecticut Militia of Cook and Lattimer to attack the elevation held by Acland's force. Out-numbered by two or three to one, the Grenadiers opened fire with musket and cannon and then Acland ordered them to fix bayonets and charge. As they swarmed down the hill the continental line first delivered a murderous volley that stopped them dead in their tracks and then, whooping and cheering, charged in with the bayonet to sweep

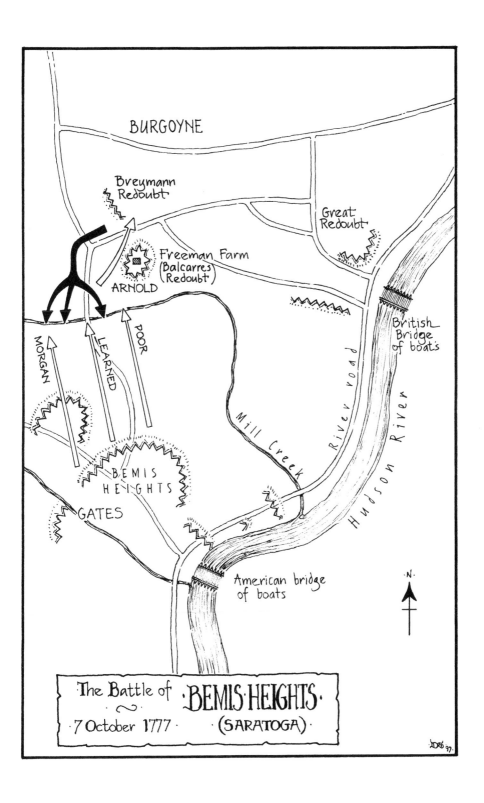

BURGOYNE

Breymann
Redoubt

Great
Redoubt

Freeman Farm
(Balcarres
Redoubt)

ARNOLD

British
Bridge
of boats

MORGAN

LEARNED

POOR

River road

Mill Creek

Hudson River

BEMIS
HEIGHTS

GATES

American bridge
of boats

·N·

The Battle of ·BEMIS·HEIGHTS·
· 7 October 1777 ·   (SARATOGA)

Bemis Heights, showing the area down towards the Hudson River, behind the trees. It was up this route that Riedesel's column came to attack the American fortifications, marked by the white posts.

over their position and send them reeling back, leaving Acland wounded on the ground.

On the other flank Morgan had routed Fraser's auxiliaries in the woods and, turning the British line, hit Balcarres in flank and rear. As the British light infantry were changing front to meet this threat they took a devastating volley from Dearborn's light infantry that sent them reeling back in rout. Before they had gone far Balcarres rallied them but was unable to prevent withdrawals from the field.

Simultaneously, General Arnold (relieved of his command and without authority) dashed at the British centre at the head of three regiments of Learned's Brigade. With both flanks uncovered, the German troops in the centre fought on, reinforced by detachments from the Rhetz and Hesse-Hanau Regiments. They drove off the first attack but, remorselessly encouraged by Arnold's overwhelming American strength, assailed them on three sides causing them to retire back to the Balcarres Redoubt in good order. General Fraser attempted a delaying action with the 24th Regiment but his conspicuous figure on a grey horse made him the target for snipers and soon he was shot from the saddle.

In the past the Americans would have been content with such a victory, but driven forward by Arnold, they made a general attack upon the British entrenchments. The light infantry and other British survivors of the action repulsed the American attackers after they had got through the abatis. Then Arnold led them and Learned's brigade in an attack that cleared the stockade between the Balcarres and Breymann Redoubts, before racing to the other flank to lead four regiments – Wesson, Livingston, Morgan and Brook's Massachusetts Regiment – in a successful assault on the redoubt. Here Breymann himself was shot dead by one of his own men after he had personally sabred four of his own soldiers 'to encourage the others'.

The Americans lost only 150 men, while Burgoyne had some 600 casualties and lost all ten guns in a defeat that forced him to ask for terms, leading to his subsequent surrender.

29 *Saratoga Today*

The Saratoga National Historical Park lies thirty miles north of Albany NY, on US4 and NY32. The Visitor Center is open daily, except Thanksgiving Day, 25 December and 1 January. Park roads are open from about 1 April to 30 November, as weather permits.

The essential first step is to go to the Visitor Center, where time spent is invaluable in familiarising oneself with the battlefield and the events that took place through study of the innumerable maps and exhibits. Obtain the guide pamphlet which details, in progressive order, the salient points of the field, keyed-in by numbers on the maps in the guide. Note the route of the short walking tour, then consider the longer autoroute, over an area of nine miles, beginning at the south end of the parking area, which takes about four hours to adequately cover, including stops at the more important marked points. Also, there are guided park tours, led by experienced park rangers, who clearly explain the principal events of the battle at the places where they occurred.

It is easy to recognise and understand the areas where the main action took place; they are liberally labelled with interpretative markers – a wonderful feature of ALL American battlefields. Should time not allow doing the full autoroute, then stops should be made at the Neilson Farm, the Barber Wheatfield, the Balcarres Redoubt and the Schuyler House.

First stop is the Freeman Farm Overlook (1) from which can be viewed the ground over which the major fighting took place on 19 September; it is where Morgan's Virginia Riflemen began the battle when, from the stout log cabin, they fired on the advance-guard of Burgoyne's centre column. In 1777, the farm was owned and the land worked by a loyalist, John Freeman, who went north to join Burgoyne's invasion force.

The second stop is the Neilson Farm on Bemis Heights (2), owned in 1777 by John Neilson who fought with the American troops opposing the British force; it has been restored to its eighteenth-century condition, when it was the American headquarters during the battle.

Next, the American River Fortifications (3). A powerful position which forced Burgoyne's men to move through the rough wooded terrain west of the valley, when they attacked the position on Bemis Heights on 7 October. In 1777 this stronghold, with its garrison of infantry and artillery supported by batteries along the near riverbank, commanded the road, the flood-plain and the river, closing-off the Hudson Valley route to Albany. Colonel Thaddeus Kosciuszko, a Polish military engineer who had thrown in his lot with the Patriot cause, commanded here.

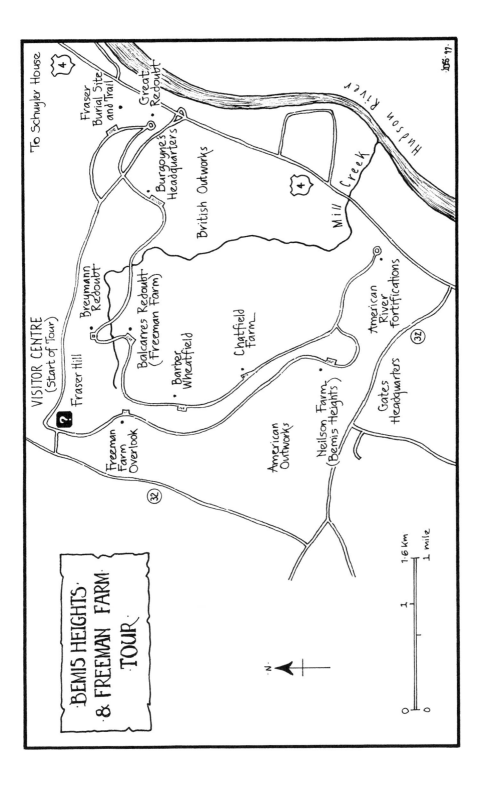

BEMIS HEIGHTS
& FREEMAN FARM
TOUR

N

0   1   1·6 Km
0   1 mile

To Schuyler House

4

Fraser Burial Site and Trail
Great Redoubt

Burgoyne's Headquarters

British Outworks

Mill Creek

Hudson River

4

VISITOR CENTRE (Start of Tour)

Fraser Hill

Breymann Redoubt

Balcarres Redoubt (Freeman Farm)

Barber Wheatfield

Chatfield Farm

American River Fortifications

32

Freeman Farm Overlook

American Outworks

Neilson Farm (Bemis Heights)

Gates Headquarters

32

JDS '97.

The John Neilson Farm, on its original site in the Saratoga National Historical Park. Built probably in 1775, it served as the headquarters of American Generals Benedict Arnold and Enoch Poor during the battle. After the battle, the farmer John Neilson and his wife returned and raised a family there.

Chatfield Farm (4), owned by Asa Chatfield at the time of the battle, sheltered an American outpost watching for an advance against the centre and left of the Patriot position. Look beyond the Ridge, to the Middle Ravine, where piquets of both armies skirmished during the lull after the Freeman Farm action of 19 September, and before the attack on Bemis Heights on 7 October.

The Barber Wheatfield (5) played no part in the events of 19 September, but on 7 October here, and in the field further west beyond the first row of trees, the Americans clashed with 1,500 British and German troops who were advancing southwards in an attempt to outflank the American left. In the fierce fighting that followed, Burgoyne's soldiers were forced back to their fortifications at the Freeman Farm. Close by, to the northwest, can be seen the spot where the British General Simon Fraser was mortally wounded by a sniper.

After the action on 19 September, Burgoyne's men hastily built a fortified line running from the river to the Breymann Redoubt; it was called the Balcarres Redoubt (6) after Lord Balcarres, who commanded the British light infantry. The area was marked by pointed stakes, and its strongest point was located at the Freeman Farm, where a long and earthen redoubt was built, 500 yards long and twelve to fourteen feet in height. Here, in the action on 7 October, Benedict Arnold led Poor's brigade, plus parts of Learned's and Paterson's commands, in a series of unsuccessful attacks.

The Breymann Redoubt (7) was a single line of breastworks about 200 yards in length and seven to eight feet high, guarding the British right flank and the road to Quaker Springs; it was held by German troops commanded by Colonel Breymann. The gap between it and the Balcarres Redoubt was defended by Canadian volunteers, in two log cabins; in the fighting of 7 October it was successfully stormed by the Americans. Here Benedict Arnold received a leg wound, which is commemorated nearby by the celebrated Boot Monument (8), so called because of American aversion to naming Arnold, the eventual traitor.

In 1777, Burgoyne's headquarters, established after the battle of 19 September, was a large tent on this site, near to a spring. After the battle of 7 October, Burgoyne withdrew his forces to the Great Redoubt (9) on this hill and two others to the north, where a system of fortifications guarded vital areas such as hospitals, artillery parks, etc. General Simon Fraser is buried to the north of the redoubt, at the end of the marked trail (10).

Later, after the Bemis Heights battle, Burgoyne retreated northwards and his dispirited army settled in a fortified camp on the heights of Saratoga, from where, on 17 October 1777, they marched out in surrender, with the Honours of War. Completed in 1883, the Saratoga Monument commemorates one of the most decisive victories in American and world history; it is 155 feet in height and, from its top floor, a fine panoramic view can be obtained.

The Saratoga Memorial, erected in 1877. 155 feet in height, it is erected on a 300-foot high mound.

30 *Mini Memories of Walking the Battlefields of the American War of Independence*

Maps Required:
Massachusetts State
New York State
North Carolina State
South Carolina State
Pennsylvania State

Walking the battlefields of American wars – the Revolution, the War of 1812, and the War Between the States – presents a debt beyond price to many well-informed American friends. For example, the following brief notes of an active day's tour with Massachusetts resident Leo Cronin indicate the full day we spent together in his native habitat (fuller details of our target-sites will be given in greater depth later):

> Into Boston. Visit USS *Constitution* and Museum Bunker Hill – column and Visitor's Center. Impressed with streets of old houses and gas-lamps.
> To Lexington, via Cambridge (Harvard) and Arlington (which resembled older parts of England).
> Lexington – pretty area around famous Common, with its surround of old houses dating from Revolutionary days.
> To Concord – Minute Man monument; Visitor's Center; film; uniformed demonstration; old well, where opposing soldiers killed each other.
> North Bridge – running-fight as Patriots came round hill and fighting breaks out at Meriam's Corner.
> Follow route of British troops retreating to Boston.

USS *Constitution*, berthed in the historic Charlestown Navy Yard, is claimed to be the oldest commissioned warship afloat in the world today, being built in 1794/7. After a tour of the ship is concluded, her story can be discovered in the museum a few yards away; here relevant exhibits are set out, a film can be seen, and regular re-enactments and demonstrations take place. Souvenirs, pictures, books, etc. can also be purchased.

Only 200 yards from the USS *Constitution* (also known as 'Old Ironsides') is the Bunker Hill Pavilion where an impressive in-the-round production, *The Whites of Their Eyes*, can be seen, a film of the Battle of

Bunker Hill involving more than a thousand slides, 14 screens, 22 life-sized costumed figures, and 7 sound channels. Following the well-marked Boston Freedom Trail, denoted by a red line marked on the sidewalk, leads to the Bunker Hill Monument, marking the summit of Breed's Hill where, on the evening of 16 June 1775, Colonel William Prescott's 1,200 Massachusetts and Connecticut soldiers fortified an earthen redoubt. Reinforced to nearly 4,000 men, the American patriots awaited attack by General Howe's British regulars, being told not to fire until they could see the whites of the British soldiers' eyes. They defied, with heavy losses, two assaults before their military inexperience caused them to be defeated, and they withdrew from the hill, after fighting the first open engagement in America's successful fight for independence. Exhibits, books, pictures, and a leaflet describing events can be obtained from the Visitors' Center at 15 State Street, across from the old State House.

Mention has been made of the Freedom Trail, a three-mile-long walking tour around Boston, embracing sixteen sites and places of historic importance, in both downtown Boston and Charlestown. The Trail can be joined at any point, but an entire day is required for the three-mile round-trip; information can be obtained at the kiosk on Boston Common, at the Park Visitor Center, and at Charlestown Navy Yard.

Along with Philadelphia, the city of Boston, certainly in its older parts

Statue of a Minuteman standing at the easterly point of Lexington Common, where the first shots of the War of Independence were fired.

such as Beacon Hill, is a real bonus to walk, with delightful old residential neighbourhoods carefully preserved with brick and cobblestoned streets and gaslights which, in places already mentioned such as Beacon Hill, Acorn Street and Louisburg Square, take the walker back to the early nineteenth century. Look out for the statue of American hero Paul Revere, gracing a small park in front of the Old North Church in the Paul Revere Mall; two lanterns hung in the church steeple in April 1775 signalled the redcoats' advance and set Revere off on his historic midnight ride to Lexington.

On Boston Waterfront lies Fort Independence, well-preserved buildings dating from 1634 when it was named Castle William, in honour of William II of England. Prior to the Revolutionary War it was used as a garrison for British troops, but was abandoned in 1776, and dedicated by President John Adams in 1799 as Fort Independence. Surrounded by immaculate lawns and flower-beds, it is an attractive site.

Today, the historic atmosphere and appearance of Lexington Green need but little imagination to transport the battlefield walker back to the morning of 19 April 1775 when a group of about seventy American militia (Minutemen) gathered on the village green to await the arrival of the expected British troops marching from Boston. Their leader, Captain John Parker, had cautioned them not to fire their muskets unless fired upon, saying: 'If war is to come, let it begin here!' When the six companies

Log City – Valley Forge.

Valley Forge

of light infantry under Major John Pitcairn arrived and formed-up on the green facing the Minutemen, they ordered the rebels to disperse, which they began to do in small and reluctant groups. Suddenly, a shot was fired – who fired the first 'shot heard around the world' at Lexington is not known, each side claiming the other fired first, but as a result of the subsequent volleys, eight Minutemen were killed and ten wounded; a British soldier was also wounded. The British then marched on to Concord, as news of the shooting spread to local communities, causing militiamen to flock to the British line of march between Boston and Concord.

The reconstructed North Bridge at Concord lies adjacent to the famous Minuteman Statue, sculpted by Daniel Chester French to memorialise the American citizen-soldier of 1775. Visitors' Centers are positioned near the North Bridge in Concord and on State Route 2A in Lexington, where fine illustrated brochures are available. The North Bridge area marks where, for the first time, Americans fired volleys into the formed ranks of British soldiers, after Major Buttrick of Concord had cried out to his men: 'Fire, fellow-soldiers! For God's sake, fire!' Regrouping, the British began their return march to Boston, harassed throughout by the fire of hundreds of militiamen from every building and bush along the Battle Road, as it is now known.

This route is now an urban highway but generally follows the same path, passing the sites of the bitterest fighting and many still existing

National Memorial Arch at Valley Forge

buildings standing nearby. The battlefield walker should reflect that it was a strange field of battle for the opening of a war that played such a vital part in the history of the world – twenty miles of hilly winding road connecting a port-city and numerous peaceful country towns and villages. But word of the events of 19 April 1775 spread throughout the American colonies, uniting men and women to the cause of independence, that lay nearly ten years ahead. It is a sensible idea to begin a tour of the area with the film and map programme at the Battle Road Visitor Center, near Fiske Hill on the road to Lexington, from Concord.

Valley Forge is perhaps the best-known place-name associated with the American Revolution, particularly to Americans, for nowhere else does one so appreciate the suffering and sacrifice endured by Washington's army in their epic struggle to survive against the unrelenting forces of nature, allied to hunger and disease. Here hundreds of American soldiers died during the winter 1777/8 without a shot being fired or a bayonet unsheathed – while the British remained snug in Philadelphia, twenty miles away. Beginning in the late summer of 1777, Sir William Howe, the British commander, had out-manoeuvred and defeated Washington in the field until early December, when the American commander led his cold and weary army into the Valley Forge encampment on 19 December 1777. Despite the hardships of living in crowded, damp, disease-ridden wooden huts, the army emerged on 19 June 1778 in far better shape so far as bearing, discipline, weapon-handling and the like were concerned, through the unrelenting training of Friedrich von Steuben, formerly on the staff of Frederick the Great of Prussia, who had offered his military skills to the patriot cause. Perhaps more than that, the army was possessed with – and never lost for the remainder of the war – the Spirit of Valley Forge, forging a will that often transcended weapons.

Today, the Valley Forge National Historical Park should be an essential venue for those walking the fields of the American Revolution; here are provided programmes, tours, and numerous other interpretative activities that bring understanding of the significant events that, in the long run, led to an independent America. The Visitors' Center, situated at the junction of North Gulph Road and PA23, is the recommended start to the tour, where a fifteen-minute film shows life in the encampment, books can be bought, descriptive brochures obtained, and relevant exhibits and artefacts studied, setting the scene for the self-guided tour that follows. This is keyed to numbered stops on the map provided to 2,800 acres of rolling hills on which can be found extensive remains, reconstructed huts, memorials, monuments, and markers, with lines of earthworks, a colonial-era Artillery Park, and the Grand Parade where von Steuben rebuilt the army. Throughout the tour, remember that it was here that the turning point of the War occurred.

Washington's HQ, Valley Forge

Steuben statue, Valley Forge

South of Valley Forge, on US1 (the Baltimore Pike) lies the battlefield of Brandywine where, on 11 September 1777, Howe inflicted upon Washington one of the defeats that resulted in the American army spending the winter at Valley Forge. Washington, with 10,500 troops, had crossed the Delaware from New Jersey and taken up a defensive position behind Brandywine Creek. Howe sent von Knyphausen with 5,000 men to make a feint at the American Center at Chad's Creek, while Cornwallis with 10,000 men circled wide to the north-west and crossed the Upper Brandywine to strike the exposed American right flank. The American General Sullivan was overwhelmed and, as Knyphausen began his assault across Chad's Ford, the American army bolted to the rear, with 1,000 casualties.

The Visitor's Center at Brandywine Battlefield Park offers a permanent interpretative exhibit and an audio-visual presentation, besides a gift-shop. Here can be purchased a brochure with map for the Battlefield Driving Tour, a twenty-three-mile route, taking forty-five to sixty minutes plus viewing times, around all the salient points of the field, including the Benjamin Ring House, Washington's battle headquarters, and the Gideon Gilpin House, where the Marquis de Lafayette, a young French volunteer later to play a leading role in the war, was quartered before seeing his first action in this battle. Also from the Visitors' Center can be obtained a leaflet and map for a self-guided tour.

While Howe was making his move for Philadelphia, General John

Burgoyne was pushing laboriously southward from Canada, through the wilderness to the Upper Hudson, ploughing slowly and doggedly forward throughout the summer of 1777. On 11 August Lieutenant-Colonel Baum with 800 men, chiefly Germans, was sent to raid the American supply depot at Bennington in Vermont, but was surrounded by General Stark's militia on 16 August and was defeated in and around the Dragoon Redoubt on a hill overlooking the Walloomsac River; Baum was mortally wounded and his force overwhelmed. Sent by Burgoyne to aid Baum, Lieutenant-Colonel Breymann's force of about 650 men nearly reached Baum's position, but were driven back by the remains of Stark's force reinforced by Seth Warner's militia.

It is possible to find the Dragoon Redoubt with a monument atop it; it is liberally adorned with stands bearing photographic panoramas illustrating the events occurring in the area and directing the visitor to different points of interest. However, all around are high trees and it is not easy to distinguish or identify salient points.

Another Revolutionary War battle fought in 1777 was at Princeton, on 3 January of that year, when Cornwallis faced Washington's 5,200-man American army east of Trenton, but was out-manoeuvred when, during the night, Washington marched his army around Cornwallis's left flank to fall on the British rearguard at Princeton. There is little recollection of ever discovering this field, but the University town of Princeton is delightful, and a tour around the old buildings of the town provide a real battlefield walker's bonus.

On 28 June 1778 the largest battle of America's War of Independence was fought in New Jersey, when 35,000 men marched, manoeuvred and fought from Manalapan Bridge to Middletown, in the Battle of Monmouth, the last great battle of the Northern Theatre of the Revolution, said to be 'Washington's Finest Hour'. On 18 June 1778, General Sir Henry Clinton (who had succeeded Howe as British commander in America) evacuated Philadelphia and began marching eastwards across New Jersey. Seizing the opportunity of ending his army's soul-destroying sojourn at Valley Forge, Washington marched out on 19 June in pursuit of the British, sending Charles Lee ahead with 6,400 men. He overtook the British rearguard (under Cornwallis) at Monmouth on 28 June, but deployed his army carelessly and, when Clinton concentrated his whole army against him, Lee ordered a total retreat, only prevented from being a disaster when Washington arrived with the main body of about 7,000 men. Re-forming quickly, the American army repulsed numerous British attacks until nightfall ended the longest battle of the war.

Monmouth Battlefield State Park is located off Route 33, Manalapan, New Jersey; its Visitors' Center and Monmouth County Historical Association Museum is at 70 Court Street, Freehold Borough, where original battlefield artefacts and exhibits can be seen. In the Park are held regular battle re-enactments, living history demonstrations, troop encampments, and there is a period sutlers, snack-bar and gift shop. The State Park includes some 1,500 acres of the battlefield, but a large proportion of it is held in private ownership, and for that reason exploration seems to be a little curtailed. However, it is possible to see over Covenhoven House which was General Clinton's headquarters, and Craig House, another surviving building, while there remain two churches – Old Tennent and St Peter's – which played a role as battlefield hospitals. In the tiny hamlet Englishtown nearby the Continental Army established its headquarters from 27 to 29 June 1778 and wounded Americans were nursed in its houses for months; the old Village Inn can be visited while nineteenth-century farm life is re-created at Longstreet Farm, Holmdel – but that is more in the nature of a bonus!

The British had captured the peninsula of Stony Point on the Hudson River in May 1779 and had begun fortifying it, cutting down trees, erecting an earthen fort and abatis, with the object of protecting the King's Ferry which crossed the Hudson at that point. Washington sent dashing General Anthony Wayne (later to achieve fame at the Battle of Fallen Timbers in 1794 in the Old North-West Indian Wars) to make a surprise midnight assault at the head of his commando-like corps of light infantry. The force was divided into three: one 300-strong column was to wade through the marshes of the Hudson River from the north; Wayne himself was to lead a second column that approached from the south after wading Havershaw Bay; while two companies would create a noisy diversion in front of the defences. On a dark and stormy night, the marshes separating Stony Point from the mainland were forded by the two attacking columns, who swept up the treeless slopes to arrive at the fort within minutes of each other. After half an hour's heavy fighting the garrison surrendered, but three days later Washington abandoned Stony Point, realising he could not defend it against the combined strength of the British army and navy.

Stony Point Battlefield State Historic Site can be reached from New York City by taking the Palisades Interstate Parkway north to exit 15; proceed on Route 106 east to Route 9W; turn left through the village of Stony Point, then right on Park Road. From the New York Thruway (exit 16 Harriman) take Route 6 east to the Bear Mountain Bridge Circle; proceed south on Route 9W approximately nine miles, then turn left on Park Road. There is a small and interesting museum, but more enterprising is the wide variety of events offered: guided and self-guided tours; artillery, musketry and camplife and cooking demonstrations, usually in period costume. A recent programme for a year's activities included: 'A Day in the Life of the 3rd New York Regiment'; eighteenth-century Re-enactment Regiments performing accurate demonstrations of eighteenth-century military camplife and military manoeuvres; Battlefield Evening Tours; plus a number of musical events by Fife and Drum bands, Drums and Bugles of the US Military Academy; ballads and folksongs of the American Revolution and traditional Irish and Scots music played by the USMC Bagpipe Band.

A unique battlefield walker's bonus was available here, in the nearby location of the United States Military Academy at West Point, very thoroughly explored during a three-night stay at the traditional Hotel Thayer, overlooking the Hudson River and at the very gates of the Military Academy. Little was missed, from the inspiring chapel, the museum, an outdoor evening band concert at the Trophy Point Amphitheatre, to getting behind the scenes through a personal introduction to a senior officer from Dr David Chandler of the Royal Military Academy Sandhurst back in England. Founded on 4 July 1802, when it began operations with ten cadets, the famed USMC West Point is the oldest US military post over which the country's flag has continuously flown.

The American War of Independence ended at 2 pm on 19 October 1781, when Cornwallis's British army marched out of Yorktown in Virginia, and laid down its arms. During that summer, the British commander had turned eastwards towards the coast so as to maintain sea communication with Clinton in New York City; reaching Yorktown on 1 August, he began fortifying the town and Gloucester, to the north, across the York River. Washington, having been joined by a large French army under Rochambeau and later by another French force under Lafayette, marched rapidly to the area and by 6 October their siege-lines, including heavy guns, were in place before Yorktown, and three days later fifty-two heavy siege guns opened fire on the British defences. Parallels were dug and two British redoubts stormed; a British sortie was repulsed on 16 October, and next day every American and French cannon opened fire on the doomed town. Realising he had no hope of holding-out, Cornwallis asked for an armistice and accepted terms of complete surrender.

There is so much to see in the Yorktown area that the battlefield walker is advised to allow plenty of time, being rewarded by bonuses in plenty! Yorktown lies at the eastern end of the Colonial Parkway (Route 238 from Williamsburg). Close around it are the remains of the British earthworks, modified by the Confederates during the Civil War, and a few hundred yards beyond are reconstructed parts of the American and French siege-lines. From the Yorktown Victory Center can be obtained leaflets and maps of the seven-mile Battlefield Tour, a forty-five-minute drive, following signs with red arrows from the Center parking-lot; and then there is the Allied Encampment Tour, a nine-mile drive beginning at Surrender Field, following the signs with yellow arrows. The first-named

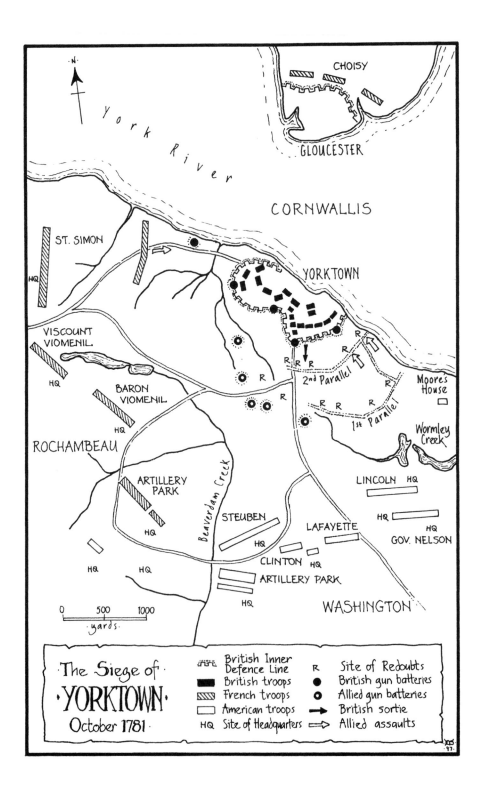

·N·

CHOISY

GLOUCESTER

York River

CORNWALLIS

ST. SIMON

HQ

YORKTOWN

VISCOUNT
VIOMENIL.

HQ

BARON
VIOMENIL

HQ

R R R

R R

2nd Parallel

R

R

R

Moores
House

R R R

1st Parallel

Wormley
Creek

ROCHAMBEAU

ARTILLERY
PARK

HQ

Beaverdam Creek

STEUBEN

HQ

LINCOLN HQ

HQ

HQ
GOV. NELSON

LAFAYETTE

CLINTON HQ

HQ HQ

ARTILLERY PARK

HQ

WASHINGTON

0   500   1000
·yards·

·The Siege of·
·YORKTOWN·
October 1781·

British Inner
Defence Line
British troops
French troops
American troops
HQ Site of Headquarters

R   Site of Redoubts
●   British gun batteries
⊙   Allied gun batteries
→   British sortie
⇒   Allied assaults

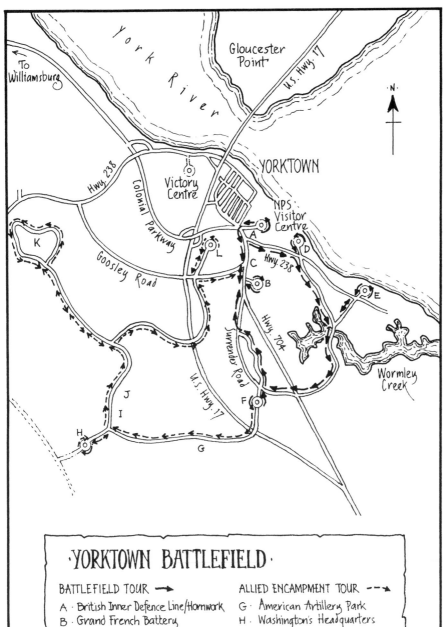

·YORKTOWN BATTLEFIELD·

BATTLEFIELD TOUR ⟶

A · British Inner Defence Line/Hornwork
B · Grand French Battery
C · Second Allied siege line
D · Redoubts 9 and 10
E · Moore House (surrender negotiated)
F · Surrender Field

ALLIED ENCAMPMENT TOUR --⟶

G · American Artillery Park
H · Washington's Headquarters
I · French cemetery
J · French Artillery Park
K · French encampment loop
L · Untouched British Redoubt

The Surrender Field at Yorktown, Virginia, where the Surrender Ceremony of
Cornwallis's British army took place in 1781, on 19 October.

tour includes: British inner defence line and ironwork; the Grand French
Battery; the second Allied siege-line; Redoubts 9 and 10; the Moore
House where surrender terms were dictated; and Surrender Field. The
second tour provides: the American Artillery Park; Washington's HQ;
the French Cemetery; French Artillery Park; French Encampment; and
an untouched British Redoubt.

A visit to the Yorktown area should begin at the Victory Center, on the
Colonial Parkway, where evocative exhibits, audio-visual programmes
and much more chronicling the American Revolution from its beginnings
in Massachusetts to its conclusion in Virginia. Along an indoor re-
creation of an eighteenth-century street – Liberty Street – voices recount
major events of the period, sights and sounds of sea and land battles bring
them to life. There is a continuously running documentary film, *The Road
to Yorktown*, telling of the events leading up to the siege and the surrender
of Cornwallis, a living-history encampment can be viewed, and there is a
gift shop. During the summer months regular history demonstrations and
presentations take place, such as ranger tours of the British inner defence
lines; artillery demonstrations, and historic houses like the Moore House
and the Nelson House can be visited.

There remain many period houses in the charming and historic streets
of Yorktown itself, and the town continues to function as an active
community circulating around the Victory Monument at the east end of

Main Street, erected in 1881 in centennial celebration. A pair of truly significant historical sites remain as bonuses, the names of both being indelibly engraved in the annals of Britain's role in the Americas: Jamestown and Williamsburg. The former lies at the western end of the Colonial Parkway and, as a town, no longer exists except in the pages of history books and the imagination. Here, in1607 landed 104 colonists to form the first English permanent settlement made in America. When the first supply ship arrived a few months later, there were only thirty-eight of them left alive, dying from starvation and disease, and it soon became apparent that the immigrants had not chosen wisely in their site for a settlement. The urge to move inland became stronger until, in 1699, the seat of government was shifted some six miles north to a crossroads, Middle Plantation, which was renamed Williamsburg.

Today, Jamestown is a reconstructed palisaded wooden fort, with three replica ships moored in the river nearby; outside the gates stands a large plaque or scroll, bearing the names of those who first landed here, with the redoubtable Captain John Smith at their head. It is a source of some satisfaction to the author of this book that halfway down the second column of names is 'Richard Featherstone – Gentleman' soon to die and be buried on an island in the Rappahannock River. The Jamestown Visitor's Center, at the edge of the original township, has a theatre, museum, and a gift shop; from it paths lead through the site of 'James Cittie', of which only one original seventeenth-century structure remains – the Old Church Tower, and near to it a statue of Captain John Smith by William Couper.

And so, in 1699, after nearly a century of relentless battling against famine, fire, pestilence and Indians, the Virginia Colony abandoned Jamestown and moved to a new town named after the King of England, William III. For more than 200 years the little town flourished, noted for its many eighteenth-century buildings, until early in the twentieth century scrupulous reconstruction restored Williamsburg to its original appearance and style, so that to step today into colonial Williamsburg is to set foot back in eighteenth-century America in what could be the perfect escape from the twentieth century into the measured cadences of the eighteenth century. It is not a museum to America's past, it is a living city where daily life is vividly re-enacted by costumed historical characters against a backcloth of militia drills, parades and eighteenth-century music and entertainments. Colonial Williamsburg is unique, presenting a singular bonus to the battlefield walker whose thoughts and imagination have been tempered in the warlike surroundings of Yorktown, but a few miles away.

Part Nine

USA – The War of 1812

31 *The Course of the War*

A war with the picturesque frontier of Canada for its arena, fought when the great American West was still a mystery and the country's forests stretched far beyond the white man's ken, could not fail to possess a high degree of colour and romance. Worthy of so vast a continent as North America, its dividing line with Canada, at the time of this war, was a long succession of mighty rivers and mightier lakes, so that many of its battles were fought amid some of the grandest scenery in the world: hills, rocks, precipitous banks, wide rivers, lakes so vast as to be inland seas, and unending forests. On a broad blue river, the fighting-chief of the Shawnees, Tecumseh, and the British General Isaac Brock rode to the capture of Fort Detroit; the muffled thunder of Niagara Falls smote the ears at Lundy's Lane, and the misty veil of its falling waters and the swirl of the river fresh from its maddening plunge were within sight of the Battle of Queenston Heights.

This, the second and last war between Great Britain and the United States of America, was fought-out twenty-nine years after the former colonies had successfully revolted against the mother country. Securing a declaration of war from the US Congress on 18 June 1812, President James Madison listed four major causes: first, the impressment of American seamen; second, the violation of the three-mile territorial limit; third, the blockade of American ports; and fourth, the British Orders in Council. They hardly seem valid reasons for what has been termed an unfortunate and criminal war, although, at the time, no doubt they seemed justifiable. Spread over three years, the war was made up of the following engagements:

1812	Fort Dearborn; Detroit; Queenston Heights
1813	Frenchtown; Sackets Harbour; Naval Engagement 'Chesapeake vs Shannon'; Stony Creek; Lake Erie; Thames River; Chateaugay River; Chrysler's Farm
1814	Chippewa River; Lundy's Lane; Fort Erie; Bladensburg; Lake Champlain; Plattsburg; Fort McHenry (Baltimore)
1815	New Orleans

This last battle, the largest of the war, occurred two weeks after peace had been signed.

Madison, President of an English-speaking Republic, seated in the chair of authority so recently vacated by Washington, chose to strike his

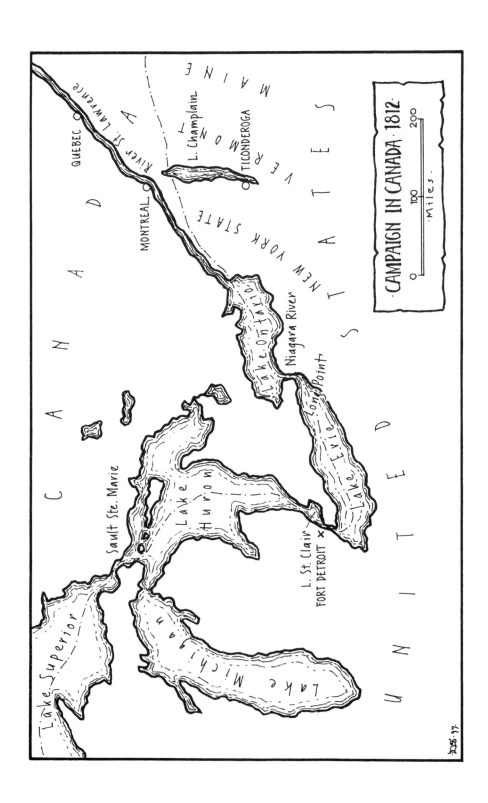

CAMPAIGN IN CANADA · 1812 ·

Miles.
0   100   200

CANADA

Lake Superior

Sault Ste. Marie

Lake Huron

Lake Michigan

UNITED

L. St. Clair
FORT DETROIT ✗

Long Point

Lake Erie

Niagara River

Lake Ontario

NEW YORK STATE

MONTREAL

River St. Lawrence

QUEBEC

VERMONT

L. Champlain

TICONDEROGA

MAINE

STATES

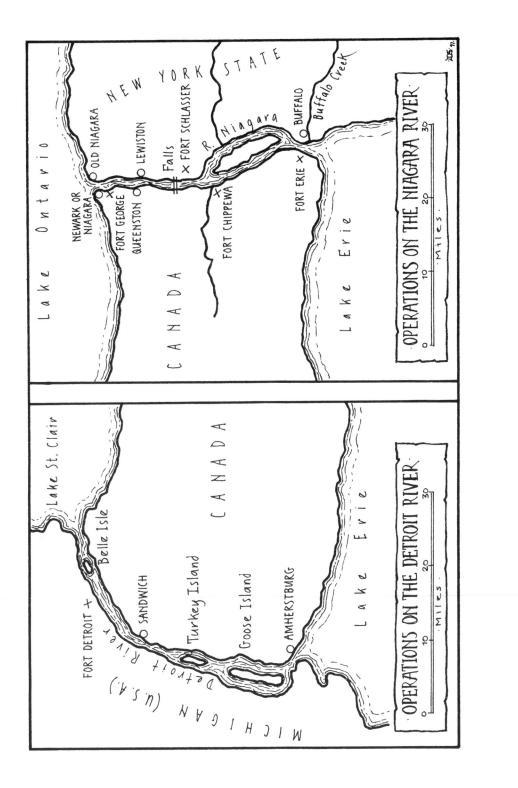

OPERATIONS ON THE DETROIT RIVER.

OPERATIONS ON THE NIAGARA RIVER.

blow at a time when the United States had no other businesses on hand save the pursuing of the war. On the other hand, so critical a state had been reached in the Napoleonic Wars in Europe, that Britain found it difficult to spare even secondary forces for this conflict in the New World.

The war began in June 1812 with the conquest of Canada entrusted by the American government to General Dearborn, who was to invade at three points simultaneously, with General Hull moving from Detroit to subdue the western peninsula of Canada and, if necessary, to march its length to Niagara, the second point of the invasion. The invasion on all fronts was a total failure, and the British captured Fort Mackinac in July and Fort Dearborn (the present site of Chicago) on 15 August. On the following day General Hull surrendered his force of 2,500 American militia, without firing a shot, to General Brock's 730 Canadians and Tecumseh's 600 Indians.

From the start, the American system of fielding armies consisting of militia was shown to be useless, with many states responding reluctantly to the call, while those men who did take up arms made bad soldiers. This was shown to be the case on 13 October 1812, when a force of some 2,270 militia and 900 regulars commanded by Militia General Van Rensselaer attempted to invade Canada across the Niagara River at Queenston. The American regulars crossed and were hotly and, to some extent successfully, engaged on the far bank, but the militia, refusing to obey orders and exercising their right to refuse to leave the territorial limits of the United States, would not cross the river to aid them. The American attack was defeated, the 600 British regulars and 400 Canadian militia caused 250 American casualties and took 700 prisoners. The militia again refused to co-operate in November when another invasion was unsuccessfully attempted across Lake Champlain.

Early in 1813 General Proctor with a force of British regulars, Canadian militia and Indians under Tecumseh attacked camps where General Harrison was recruiting and training troops. By September, Harrison had 7,000 well-trained men but could not move against Detroit until the Americans controlled Lake Erie. When the war broke out only the English had warships on Lake Erie and Ontario but by mid-1813 the Americans had constructed an inland navy manned by seamen from the Atlantic coast. On 10 September, Commodore Perry's fleet, with Harrison's riflemen acting as marines, defeated the British naval force on Lake Erie in what was the turning point of the war in the north-west. Then, moving his infantry and artillery in Perry's ships, and sending the Kentucky Mounted Riflemen round the lake, Harrison converged on Detroit and forced Proctor to withdraw to Canada, pursuing up the Thames River in small boats. On 5 October Harrison's 3,500 men attacked Proctor's force of 800 regulars and 1,000 Indians, who fled when Tecumseh was killed, so Proctor surrendered.

In April 1813 an American force of 1,600 troops under General Pike burned York (now Toronto), and in the following month Colonel Winfield Scott and Commodore Perry mounted an amphibious operation against Fort George at the mouth of the Niagara River. The fort was taken by assault when 4,000 men landed in its rear, and its garrison of 700 under General Vincent withdrew, pursued by a force of 2,000 under 'political' Generals Winder and Chandler, who were defeated when Vincent turned on them. About this time Sir John Prevost, Governor-General of Upper Canada, made a waterborne attack on Sackets Harbour and was repulsed by the small garrison of General Jacob Brown.

Later in 1813, General Wilkinson moved down the St Lawrence while General Wade Hampton pushed north from Lake Champlain to unite and assault Montreal, defended by 15,000 British troops. But attacking a much smaller British force, Hampton was persuaded, by skilfully placed buglers, that he was surrounded, so he retreated to Plattsburg and into winter quarters at the end of October. Wilkinson's 8,000 men were proceeding down the St Lawrence River with flank guards marching on both banks until he was routed by 600 British regulars and Indians. Wilkinson withdrew into winter quarters, where his troops suffered greatly during the cold weather.

On 18 December 1813 the British captured Fort Niagara and their Indian allies ravaged the countryside; on 29/30 December General Drummond with 1,500 men burned the city of Buffalo and the Black Rock Navy Yard.

In April 1814 Wilkinson was superseded by General Jacob Brown, who reorganised his forces, while the retraining of General Winfield Scott transformed them into a well-equipped and uniformed force. In early July Brown led 3,500 troops across the Niagara River into Canada, seized Fort Erie and at Chippewa was attacked by General Riall with 1,700 British regulars and a few Canadian militia and Indians. Driving in the militia and Indians on Brown's left, Riall was confronted by Scott's grey-uniformed brigade of 1,300 men who drove the British back across the river in complete defeat. The first occasion on which the regular forces of both sides had met in battle on relatively even terms, this American victory is commemorated by the grey full-dress uniform worn to this day by the cadets of the US Military Academy at West Point.

Brown with 2,600 men now found himself against Sir Gordon Drummond with 3,000 British reinforcements from Europe, veterans of Wellington's Peninsular campaign, and at Lundy's Lane on 25 July 1814 they fought the hardest battle of the war, lasting through the afternoon until long after darkness. Brown and Scott on the American side were wounded, as was General Drummond, while Riall was taken prisoner; each side had about 900 casualties and both claimed the victory. Brown's Americans fell back on Fort Erie and were besieged by Drummond until the besiegers were dispersed by an American sortie on 17 September. Fort Erie was later abandoned and no further operations of any importance occurred on the Niagara front.

Meanwhile, Prevost with 14,000 of Wellington's veteran troops came down on Lake Champlain from Montreal to Plattsburg, the last barrier to New York and the Hudson Valley, garrisoned by only 1,500 partially trained regulars and about 3,000 militia under General Macomb. Prevost planned a frontal assault while his naval force dispersed the American flotilla covering the American flank; by September 1814, both sides had hastily constructed naval squadrons. The land assault went well but the British naval squadron were completely defeated and forced to surrender in a unique and decisive naval engagement that ended all danger of British invasion from the north. Aware that command of the lake was essential, Prevost hastily withdrew in disorder, abandoning much of his stores; there were no further engagements on this front during the War.

In August 1814 a force of over 5,000 British Peninsular veterans under General Ross landed in the Chesapeake Bay area and advanced on Washington, forty miles away. General Winder with 6,500 raw militia backed by 400 sailors and marines opposed the British advance guard of 1,500 men on 24 August, and, in what became known as the 'Bladensburg Races', the militia fled, leaving the naval gunners to put up a spirited resistance before being forced to retire. Next day the British burned the White House and other public buildings in Washington. Sailing north, on 12 September Ross landed his force sixteen miles from Baltimore where the local militia, securely entrenched, repulsed the attack and Ross was mortally wounded; Fort McHenry successfully withstood a naval bombardment.

The naval rockets used by the British during the bombardment were recorded for posterity when embodied in the American National Anthem, *The Star-Spangled Banner*, written by an inspired Francis Scott Key, who was present at the bombardment.

During 1813/14, the Creek Indians in Alabama allied themselves with the British, and in the small-scale but fierce war that followed, Andrew Jackson was prominent.

In November 1814 Jackson, now a general in the regular army, organised the defences of New Orleans against a British expedition of 7,500 Peninsular War veterans under General Sir Edward Packenham, sailing from Jamaica. Landing on 13 December, British advance guards penetrated within seven miles of the city to an earthwork defence line, its right flank resting on the Mississippi River and the left on a cypress swamp, defended by a force of 700 regulars, Jackson's own Tennessee and Kentucky veteran frontiersmen, some local militia and a heavily armed party of Gulf pirates.

For two weeks, Jackson's men, armed with rifles and hunting knives, made night attacks on the British camp – the darkness giving his undisciplined men an equal chance with trained soldiers. During the day the sharp-shooting frontier riflemen harassed the British outposts from the cover of the woods. At the same time, Jackson strengthened his defences with timber and cotton bales so that a British probing attack was driven back with heavy casualties, and a heavy artillery bombardment was withstood by the defenders. These successes against the highly vaunted British force of 14,250 men (including 500 riflemen from the Light Division) elevated American morale and they awaited, with complete confidence, Packenham's assault.

On 8 January, 5,300 men made a head-on attack, advancing in close ranks on a narrow front against artillery and the Kentucky and Tennessee Riflemen, whose long-barrelled frontier rifle, deadly accurate at ranges up to 300 yards, brought down 50 per cent of the close-packed, redcoated ranks within a few minutes. When the smoke lifted, Packenham and two other generals lay dead together with 2,000 of their men. Superior British numbers had driven back the American detachment on the other bank but the whole force withdrew and Jackson, who had only lost seven men killed and six wounded, did not pursue. It was perhaps the most crushing defeat suffered by a British regular force since Bannockburn and Castillon, and was solely due to the leadership and ability of Andrew Jackson, a border captain who emerged as the best general of the war. He disciplined his troops on the battlefield and so inspired them that their high morale led to victory. The battle was actually fought after the Peace of Ghent had been signed on 4 December 1814, although the combatants were naturally not aware of this.

32 *The Battle of Queenston Heights 13 October 1812*

A t this time, lying at the beginning of a portage-route curving round Niagara Falls and ending at Chippewa, Queenston's importance rested on the fact that EVERYTHING – supplies and people – moving from the Upper Great Lakes and the rest of the colony, had to take that route. It was a strategic bridgehead, the possession of which by the Americans would cut off Canadian supplies, while control of Queenston Heights would allow Major-General Stephen Van Rensselaer, commanding American forces in the Niagara area from his headquarters at Lewiston on the American side of the river, to detect any movement of troops on the river as far as Lake Ontario. Both armies had fortified a few positions and installed guns on either side of the river, but control of the region depended upon possession of the Heights.

The latter days of September and the opening days of October 1812 were busy ones on either side of the Niagara River, where both Americans and Canadians were preparing for the inevitable struggle. Van Rensselaer had assembled in the little village of Lewiston a motley army of 3,000 untried regulars of the 13th and 16th Infantry plus about 1,700 militia of the State of New York who were decimated by disease, malnutrition and lack of enthusiasm, leading to desertions. In the Niagara region, there were 600 tried and experienced British regulars of the 41st and 49th Regiments aided by 600 combat-ready Canadian militiamen, commanded by General Isaac Brock from Fort George, with two companies of the 49th under Captain Dennis in Queenston. Believing his force to be strong enough and superior in numbers to the Queenston garrison, Van Rensselaer reasoned that here the river was narrower and less dangerous than upstream, while his own guns at Lewiston could respond to enemy cannon firing from the far bank.

Brock had been anticipating an attempted crossing and had organised the throwing-up of light earthworks and batteries all along the river from Queenston to Fort George, some seven miles away, with a sprinkling of troops posted at each, watching for the invasion boats. The night of Wednesday 13 October 1812 was a black one, with a cold and raw wind allied to drenching rain, as 600 American troops packed into a dozen boats. Skilled navigators had been pressed into service and they guided the boats through the rapid swirling water towards a narrow ledge below the village, but without the element of surprise, for 300 British

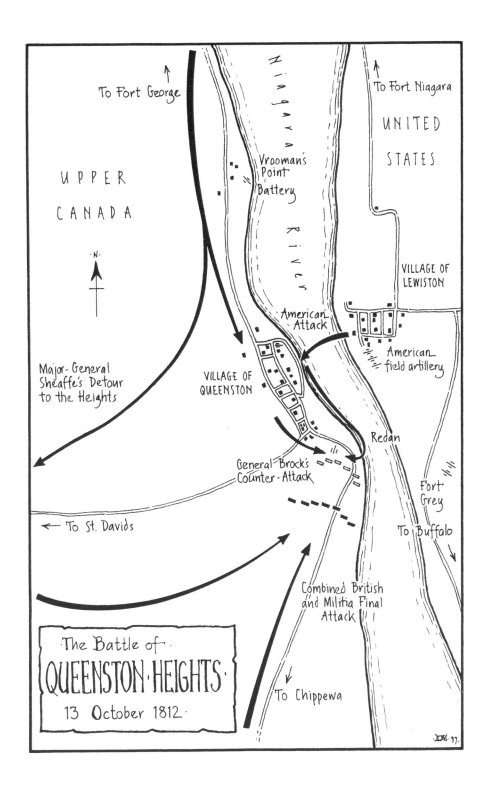

To Fort George

Niagara River

Vrooman's
Point
Battery

To Fort Niagara

UNITED

STATES

UPPER

CANADA

·N·

VILLAGE OF
LEWISTON

American
Attack

American
field artillery

Major-General
Sheaffe's Detour
to the Heights

VILLAGE OF
QUEENSTON

Redan

General-Brock's
Counter-Attack

Fort
Grey

← To St. Davids

To Buffalo

Combined British
and Militia Final
Attack

The Battle of·
QUEENSTON·HEIGHTS·
13 October 1812·

To Chippewa

·DS·97·

soldiers were resolutely awaiting them. Sharp eyes pierced the grey of the morning, the alarm was sounded and soon muskets shattered the stillness and cannonballs hissed through the night air, now diffused with a reddish hue. (Site of Plaque 1 in Self-Guided Battlefield Walk.)

The Americans effected a landing upon a narrow stretch of beach, where Captain Dennis's two companies and about a hundred militia came within musket range, despite the batteries on the American side of the river sweeping the heights they occupied. The defenders' fire forced Van Rensselaer and his men to shelter behind a high bank, where they crouched behind rocks on the narrow strip of shore, attempting to return fire. A young American officer, Captain Wool, seeking to break the deadlock, led a detachment of regulars along the face of the cliff to discover a steep fisherman's path cut into the face of the rock. At the head of sixty regulars, he led upwards slowly, hindered by the slope, bushes and over-hanging rocks, to finally establish his party in a commanding position. (This is Plaque 2 in the Self-Guided Battlefield Walk.)

Meanwhile, at Fort George, Brock heard the cannonading and, leaving General Roger Sheaffe in command, he rode towards the sound of firing at Queenston until arriving with two aides-de-camp at the redan, an earthwork with an eighteen-pounder gun. Dismounting, he surveyed the field through a telescope, but was rudely interrupted by a hail of bullets from the heights behind his party. (This is Plaque 3 in the Self-Guided Battlefield Walk.)

Wool's party had reached the escarpment ridge from where, through the bushes, could be seen the eighteen-pounder gun firing steadily on his compatriots below; it was behind earthworks shaped in the form of a half-moon or a redan, and was seemingly poorly defended, although General Brock could be seen standing directing operations. After firing a telling volley, Wool's men charged down the slope towards the redan, forcing Brock and the small party of defenders to run desperately for shelter. With the defenders caught between two fires, Brock realised that this was a crisis point in the battle and, after sending a messenger to Sheaffe at Fort George calling for reinforcements, he swiftly assembled a party made up of Captain Williams's hundred regulars with the York (Toronto) Volunteers in support, and advanced towards the earthwork. After exchanging heavy fire, he ordered a charge against Wool's Americans, tenaciously holding their ground and pouring down the hill a steady and well-directed fire.

Standing more than six feet in height, in conspicuous British officer's uniform, Brock was a target for the marksmen of Wool's force, and a bullet struck him in the right breast, killing him at once. His death brought a momentary lull to the battle, but the Canadians soon gathered themselves and, led by Brock's Provincial aide-de-camp, John Macdonell, mounted another counter-attack, which also failed when

Macdonell fell mortally wounded. The position was now abandoned to the Americans.

However, the losses were not all Canadian: the American commander Van Rensselaer and his subordinate Wadsworth were both down wounded; in fact so many officers on both sides had fallen that another momentary cessation had occurred in the fighting. But the Americans were in a much better situation at this time, Wool had been reinforced at the redan, and fresh boatloads of soldiers had successfully crossed the river.

By now day had broken, with heavy clouds rolling in and blending with the smoke of battle, and with the arrival of daylight a change was about to take place with General Sheaffe's arrival on the field, having heard of Brock's death. Covered by the Indian warriors of Iroquois chieftains Brant and Norton (Teyoninhokarawen) skirmishing with the Americans, troops of the 41st Regiment, some royal artillery (300 regulars in all) and two supporting companies of militia had arrived from Fort George. The Americans were too disorganised to intercept them, and Sheaffe was able to form on the brow of the Heights a cordon around the whole field of action, his flanks each resting on the river and, taking advantage of the ground, he began to tighten the cordon. (Plaque 4 in the Self-Guided Battlefield Walk.) General Van Rensselaer realised the need for substantial reinforcements and, despite being wounded, was taken across the river to bring over more men. In this he was totally unsuccessful, as the American militia refused pointblank to cross to the Canadian side, claiming that, as fencibles, they had not enlisted to serve outside America.

By now it was 3 pm and Sheaffe's force were reaching the top of the steep slope of the ridge. (Plaque 5 in the Self-Guided Battlefield Walk.) Out of sight of the Americans to the east of them, they halted to regroup and gain their breath. At 4 pm, joined by 150 men from Fort Chippewa, a post some miles above the Falls, Sheaffe now commanded about a thousand men, who were about to take the Americans in the rear. They fired a volley and advanced in an irresistible bayonet charge downhill that nothing could withstand, and the Americans were forced onto the shoulder of the cliffs at their back. With bayonets and tomahawks behind them, their only choices were to jump or surrender; rather than face the grim Indians, some jumped to destruction on the rocks below or into the ominous silent river; others seeking to give themselves up to the Canadians were hurled to death by Indians. Scott, one of the few remaining American officers, bearing on his sword-point a fluttering white cravat, finally surrendered what was left of the Americans to General Sheaffe.

Except for the loss of General Brock, the British/Canadian casualty list was surprising low: 14 dead, 77 injured, 21 missing. The American toll was heavy, considering they had not gained a foot of the territory they had sought to invade: 300 men killed or wounded and 925 captured.

The victory at Queenston was far reaching and went a long way towards convincing the people of Upper Canada that the Canada militia and the British regular army could withstand the American invaders; from this they gained the necessary strength to withstand the two long years of war that lay ahead of them.

33 *Queenston Today*

It is ironic to consider that nature would have been hard pressed to provide a grander setting for a battle than Queenston Heights, where the Niagara escarpment forms a steep landscape, the little town being built against a cliff some 380 feet high, from where the plain slopes gently downwards to Lake Ontario. Perched upon its ledge of rock, Queenston looks down upon a river that is deep and rapid, braided with currents and dimpled with eddies, a stretch of water speckled with the bubbles arising from the nearby Falls. Behind the town the land arises abruptly to a commanding hill that today is crowned with a column 180 feet in height, surmounted by a statue of British General Isaac Brock, looking out over the territory his troops defended and where he laid down his life. It is said that its builders went to great lengths to make it so impressive, believing that the Battle of Queenston Heights – and Brock himself – symbolised the continuance of Canada's ties with Great Britain.

Today it is set in beautiful parkland, ablaze with flowers, with an observation platform set high above the river, across which can be seen the

Queenston battle monument

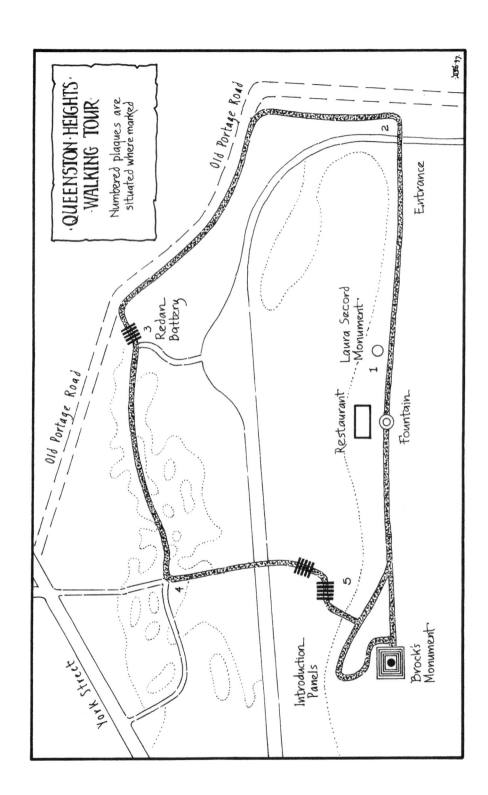

·QUEENSTON·HEIGHTS·
WALKING TOUR·
Numbered plaques are
situated where marked

Old Portage Road

Old Portage Road

York Street

Redan Battery

3

4

5

Introduction
Panels

Brock's
Monument

Restaurant

Laura Secord
Monument

1

Fountain

2

Entrance

steep American shore and a perpetual cloud of spray flung to heaven by the thundering falls of Niagara, nine miles away.

The neat little town was, in the stirring days of 1812, a place of no small importance, a place of depots for all public stores coming from Lower Canada and bound for the West, for which it was the outlet, and the focus point between Upper and Lower Canada. Two forts – Erie at the junction of Lake Erie and the Niagara River, and Malden at the mouth of the Detroit River – were both dependent upon Queenston for their stores and supplies, as were the great tracts of forested country they dominated. It was at Queenston that the civilised East touched elbows with the barbarous West, for it was the gathering place of picturesque people who lived close to nature: fur-traders, merchants, Indians, voyageurs from Lower Canada, pioneers, soldiers and hunters, all combining to form the typical frontier throng of that time. From the West came stores of rich furs; from the East many things, including rum. But trade is precarious; nature alone is unchanging, and the commercial glory has long since deserted this little town on the banks of the Niagara; the fur-laden canoes have drifted down the straits of time and the pioneer has shouldered his axe and marched into the past.

Today it is a quiet and peaceful place, set in attractive gardens, with tourists from all over the world appreciating the respect with which this historical area is afforded, as they laboriously climb the 235 steps to the

Gun on walking trail. Battle of Queenston, Niagara, 1993.

top of the Brock Column and study the pictures and exhibits in the hall below. Some emulate the author, who came back later in the day to dine in the splendid restaurant on a terrace high over the river.

An interesting illustrated handbook can be obtained which gives a succinct account of the battle, the men who fought it, and their weapons. Most valuable of all is the detailed self-guided tour of the battlefield which, in forty-five minutes, enables a very good idea to be obtained of the ground and the events of 13 October 1812. Beginning near the restaurant, the marked route describes the events of the day on inscribed plaques, posted at five separate intervals. (Noted in accompanying Battle Account.)

At the beginning of the walk stands a monument to local inhabitant Laura Secord who, on the morning of Tuesday 22 June 1812, when going to milk her cows, overheard American soldiers talking of a forthcoming attack on a small British outpost of a company of the 49th Foot commanded by Lieutenant James FitzGibbon, at Beaver Dam. To warn them, Laura Secord walked more than twelve miles on a very hot day, across country by rough and little-known backpaths. Subsequently, the American force of 600 regulars, artillery and dragoons under Lieutenant-Colonel Charles G Boerstler was ambushed at Beaver Dam by a force of 400 Indians, led by a French-Canadian Captain Dominique Ducharme, aided by FitzGibbon's soldiers, and eventually surrendered.

A battlefield bonus exists in the attractive town of Niagara-on-the-Lake a few miles up the road; in 1812 it was known as Newark, but bears little resemblance to the English town of that name! It can be reached by car from Niagara River Parkway, or Highway 405, and also from the United States by the Canadian Terminus of the Queenston–Lewiston bridge across the Niagara River.

34 *Mini Memories of Walking the Battlefields of the War of 1812*

Maps Required:
New York State & Lower Canada
Maryland

P refaced by a memorable visit to the United States Air Force Museum at Dayton, military historian Jim Getz of Columbus, Ohio, organised a trip north to Detroit, scene of General Hull's surrender of his American force on 16 August 1812. *En route* was Fort Meigs, during the War a sprawling log-and-earth fortification on the Maunes River covering nearly ten acres, with seven two-storey blockhouses, five artillery batteries, two underground powder magazines, plus a number of work and storage buildings. The garrison, ranging from 900 to 2,000 men – US regulars and militia, with some independent volunteers – under command of General William Henry Harrison, lived in tents inside the stockade as it was more an armed camp than a formal fortification. The British/Canadian forces laid siege to the fort on 1 May 1813, bombarding it for four days, but lifting the siege on 9 May after the garrison was reinforced by Kentucky militiamen. The tide of war thus turned, Harrison abandoned the fort after dismantling it.

Today Fort Meigs is a reconstruction begun by the Ohio Historical Society in 1965, re-creating exactly the fort's seven blockhouses, with walls two feet thick, four-inch deep windows, cannon-port shutters, and whitewashed interior walls. Some of the blockhouses contain exhibits and dioramas of the War of 1812, illustrating the construction and the reconstruction of the fort, besides showing how the garrison lived. There is a six-pounder cannon and accompanying instruments, and it is possible to stand at the second-floor gun-ports and imagine firing it at the enemy outside. In a stone shelterhouse built in the 1930s is a Visitors' Center and Sales Area, where can be seen announcements of battle and camp re-enactments, fife-and-drum concerts, and demonstrations of firing with cannon and muskets.

Fort Meigs lies on State Route 65 near Perrysburg, south of Toledo, and is open most days of the year, with some seasonal variations.

South-west of that area, over the Maumee River, is the Battlefield of

Re-enactment display at Fort George, Niagara

Fallen Timbers where, in 1794 during the Old North-West Indian Wars, General Anthony Wayne, a Revolutionary War hero, defeated a force of hostile Indians he had pressed back to the area of the Maumee River where they made a stand amid trees blown down by a heavy gale. Fixing the enemy with his 2,000 regulars, Wayne sent his 1,000 mounted volunteers round to strike them in the flank, routing them, with several hundred casualties; Wayne lost 33 killed and 100 wounded in the biggest victory ever won against the North-West Indians.

Proceeding to Dearborn *en route* to the Detroit area, a unique battlefield walker's bonus was enjoyed when visiting the Henry Ford Museum and Greenfield Village, founded by Henry Ford in 1929 as a national museum of American history and technology, which includes the actual original Wright brothers' home and bicycle shop and the Thomas Edison Menlo Park Laboratory. On a ninety-three-acre site, one is shown how the motorcar transformed human life. The night was spent at the Hampton Inn, Dearborn.

By-passing the city and environs of Detroit, turning eastwards, Canada was entered, following the route of the September 1813 British retreat from Amhurstburg and along the Thames Valley, leading to the British General Proctor's defeat at Moraviantown on 5 October 1813. Apart from a general awareness of these historical areas, no actual 'walking' was undertaken. Arriving in the Niagara area, we spent the next three nights at Comfort Inn, Niagara, where the serene and salubrious surroundings required great feats of imagination to achieve a return to past days when Niagara was a fiercely contested war target.

Serving as a natural border between Canada and the United States of America, the Niagara River was a vital link in the strategic water route from Montreal to the Western Frontier, vigilantly guarded and watched by the two young nations. Over a period of 150 years, the waterway became a prize of war for armies from France, Britain and America, until in 1812 inevitably it became a major battlefield, and the wooded banks echoed to the sound of battle. But the guns have long been silenced and at each of Niagara's National Historic Sites the past has been respectfully preserved and re-created, so that exploring the area becomes a battlefield walker's delight!

Built in 1796, Fort George was a major British military post after the American Revolution, when it was agreed that Niagara should be the frontier. In 1812, when the War with America began, the Fort was formed of six small bastions connected by a loopholed stockade, surrounded by a shallow dry ditch; the bastions were of solid earth, floored with solid wooden planks forming firing platforms for cannons. At that time, the armament consisted of one twelve-pounder gun, two twenty-four-pounders, and two mortars. Inside the fort were blockhouses, separate officers' quarters, a guardhouse, kitchen, and powder-magazine. In May 1813 it was captured by American forces and almost destroyed; after the War, it was allowed to tumble into ruins before being finally abandoned in 1826, remaining in a dilapidated condition until rebuilt as a tourist attraction in the twentieth century. Today, it is possible to take a self-guided walking tour of the Fort and its environs, which can be seen as one approaches the town of Niagara-on-the-Lake along the Niagara Parkway. Re-enactment displays take place frequently during summer months.

Travelling south, it is impossible to miss the impressive 180-foot Brock Monument marking the Battlefield of Queenston, considered in detail elsewhere in these pages. It was dedicated in 1853 and completed in 1856 and replaces the original simple 130-foot stone monument erected by the Province of Upper Canada to commemorate the valorous General Brock, which was destroyed in 1840 by a massive gunpowder explosion, alleged to have been set-off by an American sympathiser with the Upper Canada Rebellion.

Then comes the site of the battlefield of the Battle of Lundy's Lane, fought on 25 July 1814, and said to be the fiercest conflict in all of the War of 1812. Now a popular vacation town, the actual field has long since been built over, but is marked by a granite monument bearing a descriptive plaque in English and French set in a central churchyard. Nearby is the Lundy's Lane Historical Museum (on 5810 Ferry Street, Niagara Falls), a handsome stone building erected in 1874, featuring pioneer exhibits, glass, china and military displays. The first floor interprets the early settlement and tourism of the Falls area, and features the War of 1812 and Fenian Raid militaria; the second floor is the setting for a Victorian parlour, with an early kitchen, toys and dolls, photographs and a gallery of seasonal exhibits and displays.

South out of Lundy's Lane on Niagara Parkway, look for the small monument on the river side of the road, denoting the Chippewa battlefield, notable for being the first action of the War in which American regulars encountered British regulars who were veterans of Peninsular War battles, fought on 5 July 1814. On 3 July, General Jacob Brown with 3,500 American troops crossed the Niagara River into Canada and seized Fort Erie, making the British force under General Phineas Riall fall back sixteen miles north, to deploy his 1,500 men on a plain near the Chippewa River. Brown ordered General Winfield Scott's brigade, 1,300 strong, to attack them and, in an action lasting only half an hour, they broke the British line, killing 137 and wounding another 375, with losses to themselves of only 48 dead and 227 wounded.

The battlefield is on the west side of the road, back in the fields, lacking markers but with a small museum in a barn-like building south of the sole location sign. At the time of visiting, the museum's custodian was a very helpful lady who knew a lot about the battle.

Continue south on the Parkway to its very end, to Fort Erie, located at the most southerly end of the Parkway at the junction of Dominion and Lakeshore Roads; from the USA take the second exit off the Peace Bridge at Highway 3 and follow the direction signs. The original Fort Erie was built by the British in 1764, after the ceding of New France to Britain on the conclusion of the Seven Years War, but its damaged condition caused a second fort to be commenced in 1805, on the heights behind the original fort, and still unfinished when the war broke out in 1812. In July 1814 the fort was surrendered to the advancing American army led by General Jacob Brown, following the British withdrawal from the field of Chippewa, and after the British victory at Lundy's Lane in 1814 the Americans occupied it in force. On the night of 15/16 August 1814, General Gordon Drummond's British force launched a three-pronged assault, but lost over 1,000 men following an explosion in the north-east bastion, and withdrew. After a prolonged series of both sides attacking and counter-attacking, an American attempt to capture the British siege batteries was beaten-off with heavy losses to the attackers. Lifting the siege, the British retired to positions in Chippewa and defeated an outflanking attempt, causing the Americans to retreat to Fort Erie, which they destroyed before withdrawing to Buffalo on 5 November 1814. The British continued to occupy the ruins before abandoning them in 1823.

In 1937 reconstruction began, restoring the fort to its appearance during the American occupation period of July–November 1814; it was

Entrance to Fort Erie

officially re-opened on 1 July 1939. As one walks around the fort's impressive exterior, it is possible to discern reminders of the dramatic scenes it has witnessed: field fortifications, stone walls, a dry ditch, and a monument over a mass grave honouring the men who fought in the siege. There is much to be seen: restored rooms and exhibits, demonstrations by costumed re-enactors; from the Visitors' Center can be obtained relevant literature and a self-guided walking tour schedule; audio-tours can be hired, and audio-visual presentations take place in the Welcome Center every fifteen minutes. There is a regular demonstration schedule from 11.00 am until 3 pm which includes guided tours, musket demonstrations and a weapons-cleaning demonstration – all by authentically uniformed demonstrators.

Battlefield walkers' bonuses in the Fort Erie area are plentiful and include: Fort Erie Historical Museum; Fort Erie Railroad Museum; Doll's House Gallery; and the Antique Firefighting Museum. But, of greater interest and within the terms of reference of the beholder is the Battle of Ridgeway Scenic Drive, some ten miles west of Fort Erie, exiting at Central Avenue North, turning right onto Central Avenue North; Ridgeway itself lies on Highway 3 between Port Colborne and Fort Erie. The actual site of the battle is found above the intersection of the highway and Ridge Road, which runs north out of Ridgeway; a marker stands on the north side of Garrison Road less than a kilometre east of Ridge Road

(Garrison Road lies north of Highway 3C). This marker is at the southern end of the battleground, the centre being the intersection of Ridge Road with Bertie Road.

The battle was a small affair, fought between Anglo-Canadian forces and the Fenian Brotherhood, the American branch of the Irish Republican Brotherhood, founded in New York City in 1859 with the aim of fostering Irish independence from Great Britain. In 1866 the second of three raids into Canada culminated in an action at Ridgeway on 1–3 June 1866, when they defeated the Anglo-Canadian Militia, but withdrew when America enforced Neutrality Laws and prevented reinforcements and supplies reaching them. A Ridgeway Battlefield Museum can be visited on Highway 3, Ridgeway, Ontario, Canada.

On the American side of the Niagara River, near Youngstown in New York State, in a picturesque setting on the Lake Front, is Old Fort Niagara, with a history spanning more than 300 years. A fort at the mouth of the Niagara River was vital during the colonial wars in North America, for it controlled both the westward route to the heartland of the continent and access to the Great Lakes. Its strategic value lessened with the completion of the Erie Canal in 1825, but it remained a working military post until well into the twentieth century, being an active barracks and training station for the American army during both World Wars; the last army units did not leave the fort until 1963. Three flags are flown daily above its parade ground to symbolise the nations which held the fort in turn, with each seeking the support of the powerful Indian Iroquois Confederacy. Early forts of Conti and Denonville were held by the French in 1679 and 1687/8 respectively, until in 1726 with the construction of the still-standing impressive French castle, France erected a permanent fortification. They lost it after a nineteen-day siege in 1759 during the French and Indian War, and the British held it throughout the American Revolution but were forced to cede it to the United States in 1796. During the War of 1812, Niagara was recaptured by the British in 1813, and ceded back to America at the end of the War in 1815.

The Old Fort was restored between 1927 and 1934 and is a very worthwhile place to visit today, with a trading post where souvenirs can be purchased and snacks obtained. Within its immaculate bounds are many guns and artefacts, and military re-enactments take place during the day throughout the summer months. A very comprehensive illustrated guide is available and, for the most enjoyable and comprehensive visit, it is advisable to follow the tour outlined in the guide; members of the Old Fort Niagara staff are on the spot to give descriptions and answer questions.

A Canadian-based organisation known as 1812 Battlefield Tours can be contacted at PO Box 2061, Niagara Falls, Ontario L2E 6Z2

Fort McHenry, Baltimore

(416 356–3139) and conduct guided tours of all the main historical sites in the area.

It is doubtful if the battlefield walker will ever find a greater 'bonus' than all that will surround him or her in the Niagara region, with its unique stupendous waterfalls which, together with the superb parklands, make it a place of beauty, history and natural power. The Niagara Parkway is a 'must' to be driven, enjoying what Sir Winston Churchill described as 'the prettiest Sunday afternoon drive in the world'. Truly, it makes the War of 1812 among the most memorable of all conflicts to explore, if only through the softening influences of the surroundings.

And that is not all the War of 1812 has to offer: there remains a singularly colourful piece of American history evolving around a battle at Baltimore in September 1814, and subsequent events at nearby Fort McHenry. The battle at Baltimore would make its mark in history as one of the few American victories of consequence in the War of 1812, but truly hallmarked by the presence of 35-year-old Francis Scott Key who, from a prisoner-exchange boat in Baltimore Harbour, saw the night-long bombardment of the Fort by British warships. During the darkness, he anxiously watched events and, when morning came, was so happy to see the huge forty-two by thirty-foot National flag flying defiantly over the

battered fort that he spontaneously wrote down, on the back of an unfinished letter, the words of *The Star-Spangled Banner* which
subsequently became the American National Anthem.

Fort McHenry is a battlefield walker's delight, a national monument
and historic shrine, situated three miles south-east of the town of
Baltimore's Inner Harbour, just off I-95, following the blue-green direc-
tional signs on all major routes. It lies in historic splendour, seemingly
exactly as it was in 1814, but with scars of war cleared up; over it flies a
huge star-spangled flag, still with fifteen bright stars and broad stripes as
when it inspired Francis Scott Key. The Visitors' Center is highly comprehensive, with an impressive programme of films, daily demonstrations,
living history programmes, backed by a large coloured folding brochure,
provided free of charge. Don't miss Fort Henry!

Part Ten

USA: The War Between the States (The American Civil War) 1861–65

35 *The Course of the War*

This conflict, big in its every aspect, was fought by citizen-soldiers in armies that progressively increased in size, firepower and standards of leadership. In both tactics and weapons it was the first conflict in history to be readily identified with present-day warfare, with railways and telegraphs playing important parts, steamships fighting and transporting armies, the first metallic cartridges produced for the first breech-loading repeating rifle, while the machine-gun, the revolver and the rifled gun made their appearance on the battlefield. Because of improvements in weapons that revolutionised tactics, this war saw the disappearance of the solid infantry formations of past wars, and the old type of cavalry warfare involving shock action against infantry, with frontal assaults ruled-out, formations dispersed and becoming more flexible. It was a conflict where, more than in any previous war, the soldier was subordinated to his firepower, with battles frequently decided by one side being armed with superior numbers of modern weapons rather than by any well-planned tactics evolved by generals. The sheer volume of fire prevented attackers coming to close quarters so that the bayonet lost its importance and infantry, in mass formation, emerged from cover to be torn to shreds by case-shot and shell, fired by concentrated and untouched artillery. The enthusiasm and fervour of the charge, aroused by drums, bugles, shouts and the 'rebel yell', frequently lost momentum, to peter out in a fire-fight long before reaching the enemy. Cavalry charges against weapons which, even in ill-trained hands, could kill at 500 yards were a crude form of suicide.

Both sides quickly learned to throw-up log-faced earthworks, and the Confederate armies, struggling to match the firepower of the North, showed great ingenuity in defensive warfare featuring the use of artillery and defensive foxholes dug by riflemen. These foxholes and rifle-pits expanded into trench systems, used as a base for both defensive and offensive operations; in front of Petersburg in 1864–65, both sides were entrenched sometimes only fifty yards apart. World War I veterans of the Western Front would have felt quite at home among the wire entanglements, the trenches, dug-outs, listening-posts, bomb-proof shelters and rifle-pits of 1864.

When considering the style of warfare in the American Civil War, it is necessary to understand that the terrain created three separate and distinct theatres of war. In the East, the rolling countryside of Virginia, with its deeply fretted coastline, was the area which both sides regarded as the most important, and in which each could give to their commanders the least freedom of action, because the capital cities – Richmond and Washington – were only eighty miles apart. In the centre was the wild mountain country of Tennessee and Kentucky guarding the passes to the Deep South. And in the West, the rich Mississippi Valley controlled much of the commerce of the country.

In a sense, it was a curiosity of the war between two halves of such a vast country, that the most bitter fighting occurred within the confined area of northern Virginia, much of it taking place in the well-populated 150 square miles containing the two capitals and marked by woods, valleys, rivers and railways. Thus, it was in Virginia that the two hastily formed armies of a divided nation clashed for the first time on a field overlooking Bull Run, on a warm July day in 1861. The Union commander, General McDowell's army of 35,000 ninety-day volunteers aimed for control of the vital railroad junction at Manassas, the best overland approach to the Confederate capital, but ended the day in retreat. Soldiers of both sides were stunned by the violence and destruction in ten hours of heavy fighting that swept away any notions that the war's outcome would be quickly decided.

More than 2,000 engagements and over 100 major battles were to be fought before, on 9 April 1865, Robert E Lee, commanding the Confederate Army of Northern Virginia, surrendered his army to the Union commander General Ulysses S Grant at Appomattox Courthouse. And so the long war ended where it had begun – in Virginia.

The Battles of the War 1861–65

1861		Victory to
14 April	Fort Sumter	Confederate
1 June	Booneville	Federal
3 June	Philippi, W Va	Fed
10 June	Big Bethel	Con
11–14 July	Rich Mountain	Fed
21 July	Bull Run (1st Manassas)	Con
10 August	Wilson's Creek	Con
10–15 Sept	Cheat Mountain	Fed
21 October	Balls Bluff	Con
7 November	Belmont	Fed
1862		
19 January	Mill Springs	Fed
6 February	Fort Henry	Fed
8 February	Roanoke Island	Fed
February	Fort Donelson	Fed

1862 *(cont.)*		Victory to
7–8 March	Pea Ridge	Fed
8 March	Hampton Roads	Con
23 March	Kernstown I	Fed
Feb–March	Island No 10	
	New Madrid	Fed
6–7 April	Shiloh	Fed
15 April	Peralta	Fed
4 Apr–4 May	Yorktown II	Fed
25 April	New Orleans II	Fed
5 May	Williamsburg	Con
8 May	McDowell	Con
23 May	Front Royal	Con
25 May	Winchester I	Con
31 May–1 June	Fair Oaks (Seven Pines)	Fed
6 June	Memphis	Fed
8/9 June	Cross Keys–Fort Republic	Con
26 June	Mechanicsville	Fed
27 June	Gaines Mill	Con
29/30 June	Peach Orchard	Fed
29/30 June	White Oaks Swamp	Fed
30 June	Savage's Station	Fed
30 June	Frayser's Farm	Fed
1 July	Malvern Hill	Fed
9 August	Cedar Mountain	Con
29/30 Aug	2nd Bull Run (2nd Manassas)	Con
28 August	Groveton	Con
31 August	Chantilly	Fed
29/30 Aug	Richmond Ky	Con
14/15 Sept	Harper's Ferry	Con
17 Sept	Antietam Creek	Con
14 Sept	South Mountain	Con
14 Sept	Crampton's Gap	Con
19/20 Sept	Iuka	Fed
3/4 October	Corinth, Mississippi	Fed
8 October	Perryville	Con
7 December	Prairie Grove	Fed
13 December	Fredericksburg	Con
25–29 Dec	Chickasaw Bluffs	Con
31 December	Stones River	Fed
1863		
4/12 January	Arkansas Post	Fed
14 Mar–9 July	Port Hudson	Fed
1–6 May	Chancellorsville	Con
1 May	Port Gibson	Fed
14 May	Jackson	Fed

1863 *(cont.)*   **Victory to**

16 May	Champions Hill	Fed
7/9 May	Big Black River	Fed
4 May	Salem Church	Con
9 June	Brandy Station	Con
13/14 June	Winchester II	Con
1–3 July	Gettysburg	Fed
Jan–July	*Siege of Vicksburg*	Fed
19/20 Sept	Chickamauga	Fed
September–Oct	Chattanooga	Fed
14 October	Bristoe Station	Fed
24 Nov	Lookout Mountain	Fed
25 Nov	Missionary Ridge	Fed
Nov/Dec	Knoxville	Fed

1864

20 February	Olustee	Con
22 February	Okolona	Con
8 April	Sabine Crossroads – Pleasant Hill	Con
12 April	Fort Pillow	Con
14 May	Alexandria LA	Con
5/6 May	Wilderness	Drawn
8–18 May	Spotsylvania	Con
11 May	Yellow Tavern	Fed
15 May	Drewry's Bluff	Con
15 May	Resaca	Fed
15 May	New Market	Con
23/25 May	North Anna River	Fed
25 May	New Hope Church	Con
3/12 June	Cold Harbor	Con
5 June	Piedmont	Fed
10 June	Brice's Cross Roads	Con
11/12 June	Trevilian Station	Con
15/18 June	Petersburg	Con
17/18 June	Lynchburg	Con
27 June	Kenesaw Mountain	Con
9 July	Monocacy River	Con
14/15 July	Tupelo	Drawn
22 July	Atlanta	Fed
20 July	Peach Tree Creek	Fed
23/24 July	Kernstown II	Con
28 July	Ezra Church	Fed
30 July	The Crater (Petersburg)	Con
3 August	Mobile Bay	Fed
19 September	Opequon Creek (Winchester III)	Fed
22 September	Fisher's Hill	Fed
19 October	Cedar Creek	Fed
23 October	Westport	Fed

1864 *(cont.)*		Victory to
29 November	Spring Hill	Fed
30 November	Franklin	Fed
15/16 Dec	Nashville	Fed
23/25 Dec	Fort Fisher	Con
1865		
13/15 Jan	Fort Fisher	Fed
2 March	Waynesboro	Fed
19/20 March	Bentonville	Fed
25 March	Fort Stedman (Petersburg)	Fed
29/31 March	Dinwiddie C H and White Oak Road	Fed
2 April	Selma	Fed
6/7 April	Sayler's Creek	Fed
9 April	Appomattox River	Fed

Influencing the future shape of the world, this epic conflict began when Abraham Lincoln was inaugurated as President of the United States of America in March 1861, after his anti-slavery Republicans had won the previous year's election, hoping to bring to an end the strain of growing rifts in the Union. Before this, in the last four months of President James Buchanan's presidency, the Union had begun to disintegrate and, in Washington, senators and representatives from the South had met repeatedly to discuss whether their states could remain in a union hostile to slavery. At the same time, officers of the small US Army considered their allegiancies, wondering whether they would side with the North or the South, if the worst occurred. When that happened, some of the best of them, after hours of painful consideration, resigned their US commissions and chose the South.

Six weeks after the election, South Carolina seceded, followed by the states of Florida, Georgia, Alabama, Lousiana, Mississippi and Texas; they met in Alabama on 4 February 1861 to organise themselves into the Confederate States of America, electing Jefferson Davis, a senator from Mississippi, as their president.

In January, guns on the shore had driven-off a government steamer, *Star of the West*, trying to unload supplies for Fort Sumter, a US Army garrison in Charleston Harbour, in South Carolina. A few weeks after taking office, President Lincoln ordered supplies to be sent again to Sumter, telling the governor of South Carolina what he planned. Subsequently, on 12 April, Brigadier-General Pierre Beauregard, commanding the harbour batteries, ordered them to shell the fort, forcing it to surrender and so start the War. By June, Virginia, North Carolina, Arkansas and Tennessee had joined the Confederacy; while the border states of Delaware, Maryland, Missouri and Kentucky, with bitter and divided populations, agonised over their choice. By the autumn of 1861, skilful negotiation, backed by a show of force when required, brought all four under the control of the North.

At the beginning neither side had an army, both having to frantically build striking forces from their respective cadres of the small pre-war US Army – the North with 15,000 regulars (but only about 3,000 available in the East), while the South had only 314 regular army personnel, all officers. Lincoln called for 75,000 militia to serve for three months, with 65,000 on longer engagements; the Confederacy called for 170,000 volunteers. In the event, by June 1861 the Union army was about 152,000 strong, and the Confederacy about 112,000. The Union navy had an assortment of ninety ships, but many were obsolete and others were stationed overseas; the Confederates had no navy, but seized Federal ships from surrendered Union dockyards, and also began a building programme. All in all, in the beginning the North possessed long-term advantages of superior equipment and an extensive industrial plant, whilst the South had immediate advantages in a population of men experienced in shooting, riding and living off the country. When the war began, the army raised by the South took the field equipped with nearly every military quality, particularly in their cavalry arm.

The available manpower ratio favoured the North by 5:2; the twenty-two Northern states (including three Border states with divided loyalties) had a population of some 22 million; the eleven seceding states had 5.5

An original photograph taken in 1862 of Confederate Volunteers at Pensacola in Florida.

million whites and 3.5 million Negro slaves. Both sides turned to militia and poorly trained volunteers on short enlistments, formed into regiments going almost untrained into battle; lacking veterans and regimental loyalties, commanded by men knowing no more of war than the men in the ranks, it is surprising that they performed so well. In this sphere, throughout the war the Confederacy held a superiority in leadership because in 1861 the best and most experienced officers of the US Army pledged allegiance to the Confederacy; in the early days many Federal officers were inefficient political appointees, lacking any military experience. It was a unique facet that most of the opposing commanders were intimately acquainted with each other's strengths and weaknesses through their associations at West Point and when serving in the Mexican War of 1846.

The Southern commanders at the beginning of the war – Lee, Longstreet, Bragg and Forrest – were still commanding at the end; Lee did not begin the war as Confederate Commander-in-Chief; at that time it was considered that the best soldier in the South was General A S Johnston, killed at Shiloh in 1862. General Robert E Lee was possibly the best American military thinker and organiser of his time; his Federal counterpart Ulysses S Grant, alone of all the generals on both sides, demonstrated the capacity to command small forces as well as large ones in battle under a great variety of conditions. As the war ran its course, the Union threw up a host of aggressive young generals like Sheridan, Custer, Wilson, Upton and Kilpatrick; Reynolds, said to be 'the most complete soldier in the army' was killed on the first day at Gettysburg. Then there were Sherman, Thomas and Hancock, all first-class soldiers and commanders who would have made their mark in any war. So would General Thomas J Jackson of the Confederacy, killed at Chancellorsville in 1863, who won the nickname of 'Stonewall' at First Bull Run, where he displayed all the military pleasure of an Old Testament warrior in the skill and cunning of warfare. When J E B Stuart, the renowned Confederate cavalry leader, was killed at Yellow Tavern in 1864, the Army of Northern Virginia stumbled along in half-blinded condition for weeks. It can reasonably be said that at least three commanders on each side were more able than most generals of the Napoleonic Wars.

Both armies were similarly organised, with the regiment as the basic infantry and cavalry unit, known by their number and state, thus the 2nd Vermont or the 7th Alabama; regiments were grouped into brigades, with three brigades in a division, and three divisions in a corps; corps made up armies. Union army corps and divisions were only about half as strong as those of the Confederates – eleven of their divisions equalled seventeen Federal corps. In the Confederate army regiments from the same state were brigaded together, and formations bore the names of their original leaders, even after the command had passed to another; Federal corps were more likely to be known by numbers. Armies were usually referred to by locality, such as the Union Armies of the Potomac, the Ohio and the Cumberland; the Confederate armies were the Armies of Northern Virginia, Tennessee, and the West of the Confederacy. There were distinctive flags for armies, corps, divisions, brigades and regiments carried into action by Colour Guards who served their purpose as a rallying point, maintaining morale and indicating the formation's position and progress; doing this, they invariably suffered heavy losses.

The basic uniform worn by the Federal troops was a dark-blue tunic and light-blue pants, topped by a dark-blue forage cap (kepi); Southern soldiers wore uniforms varying from the elegant to the ragged, and often they lacked shoes. Without realisation or intention, the Confederate soldiers became the first major army of history to wear camouflage-coloured uniforms, wearing, for want of anything else being available, tunics of butt-nut-brown homespun, which reduced casualties by allowing concealment and surprise. At the outbreak of hostilities, both sides fielded units wearing fanciful garb such as baggy Zouave pants, boleros, and fezzes, along with fanciful names to match; the first few months of campaigning saw them disappear.

Lacking the officers to supervise training and without the national characteristics that produced the machine-like obedience of the European soldier, Johnny Reb and Billy Yank fought like demons but strayed like schoolboys. The men of both sides displayed the highest standards of bravery, fortitude and self-reliance, but lack of discipline liquidated the results of many hard-fought battles, with perhaps the only advantage possessed by the Union soldier over his Confederate counterpart being a certain innate capacity for discipline. Throughout the long war, the Northern soldier had everything to learn in a military sense, not knowing how to adapt himself to outdoor life, as did his enemy, and subsequently suffering heavily through sickness. After being out-generalled, out-fought and defeated, the Federal soldiers who made up the Army of the Potomac persistently bounced back under some new commander until, at Gettysburg in July 1863, the city dwellers and farm lads from the East found a new degree of morale grafted upon them by their newly appointed commander, General Meade, backed by some competent corps and divisional leaders such as Sedgwick, McPherson, Hancock and Slocum. In other theatres of war it was different – the men from Minnesota and Iowa in the Army of the Tennessee possessed a proficiency with weapons that more than equalled that of the Southerners, and they were infinitely better at obeying their officers. In the West the men facing the Confederacy were mostly farmers, possessing many of the attributes that go to form a capable soldier.

In the early days of the war the Confederate cavalry literally rode rings around the Northern horsemen, to burn, raid and loot, almost without loss to themselves, under such competent leaders as J E B Stuart, Wade Hampton, Wheeler, S D Lee and Fitz-Lee. In addition, there were the semi-guerrilla cavalry leaders Bedford Forrest and Morgan, who led seemingly undisciplined and disorganised forces that, wearing no recognised uniforms, must have resembled Boer commandos; spreading alarm and confusion in rear areas, the raiders tore up railway track and burned Union supply depots. In time the Union produced increasingly proficient cavalry units, those of the Army of the Potomac organised into a corps; always better equipped than the Southerners, the Federal cavalry steadily overtook, then bettered their Southern counterpart. By early 1863, the North's cavalry arm had established itself, with recruited plainsmen from the West and lively new leaders like Pleasanton, Buford, Gregg, Kilpatrick, Farnsworth (killed at Gettysburg), Merritt, Custer, Wilson, and the redoubtable Sheridan. In the last two years of the war, no one in the Army of the Potomac did more to overthrow Lee than the cavalry operating in the Valley of the Shenandoah and at Petersburg.

The Southern cavalry trooper provided his own horse, being paid for its use and recompensed if the mount was killed in action; but if it died in any other way, no compensation was given. As horses became scarce and more costly, large numbers of Confederate horsemen had to go into infantry units as they could not replace their mounts; this penalised bravery because courageous troopers got their horses killed and, being unable to replace them, were lost to the cavalry.

Commanding the Army of Northern Virginia, Lee was unable to affect the fatal disasters suffered by the Confederacy in the West, where even the technical victory of Chickamauga in 1863 was, in reality, a fateful defeat. Confederate General D H Hill said: 'After that battle the élan of the Southern soldier was never seen again; he fought stoutly to the last but, after Chickamauga, with the sullenness of despair, without enthusiasm or hope.'

It has been suggested that, failing to win the war in its early stages, the Confederacy were bound to lose eventually because they could never hope to improve upon the genius of Robert E Lee as a commander, whereas the Union, by a process of elimination of commanders, might throw up a leader who could approach Lee's brilliance – which occurred when U S Grant rose to the top. In fact, by capturing Vicksburg on the same days as Meade defeated Lee at Gettysburg in July 1863, Grant won the Civil War for the Union because, as Sherman said: 'The possession of Vicksburg is the possession of America.'

A very powerful argument for a Union victory was that the South could not greatly increase the numbers of its soldiers, whereas the Union had an almost unlimited supply of manpower, although not as great as is generally stated, certainly not the often claimed 3 to 1. But it was not numerical inferiority that defeated the barefooted and ragged army of

Virginia, it was lack of supplies – logistics were the great deficiency in Lee's generalship. Even the overwhelming Confederate victory at Fredericksburg in 1862 did not teach him that the severely battered Union army still possessed both the will and physical capacity to return for another battle. Had he taken Jackson's advice and pursued the enemy while they were disorganised by retreat and backed-up against a river without artillery support, then he might have emulated Napoleon who, at Friedland in 1807, under very similar circumstances, mercilessly destroyed the Russian army, and ended the war.

Perhaps the morale of the Southern soldier, defending his home against an invader, stimulated by early success and led by an excellent and much-loved commander, was higher. In the face of great numerical superiority, or when tactically defeated, he knew himself to be capable of holding his ground.

36 *The Battle of Gettysburg 1–3 July 1863*

At the end of June 1863, the future seemed to hold great promise to the 75,000 men of the Confederate Army of Northern Virginia marching along the dusty lanes towards Gettysburg; although ragged, ill shod and badly equipped, they were a well-organised and trained formation who had not met a major reverse in two years of fighting. They knew that their beloved commander Robert E Lee had side-stepped Federal leader 'Fighting Joe' Hooker after Chancellorsville in early May, and had brought them safely across the River Potomac, out of the ruined countryside of Central Virginia into this lush paradise, where they would find food, and fresh clothing and footwear, before striking for the rich, undamaged cities of the North. Using the Shenandoah Valley as an approach into Pennsylvania, Lee's army had begun moving northward from Fredericksburg on 3 June, crossed the Potomac at Williamsport and Shepherdstown, and made for the Pennsylvanian town of Harrisburg. However, the tide was about to turn, although there was not a Confederate soldier who would have failed to laugh derisively had he been told this.

It began when Lee allowed J E B Stuart, after crossing the Potomac, to take the Confederate cavalry on a long raiding march towards Baltimore, thus depriving the army of its eyes and dealing a deadly blow to the advantages Lee hoped to gain by his daring march North. Nor was Lee to know that Hooker had been relieved of command of the Army of the Potomac and replaced by the more dynamic Meade, who was pounding northward across Maryland by forced marches, to reach Frederick in Maryland before Lee, across the mountains at Chambersburg. It was on 28 June that Lee learned of Meade's nearness. Immediately, the Confederate leader changed his plans, abandoning his intended movement towards Harrisburg, and directing a concentration of his entire force at the eastern base of South Mountain, at Cashtown, about eight miles from Gettysburg.

In the two days since assuming command of the Union forces, Meade had moved northward, with the idea of taking up a battle position near Taneytown in northern Maryland. He needed information of Lee's movements and whereabouts, and sent out Buford's cavalry division on 30 June to make a reconnaissance in the Gettysburg area, and on the morning of 1 July, they reached McPherson Ridge just west of the town.

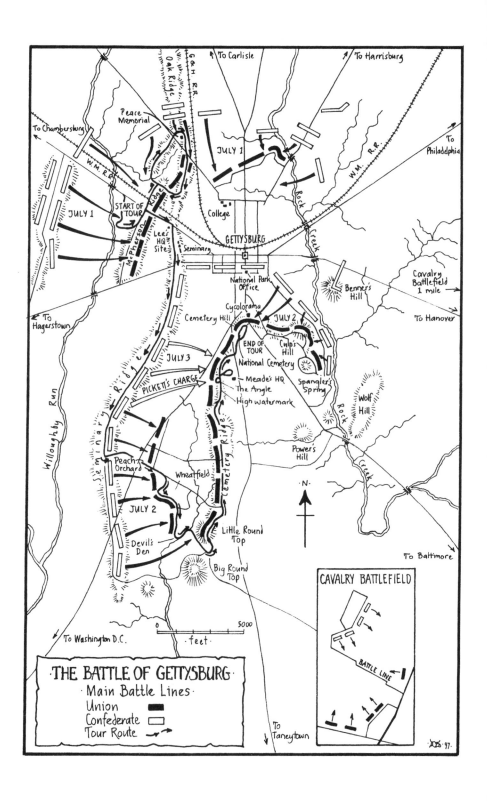

To Carlisle
To Harrisburg
To Philadelphia
To Chambersburg
G & H R.R.
W.M. R.R.
Oak Ridge
Peace Memorial
JULY 1
JULY 1
W.M. R.R.
START OF TOUR
McPherson Ridge
College
Rock Creek
Lee's HQ Site
Seminary
GETTYSBURG
To Hagerstown
National Park Office
Cemetery Hill
Cyclorama
JULY 2
Benner's Hill
Cavalry Battlefield 1 mile
To Hanover
JULY 3
END OF TOUR
National Cemetery
Culp's Hill
Spangler's Spring
PICKETT'S CHARGE
Meade's HQ
The Angle
High watermark
Wolf Hill
Willoughby Run
Seminary Ridge
Cemetery Ridge
Power's Hill
Rock Creek
Peach Orchard
Wheatfield
N
JULY 2
Devil's Den
Little Round Top
To Baltimore
Big Round Top
5000
To Washington D.C.
feet
To Taneytown

THE BATTLE OF GETTYSBURG
Main Battle Lines
Union
Confederate
Tour Route

CAVALRY BATTLEFIELD

BATTLE LINE

DO·97.

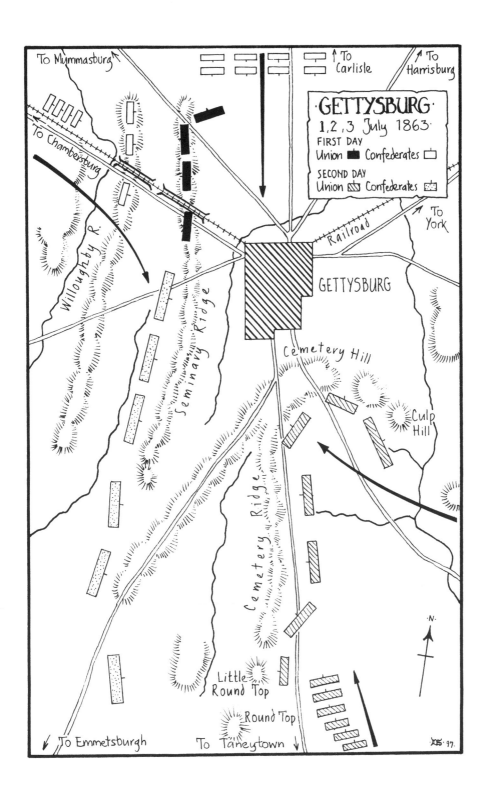

At the same time, Pettigrew's brigade of Heth's Confederate infantry division, was sent to Gettysburg to obtain supplies, but on reaching a ridge a mile west of the town, observed Federal cavalry scouts posted along the roads, so Pettigrew returned to Cashtown. Both Lee and Meade expected to take a strong defensive position and force the enemy to attack, and neither at that stage foresaw Gettysburg as the field of battle. But Lee was still beyond the mountains and General A P Hill was in command in the area; he took the initiative and at daybreak on 1 July ordered the brigades of Archer and Davis, of Heth's division, to advance along the Chambersburg Road towards Gettysburg to test the strength of the Union forces. Thus, subordinate field commanders had chosen the ground on which the armies were to clash.

Taking fire at Marsh Creek from cavalry piquets, Archer on the right and Davis on the left of the Chambersburg Road deployed on Herr Ridge and, supported by Pegram's artillery, charged down the long slope and across Willoughby Run against Buford's cavalry troopers, dismounted and fighting as infantry. They had recently been issued with Spencer repeating carbines, which enabled them to hold their ground against the spirited attacks of the Confederate infantry, until timely aid arrived at 10 o'clock when Federal General John F Reynold's 1st Infantry Corps began streaming over Seminary Ridge from the south. At the head of his men, Reynolds was almost immediately killed by a sharpshooter's bullet.

Forces of both sides were now reaching the field and when Archer's Confederates, who had been momentarily checked, renewed their attack across Willoughby Run, they were struck in the flank by Meredith's Iron Brigade, many of them being captured, including Archer, their commander. Further Federal reinforcements steadily pressed the Southerners until they withdrew beyond striking distance, and a lull ensued during the noon hour. While these advance units were battling it out west of Gettysburg, the main armies were rushing to the scene over roads from north and south. Rodes's Confederates were marching from Biglerville and Early's force was approaching on the Harrisburg Road. Rodes, using the wooded ridge as a screen, positioned his guns on Oak Ridge at about 1 o'clock and opened fire on the flank of General Abner Doubleday – Reynolds's successor – on McPherson Ridge, forcing the Union troops on to Oak Ridge and the Mummasburg Road, where they held off the attack. Meanwhile, two divisions of Howard's Corps were endeavouring to make contact with Doubleday on Oak Ridge, having arrived by way of the Taneytown Road.

Howard was temporarily forced back, but it was the arrival of Early's division, from the south-east on the Harrisburg Road, in the early afternoon that broke the Union line west of Gettysburg, forcing them to retreat in disorder through the streets of the town, exposing the Union flank on the north-west and west, which soon collapsed. The Union forces retreated first to Seminary Ridge, then across the fields to Cemetery Hill, which had earlier been selected as a rallying ground if the area west and north-west of the town was lost. So, by 5 o'clock the remnants of the Union forces engaged in that first day's struggle (some 6,000 out of the 18,000 engaged) were hastily occupying defence positions on Cemetery Hill, Culp's Hill and a part of Cemetery Ridge. In possession of the town, Ewell extended his line from the streets eastward to Rock Creek.

Lee had reached the field at 3 o'clock, in time to witness the retreat of the disorganised Union troops through the streets of Gettysburg and, through his glasses, watched their attempts to re-establish their lines on Cemetery Hill. He sent orders to Ewell to 'press those people' and secure the hill they occupied. However, two of Ewell's divisions (Rodes and Early) had been heavily engaged throughout the afternoon and were not well in hand and Johnson's division would not reach the area until late in the evening. Lacking cavalry reconnaissance through Stuart's absence and uninformed of Union strength in the hills south of the town, Ewell decided to wait until Johnson's arrival, but he stopped at the base of Culp's Hill, so Cemetery Hill was not attacked that night. Lee had made a momentous decision without ensuring his wishes were carried out by his subordinates – so passed the first of the Confederate commander's opportunities at Gettysburg.

As the day ended, Union formations began to arrive on the scene, Slocum by the Baltimore Pike and Sickles along the Emmitsburg Road, to consolidate the Federal right flank at Culp's Hill and Spangler's Spring and on the left the important position at Little Round Top, thus forming a strong defensive battle-line shaped like a fish-hook, about three miles long, and with the advantage of interior lines and higher ground. Meade at Taneytown sent General Hancock forward to size up the situation, and he arrived in time to rally the troops, returning to recommend that the battle be fought on and around the ground they were occupying.

Opposite, in a semicircle about six miles long, extending down Seminary Ridge and eastward into the streets of Gettysburg, Lee was preparing his battle-line as troops marched onto the scene from north and west. Throughout the night and into the morning of the second day, 2 July, both armies marshalled their forces, set up defences and positioned their artillery, and not until early afternoon was either prepared to take the first step. By then, onto the stage set for this epoch-making battle had gathered 172,000 men, from eighteen states of the Union and twelve of the Confederacy. They were spread out on Cemetery Hill, rising abruptly from lower ground south of the town, hardly more than a musket-shot from houses on its outer edge; they extended southward on Cemetery Ridge, a two-mile-long roll of land with, at its southern extremity, a sharp incline terminating in the wooded crest of Little Round Top, and half a

mile beyond it was the sugar-loaf peak of Big Round Top. From this undulating line the Union defenders could look out at Seminary Ridge, at
an average distance of two-thirds of a mile west, named for the Lutheran
Seminary on its crest half a mile from Gettysburg, where stood their
Confederate enemy.

The Union General Sickles set the ball rolling; commanding 3rd Corps
lying north of Little Round Top, he believed his left flank to be insecure,
so advanced towards the advantageous higher ground at the Peach
Orchard so that by 3.30 pm his battle-front extended from Devil's End
north-west to the Orchard, and north on the Emmitsburg Road, but left
unoccupied a strong position on the crest of Little Round Top. Lee sent
Longstreet forward on the Confederate right, moving out from his
encampment on the Chambersburg Road, three miles west of Gettysburg,
through Willoughby Run Valley to a position on the Emmitsburg Road
facing the Peach Orchard and Sickles's force 700 yards away; at the same
time he saw that Little Round Top was unoccupied and sent troops to
secure it, the 'key to the Union position'. However, General G K Warren,
Meade's Chief of Engineers, on the spot, summed-up the situation and
hastily brought forward artillery and infantry, and a desperate struggle
surged back and forth on the slopes and, at the end of the afternoon, Little
Round Top remained in possession of the Union.

Meanwhile, Longstreet had directed his entire line to attack, by nine
brigades in turn, against two Union brigades in the Wheatfield, the Peach
Orchard and along the Emmitsburg Road. Sickles's men were driven back
and by late afternoon the Confederacy held the west slope of Big Round
top, Devil's Den and the Peach Orchard, with the Union forces back at
the foot of Cemetery Ridge.

On the Confederate left, Ewell had been ordered to attack and take
Cemetery Ridge and Culp's Hill, beginning with an artillery duel eventually won by Union guns. After delays, Early's men attacked at dusk,
reached the crest of East Cemetery Hill to engage in a desperate hand-to-
hand struggle with the defenders that went on late into darkness, with
Early sullenly giving way at ten o'clock and returning to his old position.
Closely timed with this assault, Johnston's division attacked Culp's Hill
but found the steep slopes and strong Union defences too much for them,
fell back across Rock Creek, and attacked the thinly manned southern
slope of the hill, taking possession of the position but failing to press
further forward. Here another opportunity was lost to strike a telling
blow at the Union, for on a few hundred yards, beyond on the Baltimore
Pike, lay the Union supply trains.

Night brought the bloody conflict to a temporary end on East
Cemetery Hill; during the hours of darkness Meade, backed by his corps
commanders, determined to hold his position and, at daybreak began to
fortify Cemetery Ridge, bringing up artillery and shifting formations until

he had formed a very strong defensive position along the stone walls on the crest of the ridge, backed by impressive reserve power. Meade had correctly assessed Lee's intention of attacking the Union centre, but it was not here that the first fighting heralded the third day of the battle. Dawn was ushered in by the thunder of Union guns on their right, in the area of Spangler's Spring and Culp's Hill, followed by strong Union infantry attacks on the positions they had lost on the first day. Seven hours of furious fighting saw the Confederates retiring across Rock Creek and Union troops again in possession of their earthworks at Spangler's Spring.

Now ensued the lull before the storm as an ominous calm fell over the battlefield, the quiet being only occasionally shattered by sporadic sharp-shooting activity, casual skirmishing and a brisk cavalry action in the rear of the Union position, where Federal cavalry saw off the Con-federate horsemen of J E B Stuart, who had returned to the area and was seeking to prevent a possible Union retreat if Lee's centre attack succeeded.

Assessing that Union strength on both flanks was probably at the expense of weakening their centre, Lee decided on an all-out drive on that area, well aware that it meant a charge across extensive open fields in the face of flank and frontal artillery fire, and in the face of Longstreet's strongly voiced objections. By noon, Lee had 138 guns in line from the Peach Orchard northward to the Seminary buildings, many of them only 800 yards from the Union centre. At one o'clock, they opened fire, in salvos and in succession until the sky was darkened by smoke and heavy dust; eighty Union guns on Cemetery Ridge immediately responded and for two hours an ear-splitting duel was carried on. With Union fire slack-ening and Confederate ammunition running low, the order was given to the waiting infantry to go forward in attack.

Then, in what was to become a salient point in American history, more than 15,000 Confederate foot soldiers advanced in magnificent array, Pickett's division at their head. In front of the Union defensive stone walls, clouds of smoke momentarily obscured the enemy's advance, but it was detected by observers on Little Round Top, who signalled to the Union centre, and their artillery renewed their firing, supported by guns as far south as Little Round Top and on Cemetery Hill, on both flanks of the advancing Confederates. Their advancing lines recoiled, re-formed and again pressed forward, heads down as thought moving into a rain-storm, to press ahead into the hail of shot, shell and bullets. On nearing the Union line at the stone wall on Cemetery Ridge, the withering fire of double-canister and infantry volleys doubled. Only a hundred men crossed the stone wall at the Angle on the Ridge, the remnants of the proud divisions, and singly and in little clumps reluctantly retreated back to Seminary Ridge, whence they had come. It was a repulse that became known as the highwater mark of the tide of the Confederacy, which had 'swept to its crest, paused and receded'.

Lee rode out to meet his men, saying: 'All this has been my fault . . . it is I that have lost this fight, and you must help me out of it the best way you can.' Meade did not counter-attack, and the two armies lay facing each other, too exhausted and shattered to move, until late in the afternoon of 4 July, the Confederates began an orderly retreat south-west over the Hagerstown Road, and on the night of 13 July, crossed the Potomac into Virginia, Stuart's cavalry skilfully covering the retreat. The critics of General Meade, the victor, said he had permitted the Confederate Army to slip from the Union grasp.

Lee's irreparable loss at Chancellorsville, when Stonewall Jackson was mortally wounded, caused his virtues to become defects at Gettysburg, where the gentle and informal style of command that marked their relationship did not work with Longstreet, who lacked both Jackson's ability and loyalty. Longstreet and Ewell failed to get underway the attacks on Meade's left and right wings until late in the afternoon of 2 July, and both failed. With difficulty, Longstreet was persuaded to renew it next day – on Meade's centre – with a force led by Pickett, and by then the Federals were ready and waiting for it.

In the light of subsequent events connected with the charge, and Lee's impassioned acceptance of blame, could it be said that Longstreet was perhaps right?

Of the 97,000 Union troops engaged, 23,000 were killed, wounded or captured; Confederate losses were 28,000 from a force of 75,000. The bodies of about 7,000 of both armies were temporarily buried on the battlefield, and of these 3,706 Federal soldiers were subsequently interred in Gettysburg National Cemetery. Gettysburg is immortalised not only by the heroism of the men who fought there, brother against brother, father against son, but by President Abraham Lincoln's incomparable address, given a few months after the battle, when he came to dedicate a portion of the field as a burial ground for those who fell there.

37 *Gettysburg Today*

The official guidebook to Gettysburg town (published and available from The Gettysburg Travel Council, 35 Carlisle Street, Gettysburg, PA 17325 USA) claims that:

> the Gettysburg battlefield is the most visited, most written about, and most intensely studied battle ever recorded. Today the Gettysburg National Military Park stands supreme as the largest battlefield shrine in America, with over 1,000 monuments and cannon along 40 miles of scenic avenues. In addition, the area offers outstanding scenic beauty, entertainment and recreation.

The Gettysburg National Military Park is accessible by US30 from the east and west; US15 from north and south; US140 from Baltimore; State Route 34 from Carlisle PA; and State Route 116 from Hagerstown MD: and Hanover PA.

The situation of the Eastern Theatre of the American Civil War made it almost inevitable that the war should eventually come to Gettysburg, simply because through the rolling Pennsylvania countryside, all roads led to it, they did then and they do now, all ten of them. These routes roll in from Washington in the south, Baltimore to the south-east, and cut across the rolling landscape south-west from the Susquehanna River, and today's tourists use them by the thousand. Some are well briefed and know what they are looking for, but that is not essential because starting with the lavish Visitors' Center, everything is geared-up to guide and inform. Theirs is a distant acquaintance, unlike that of those 'special' tourists – their forebears – who came to the field over seven decades, until 1939, when the last Gettysburg Veteran died. Looking suitably pensive, one would say: 'I was standing here when Pickett's charge began'; or 'It was about here that I got hit.' Their memories peopled the peaceful terrain with the ear-splitting sound of gunfire, and yelling and cursing soldiers. Just as it is doing in Normandy today, the passing years cause such veteran visitors to dwindle.

Soon after the war, Gettysburg became a national shrine, as grateful states placed monuments there in abundance; in 1895 the battlefield became a National Park. Veterans of both armies returned to visit the field, holding special observances on the 25th (1888), 50th (1913), and 75th (1938) anniversaries of the battle; it was at this final gathering that the Eternal Light Peace Memorial was dedicated as a symbol of reunion, national unity and peace.

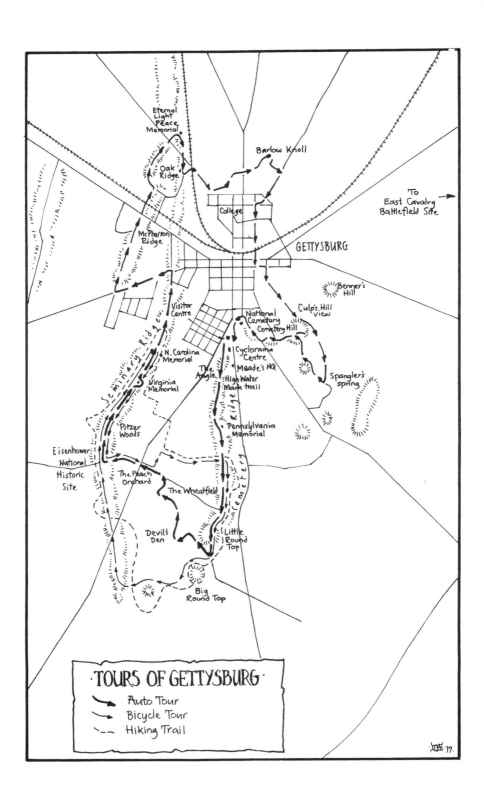

TOURS OF GETTYSBURG

➤ Auto Tour
→ Bicycle Tour
-- Hiking Trail

In 1863 Gettysburg was a thriving market town with 2,400 inhabitants. Except that it has now grown to 8,000–10,000 residents, the sweep of the immortal battlefield is largely unchanged. From the northern edge of the field, stand on Oak Ridge and look south towards Seminary Ridge to the right, Cemetery Ridge to the left, all the way to the dark rocky hills appropriately named Little and Big Round Tops. The first day's fighting swirled in from the left and down through the town, whose houses begin half a mile south. As they were in 1863, just beyond the town are Culp's Hill, Cemetery Hill and Cemetery Ridge.

Also from a standpoint on Oak Ridge can be seen the field of a far lesser, ignoble battle, where scores of newly built suburban homes have

Virginia State Monument, at Gettysburg.

East Cemetery Hill, Gettysburg.

encroached upon the sacred acres, simply because within the Park lay dotted areas of privately owned land.

Each year more than 2 million visitors come to tour the Park at Gettysburg, which extends over more than 25 square miles, has 32 entrances and 31 miles of avenues, many running along the battle-lines; there are claimed to be more than 3,000 monuments and markers, and almost 450 cannon, which are painted every three years, along with the pyramids of cannon balls alongside each gun. The scene is preserved and the battle-lines traced by 93 miles of fence, some around the old farm buildings still standing on the field, and maintained by the National Park Service. Leasing the land and living in the old houses, farmers today raise the same crops – wheat, corn, hay, peaches – that were growing when the battle raged around them.

Visiting the Park

The Park can be seen by car – it takes 2 to 3 hours to tour, with numbered stops along the way indicating significant areas. An Auto Tour map can be obtained from the Visitors' Center. It is also possible for a licensed *Battlefield Guide* of the National Park Service to travel in the tourist's own car and provide a personal two-hour tour. Guides can also be booked for bus tours. A fee is payable and enquiries should be made at the Visitors' Center.

For those wishing to see the Park on foot, the High Water Mark Trail is a walk about 1.6 km (1 mile) in length and begins at the Cyclorama Center, where a free trail-guide can be obtained. There is also the Big Round Top Loop Trail, a 1.6 km (1 mile) trail that takes about an hour to walk, and begins in the Big Round Top Parking Lot.

For more comprehensive coverage, there are the Billy Yank Trail of 14.5 km (9 miles) and the Johnny Reb Trail of 5.6 km (3.5 miles) – ask at the Visitors' Center for details.

Park Rangers give talks and lead walks and, at various locations on the battlefield they present detailed programmes of the events occurring at that spot. Details can be obtained from the Visitors' Center. In fact, it all circulates around the impressive Visitors' Center, the best place from which to begin sightseeing after obtaining from the information desk the current events schedules. The small museum contains a collection of artefacts and exhibits pertaining to the battle, and the Electric Map provides an ideal introduction to the battlefield, bringing the sweep of the conflict into perspective as the 750 square foot map accurately presents the field as it looked in 1863. In a thirty-minute programme, its 600 coloured lights indicate salient points of the field, and the movements of

Gettysburg, near High Water Mark of the Confederacy. In the background is the field of Pickett's Charge.

New York State
Monument in the
National Cemetery at
Gettysburg.

formations at critical points, all co-ordinated with a taped narration to vividly present the course of the battle.

Also available are Battlefield Bus Tours, over a twenty-three-mile route taking two hours, with dramatised living stereo sound; the buses run regularly from the Gettysburg Tour Center.

One thing not to be missed at Gettysburg is the *Cyclorama*, a large (356 ft by 26 ft) painting of Pickett's charge by the artist Paul Philippoteaux, who came to America in 1881, and made sketches of the terrain from a platform in the rear of the Angle. In 1884, after three years' work, the painting was finished and today is displayed in the Cyclorama Center where, for the viewer standing in the middle of the circular painting, a sound and light programme re-creates the fighting.

The Gettysburg Address

Almost as the conflicting armies marched away, work was begun on the Gettysburg National Cemetery and, on 19 November 1863 – a mere 139 days after the last shots were fired – the President, Abraham Lincoln, came to dedicate the shrine. He was preceded by an oration lasting two and a quarter hours, by Edward Everett. Lincoln delivered in two brief minutes the immortal Address which, although not recognised as such at the time, has since been accepted as one of the most outstanding orations in the English language. The Address is given below:

> Fourscore and seven years ago our fathers brought forth on this continent, a new nation, conceived in Liberty, and dedicated to the proposition that all men are created equal.
>
> Now we are engaged in a great civil war, testing whether that nation or any nation so conceived and so dedicated can long endure. We are met on a great battlefield of that war. We have come to dedicate a portion of that field, as a final resting place for those who here gave their lives that that nation might live. It is altogether fitting and proper that we should do this.
>
> But, in a larger sense, we cannot dedicate – we cannot consecrate – we cannot hallow – this ground. The brave men, living and dead, who struggled here, have consecrated it far above our poor power to add or detract. The world will little note nor long remember what we say here, but it can never forget what they did here. It is for us, the living, rather to be dedicated here to the unfinished work which they who fought here have thus far so nobly advanced. It is rather for us to be here dedicated to the great task remaining before us – that from these honored dead we take increased devotion to that cause for which they here gave the last full measure of devotion; that we here highly resolve that these dead shall not have died in vain; that this nation, under God, shall have a new birth of freedom; and that government of the people, by the people, for the people, shall not perish from the earth.

In January 1912 the Park Commission erected the Lincoln Address Memorial, near the West Gate of the National Cemetery.

Another American President retired to the battlefield area in later life, when ex-President Dwight Eisenhower and his wife Mamie lived close by at what is now the Eisenhower National Historic Site.

38 *Mini Memories of Walking the Battlefields of the American Civil War*

Maps Required:
States of Arkansas
Georgia
Kansas
Kentucky
Louisiana
Maryland
Missouri
Pennsylvania
South Carolina
Tennessee
Virginia
West Virginia

Two tours of America, in successive years, which included most of the major battlefields of the War in the East and the South, seem to encapsulate the struggle between the Union and the Confederacy which occupied the years 1861–65. Arriving appropriately on 4 July – American Independence Day – in Boston, an immediate 'bonus' occurred when American hosts drove the party on a round trip of about 750 miles, north through Massachusetts, New York State, Vermont and New Hampshire, to historic Fort Ticonderoga, and Fort William Henry on Lake George, in north-east New York State. *En route*, the Battlefield of Saratoga, vital field of the War of Independence, was walked, as was Bennington, another field of that War – both are considered in the section dealing with that conflict. Also encountered – and a bonus within a bonus so to speak – was the living history museum of Old Sturbridge Village in Massachusetts, where is presented the story of the life in a rural New England town during the 1830s, with a landscape re-created with restored buildings where historically dressed men, women and children demonstrate and share the daily life, work, amusements and celebrations of early nineteenth-century America. The very antithesis of conflict and warfare, it presents a welcome change without departing from the battlefield walker's historical terms of reference.

Known in its day as 'the key to a Continent', Fort Ticonderoga, first built as Fort Carillon by the French in 1755, was held in turn by France, Britain and the United States, dominating disputed territory. From 1755 until 1777, the fortress was attacked six times: three times it fell and three times it was successfully held, during times when it was the southern outpost of New France, the northern bastion of the British Colonies, and the first British stronghold captured by the rebellious colonies during the American Revolution. On the shores of Lake Champlain, the Fort Ticonderoga Military Complex today comprises the fort itself, magnificently restored, the Mount Hope Battery which guarded communications between Lakes George and Champlain, Mount Defiance on the New York shoreline, and Ticonderoga's sister-fort, Mount Independence on the Vermont shore. The whole can be reached from the south via New York State Route 74, and is at the junction of the two lakes.

South of Ticonderoga lies Fort William Henry, at Lake George Village, which was built by British General William Johnson in 1755 to prevent a possible French invasion from Canada, and was besieged throughout the summer of 1757 by French General Montcalm, leading a force of French and Indians. Following a six-day artillery pounding, the fort surrendered, being completely burnt-out; the Indians slaughtered the survivors. It is well known as the central theme of James Fennimore Cooper's book, *The Last of the Mohicans*, made into a feature film in 1936 and again recently. Totally reconstructed, it offers audio-visual displays, period demonstrations and theme displays.

Notes written during this tour arouse happy memories and not a little nostalgia, revealing all that wonderfully organised American hospitality and international comradeship which has invariably made walking American battlefields so memorable. The notes continue with details of two hectic days touring Boston, considered in detail in the section dealing with the War of Independence; again, bearing no relation at all to wars and warfare, the streets and houses around Beacon Hill are a delight, a throwback to days of British rule.

The party then moved west to Harrisburg in Pennsylvania where, for three days, a convention was enjoyed – with plenty of interest, laughs and good fellowship. Then, in hired cars, south to Gettysburg where very comfortable accommodation was booked at Doubleday's Inn, situated on the ridge occupied by the General of that name during the Battle. Much is written elsewhere in these pages of the incomparable hours spent walking this field, which should be a Mecca for every battlefield walker worthy of the name!

Now followed a hectic, never to be forgotten pilgrimage to as many Virginian Civil War battlefields as could be humanly and realistically reached – and, at the end of the day, we sat back in the aircraft returning us to London, weary but very satisfied with what had been achieved in less than twenty-one days. From Gettysburg, we drove south to Antietam field in Maryland, where on 17 September 1862 was fought the conflict that ended Lee's first invasion of the North, when 41,000 Confederate soldiers fought McClellan's 87,000 Federals to an indecisive end. Known as the field on which more men were killed and wounded in a single day than in any other battle of the War, today its 183 acres include all the salient points of 1862, little changed. And, of course, it possesses the invariably superb Visitors' Center where literature can be obtained, films seen, exhibits studied, and maps consulted. Much of the Antietam Battlefield can be viewed from the well-placed and lofty observation tower.

South again to the scenic confluence of the Shenandoah and Potomac Rivers, to Harper's Ferry, where the stone and brick houses and narrow streets have been much restored to how it looked in 1859, when John Brown's raiders made their violent demonstration against slavery by seizing the arsenal. Strategically important, it changed hands many times during the War, and its capture by 'Stonewall' Jackson in 1862 was a dramatic prelude to the Battle of Antietam Creek. The area around the quiet little town is extraordinarily beautiful, and from a vantage-point above the town, the rivers can be seen flowing together near where Virginia, Maryland and West Virginia meet. A National Historical Park,

Burnside's Bridge at Antietam National Military Park.

Originally the US Arsenal Fire Engine House at Harper's Ferry, the building was
defended by John Brown and his men during the 1850 raid.

there are numerous historic houses on show, museums and a waxworks; coloured literature and maps are available.

Continuing south to Winchester, where Jackson's army quartered in the winter 1862/3, the house Jackson occupied (415 North Braddock Street) can be viewed. Another Civil War site is where Federal General Philip Sheridan wintered in 1864/5 after his campaign through the Valley of Virginia. The house he occupied is now the Elks Club at the intersection of Piccadilly and Braddock Streets. Winchester was the scene of more than one Civil War battle; during Jackson's Valley Campaign of 1862, he attacked McDowell's Union armies six times – Kernstown, McDowell, Front Royal, Winchester, Cross Keys, and Port Republic, winning all but the first named. Still going south, between Winchester and Lexington is the New Market Battlefield Park, formed of 160 acres of the historic Bushong Farm on which Confederates repulsed invading Federal forces at the Battle of New Market, fought on a rainy Sunday afternoon on 15 May 1864. Here can be seen the remarkable Hall of Valor, a very modern two-storey building which displays exhibits, battlefield dioramas and films, and a 28-foot stained glass window bearing the names of the ten cadets killed when, in May 1864, 247 teenage cadets of the Virginia Military Academy advanced under fire to hold a section of the Confederate line against the assault of seasoned troops. Moving on, the party travelled on the scenic Blue Ridge Parkway, through the battlefield of Staunton, to bed-down for the night in a previously visited motel at Waynsboro.

Travelling south and slightly west on the Blue Ridge Parkway and Skyline Route, Lexington came next; one of the most interesting Civil War towns in the Valley of Virginia, it is where both Robert E Lee and Stonewall Jackson are buried. Lee, who died on 12 October 1870, is buried in a family crypt marked by an imposing statue in the Chapel of the Washington and Lee University at Lexington, Virginia. Marked by a monument, Jackson is buried in the Lexington Cemetery on Main Street. The Virginia Military Institute was established at Lexington in 1839 and was the nation's first state-supported military college, and is still occupied as such, in an impressive complex of historic and attractive buildings; the cadets wear uniform and are subject to military discipline besides obtaining degrees in chosen subjects. Redolent with American history, the VMI has, in addition to numerous other sites of interest, a very good museum.

In April 1865 the American Civil War ended at Appomattox, the next town on our route but, because our tour was more or less in a circular direction, this quiet Virginia town did not see the conclusion of our travels. Aware of the history of the momentuous events occurring there and the impact upon the American people even today, Appomattox was approached in a noticeably more restrained manner than was perhaps the case when trudging over other battlefields, albeit the ground beneath our feet was equally hallowed and historic. Although much rebuilt after fires and destruction, it resembles today almost exactly what it was in 1865, and in April 1954 was designated Appomattox Courthouse National Historical Park. Pushing that into the back of the mind, it is a privilege to stand looking at the parlour of the McLean House, and picture the figures of the sad but dignified Robert E Lee and the more down-to-earth Ulysses S Grant, amid their generals, facing each other in that room.

Immediately prior to the Appomattox Surrender, one of the very last battles of the War was fought on 6 April 1865, at Sayler's Creek, which is now a Battlefield Historical State Park, which can be visited and indeed was walked by our party *en route* to Petersburg, a few miles east. It was in a semicircle around this town, covering approximately 170 square miles – the largest single battlefield in America – that for ten months from the summer of 1864 until spring 1865, Lee and Grant fought out the military struggle between the Confederate Army of Northern Virginia and the Union Army of the Potomac for control of lines of communication. Today, Petersburg National Military Park, established in 1926, covers nearly two and a half square miles, preserving parts of seven battlefields, and the remains of both Union and Confederate fortifications. There is an excellent Visitors' Center, with maps of the tour route, plus a 20-minute map show; it is possible to halt during the self-guided tour to hear a recorded talk. Recently opened is the Siege Museum, housed in the former Exchange; guided walking tours are offered in summer, on Saturday and Sunday afternoons, and special evening programmes involving 'first-person' interpretation. It is said that downtown Petersburg preserves its Civil War appearance more clearly than any other Virginian town. Our notes indicate that our party visited such prominent features as the Crater, Batteries 8 and 9, and Fort Stedman, where an artillery firing demonstration was seen.

The notes also indicate that the party spent some time enjoying a couple of 'bonus-sites' at the famous historical re-enactment town of Colonial Williamsburg, and at Jamestown, where British adventurers settled in the early seventeenth century. Along with our other noted visit to Yorktown, these three sites are fully considered elsewhere in this book.

In their seventh day on the road, the party now turned its footsteps northward on the final lap of its odyssey, and less than six days before flying out from Dulles Airport in Washington – and with among half a dozen of the War's most important battlefields still to be walked! Almost at once – over breakfast in fact – this was discovered to be a delusion in that, here in Richmond, the party had not allowed for the Federal General McClellan's battles of the Seven Days: Mechanicsville (Beaver Dam Creek); Gaines Mill; Savage's Station; Glendale (Frayser's Farm) and Malvern Hill, all fought between 26 June and 1 July 1862, and preceded by the Battle of Seven Pines (Fair Oaks) on 31 May. Worst was to follow: nor had Grant's battle at Cold Harbor on 3–12 June 1864 been included! More than that, how could one come to the famed capital of the Confederacy and not visit the Virginia State Capital in Richmond, the first public building in the New World to be built in the Classical Revival style of architecture, or the Museum of the Confederacy and the Richmond Battlefield Parks Museum? The notes indicate that both were visited, but no comments are given; also one learns how the seemingly insuperable problem of walking SEVEN battlefields in a single day was solved – and solved it was!

The official guidebook told how the Park occupies nearly 800 acres of land in ten separate park units, and included a map showing a marked 57-mile drive to take them all in, beginning at the main Visitors' Center in Chimborazo Park and with markers, maps and interpretative devices along the route to aid in understanding the military operations. And, as the guide claimed, they DID do their job, as our party cruised through fields of combat, massive forts and intricate field fortifications. Obviously, not the *best* way to conscientiously walk battlefields, but preferable to coming home and admitting to not seeing them! Notes hastily taken at the time reveal our feelings on the battlefields: Seven Pines and Savage's Station – 'not much to see'; Gaines Mill, Mechanicsville and

Cold Harbor – 'reasonable'; while we seemed to feel that Glendale and Malvern Hill were good.

By this time, the hectic tempo of our tour seemed to be increasing rather than easing-off; although likely to be confusing, life was perhaps made easier by FOUR major battlefields all being concentrated within *one* National Military Park of Fredericksburg and Spotsylvania, which memorialises the Battles of Fredericksburg, Chancellorsville, the Wilderness and Spotsylvania Courthouse. No other area of comparable size on the American continent has witnessed such heavy and continuous fighting. All have excellent Visitors' Centers, with films, museums, maps, and details of self-guided tours or Ranger-assisted programmes. Far too prevalent to give in detail are the innumerable fascinating aspects of these fields, with miles of original, well-preserved trench remains and gun-pits, along with such notable historical sites as the Sunken Road, Marye's Heights, Hamilton's Crossing, the Jackson Trail, Jackson Shrine, and the Bloody Angle. Of course, some of them were a MUST, like the monument near the Chancellorsville battlefield where Stonewall Jackson was mortally wounded by his own men in a dusky wood, or the Bloody Angle at Spotsylvania, looking much today as it did in 1864 when cleared fields and open farmland separated the opposing lines. For the informed and interested military historian, a tour through these closely knit battlefields of 1862 and 1864 is a memorable experience, a tour of areas carefully preserved by caring countrymen to commemorate the sacrifices made by their ancestors in the Civil War.

Our enforced route to Washington and the Airport meant that the last of these fields encountered was Fredericksburg, fought 11–13 December 1862, when a proud Union army met with complete disaster in a pitched battle fought over many square miles of territory. Numerous important sites are outside the boundaries of the National Military Park, but a tour-guide is available at the Visitors' Center directing to four key sites on the battlefield, and explains the historic events associated with each location. At the Fredericksburg National Cemetery there is a large painting depicting the scene on the day and a recorded message explaining the dramatic story. Walking the Sunken Road is an evocative affair as it is not hard to put oneself into the shoes of the advancing Federal infantry being mown down in World War I fashion as they went against the well-entrenched Confederates behind their stone wall.

The notes refresh the memory of a disappointing ending to the day as, completing our walking of the battlefield, the party hastened up the road in late afternoon to visit the United States Marine Base at Quantico. Arriving at the entrance barrier, the car was halted by an archetypal crew-cut, immaculately uniformed Marine sentry, who seemed to achieve a certain degree of satisfaction in telling four Brits that the museum closed at 16.00 hours. So, we meandered north-west across very pleasant countryside on a glorious summer's evening until reaching Warrenton, where the Comfort Inn saw to our needs. Our purpose in diverging from the direct route to Washington was, of course, governed by the desire to walk the two fields of Manassas – 1st and 2nd Bull Run.

Not unfamiliar with our own seventeenth-century Civil War, members of the party did not find it hard to envisage the sudden and dramatic clash of fellow countrymen, as ill-formed and untrained, although fervent and committed, men marched resolutely out to the first battle of the war at a small stream, Bull Run, about twenty-six miles from Washington DC. First-Manassas is a satisfactory field to walk, easily understood and through its still existing landmarks, clearly pictured; from the Henry House Hill, the most significant site within the Park, it is possible to obtain a panoramic sweep of the whole battle area. The House contains a museum and is adjacent to the impressive statue of Stonewall Jackson; the Visitors' Center is not far away and is, as usual, first-class. From it can be obtained maps and details of the Henry Hill Walking Tour of about one mile, which includes all the vital spots and areas concerned with the battle, such as the dramatic first encounter of the American Civil War, fought on 21 July 1861. The Stone Bridge Trail covers about five miles and, of course, is far more comprehensive.

About a year later, both armies, now composed of seasoned veterans, were locked in a bitter struggle on the same field, on 28–30 August 1862. Second-Manassas can be covered by using the Deep Cut Trail of six miles, which focuses on the third and last day of the battle. Our notes recall an exercise where the party paced-out the distance between opposing lines of infantry firing steadily at each other for a long period – at sixty paces' range, standing upright and without any sort of cover. There is also a map and details available of the Second-Manassas Driving Tour taking in Sudley, Groveton, the Unfinished Railroad, New York Monuments, Battery Heights, the Stone House, Dogan Ridge, Deep Cut and the Chinn House (Hazel Plain). The tour covers about twelve miles and, by following numbered stops marked by blue bullet-shaped tour signs, enables points of interest to be seen in the approximate chronological order that the events occurred in the battle.

Thus ended the marathon battlefield tour, but it by no means put an end to other desirable sites and places, to fill in the two remaining days before take-off. That night we spent in the very pleasant suburb of Washington, Alexandria, a very congenial small town of lovely houses and interesting streets. On our penultimate day in America, the party sallied forth into Washington, the capital of the United States of America, where we paid hasty homage to the usual tourist attractions, like the White House, the Capitol, Ford's Theatre, the Iwo Jima Statue (the Marine Corps Memorial, where that evening we were privileged to see a Marine Sunset Ceremony), the Memorials for Jefferson, Lincoln and

Roosevelt, the Vietnam Veterans Memorial, and the Washington monument. We went to the Washington Navy Yard, where we browsed in the US Navy Museum and the US Marines Museum, who rewarded our obvious interest by inviting us to the Officer's Club for drinks!

Arlington National Cemetery is quite rightly a shrine to Americans; to Britons it is a place arousing awe and respect, bringing us into the closest proximity with the remains of notable figures who, in their day, changed the face of history. To stand before the graves of such eminent Civil War leaders as Sheridan, Berdan, and Crook, or before the memorials to the Kennedy brothers, and a veritable host of names known and unknown of 175,000 American soldiers who fought from the Revolutionary War to the present, is a very humbling experience. There are but two men of British birth buried at Arlington, and to read their names aroused patriotic pride – they are Field Marshal Sir John Dill, who died in Washington whilst serving in a military capacity and was buried there by an act of official recognition (he also has a large mounted statue there), and General Orde Wingate, the soldier who made his name in Burma during World War II and who rests in a grave with the six or seven American comrades who were in the same aircraft when it crashed.

The American Unknown Soldier's tomb is in Arlington Cemetery, permanently watched over by a Guard of American Servicemen, who are changed hourly in an impressive ceremony, which we had the privilege of witnessing. On a hill above the Cemetery stands Arlington House, family home of Robert E Lee before the transference of allegiance to the South in 1861, but today a memorial to him.

On the following, and last day of our pilgrimage, booking-in time at Dulles Airport was 15.00 hours, so the morning was spent extracting the very last ounce of satisfaction from the innumerable battlefield bonuses offered by Washington DC. We hastened to the world-famous Smithsonian Museum Group to wonder at the mind-boggling exhibits in the National Air and Space Museum, claimed to be the most visited museum in the world. There was just time for a fleeting visit to the American History Museum, to put an appropriate 'cap' on that host of unique sites and sights that had been enjoyed in the northern part of the United States of America.

Back home, we worked out the sheer statistics of it all, wondering how time was found for food and rest. Seemingly, in America for nineteen days, three and a half days were spent static at the Convention in Harrisburg, Pennsylvania; and more or less two days were spent flying in-and-out of Britain/America. In the remaining days our party travelled with Americans before the Convention 1,275 miles; the all-Brit party then took off to Gettysburg and the host of places here described in a round mileage of 1,300 miles, totalling 2,575 miles. If that arouses opinions that we did not truly see what there was to be seen in all the sites visited, rest assured that not much was missed, to the extent that, nearly six years later, backed by our notes, we can still recall and discuss – with some authority – all we did and saw!

A year later, as we had promised ourselves, last year's party (with two members replaced by other Brits) went to America to take in those major Southern Battles which, along with last year's wide selection of Northern battles, enabled us to claim seeing most of the major battlefields of the American Civil War. We flew into Atlanta, Georgia, and our first targeted battlefield was that of Kennesaw Mountain, in the National Battlefield Park established to commemorate the 1854 Atlanta Campaign: it was fought on 27 June 1864. The Union General Sherman had begun his drive on Atlanta in early May, moving with 100,000 men against Johnston's 50,000, who was being pressed deeper and deeper into Georgia and closer to Atlanta, to a position in the vicinity of the town of Marietta, on and around Kennesaw Mountain, 1,806 feet above sea-level. Sherman planned a two-pronged attack against the Confederate centre, after an artillery bombardment; both were brief and bloody failures, inflicted by experienced Confederate soldiers fighting with courage and determination from behind barricades, field fortifications and trenches.

After spending a little introductory time in the well-organised Visitors' Center, which included a demonstration by a Park Ranger in Confederate uniform of drill and musketry, the party undertook a self-guided auto-tour, using maps provided. There were four main stops, each with a parking area and wayside marker and exhibits; on top of Kennesaw Mountain and Cheatham Hill short interpretative trails were available. Stop 1 on Kennesaw Mountain gave sweeping panoramic views of the terrain in northern Georgia over which Sherman was advancing; along the short trail to the top are explanatory markers and gun emplacements. Stop 2 on Pigeon Hill, where one of Sherman's two main attacks was repulsed, still has existing entrenchments. Stop 3 on Cheatham Hill (named for its Confederate defender) takes one to the area of fiercest fighting, and is marked by the imposing Illinois Monument, with Confederate entrenchments and numerous markers. At the base of the monument are Union entrenchments, held for six days whilst they attempted to dig a mine under the Confederate position – the mine entrance can be seen near the base of the Monument. Stop 4 is at Kolb's Farm, restored to its original appearance but not open to the public. If time permits, there are two walking tours to the crest of the Mountain and to the Cheatham Hill area. Throughout summer and autumn are held regular Historical Interpretative Programmes, of talks, demonstrations, camp-life and the like.

Sherman resumed his flanking strategy, causing the Confederates to abandon their Kennesaw Mountain lines during the night of 2 July, with-drawing to the fortifications of Atlanta, some twenty miles east.

Cannon on Lookout Mountain, Tennessee.

Subsequently, Lee replaced Johnston with General J B Hood, who lost three battles to Sherman in quick succession, then Sherman cut the railroad in a fourth battle, and the Confederates evacuated Atlanta; Sherman entered the city on 2 September 1864. Not only was this a crippling blow to Confederate will to make war but it also opened the road for Sherman's 'March to the Sea', a devastating sweep across Georgia to Savananah.

Although the party was based on Atlanta, the modern growth of the city and its environs made further battlefield walking out of the question and, with an ultimate destination due north, we left the Atlanta Campaign and stepped back a year in time, to autumn 1863, to the fields of Chickamauga, fought 19/20 September 1863, and Chattanooga 23/25 November 1863. Between 1890 and 1899, were established the first four National Military Parks, Chickamauga and Chattanooga being the first (the others Shiloh, Gettysburg and Vicksburg). The Park is composed of several separate areas, the most important being Chickamauga Battlefield in Georgia; Point Park and the Battlefield of Lookout Mountain in Tennessee; Orchard Knob in Chattanooga; a chain of small reservations located on Missionary Ridge; and Signal Post on Signal Mountain – all in an area of 8,190 acres.

In and around strategically important Chattanooga in Tennessee, there occurred in the autumn of 1863 some of the most complex manoeuvres and fighting of the entire war. The Confederate victory at Chickamauga in September raised Southern hopes, low after the reverses at Gettysburg and Vicksburg during the summer, but at Chattanooga in November Union leader Ulysses S Grant's victory destroyed these hopes, preparing the way for the fall of Atlanta and Sherman's March to the Sea. During the summer and autumn of 1863 Union General Rosecrans's Army of the Cumberland, by skilful manoeuvres, forced Confederate General Bragg's Southern Army of Tennessee out of Tennessee and Chattanooga. But Bragg, taking up a position along Chickamauga Creek gave battle and, on 19 and 20 September, the two armies fought one of the fiercest battles of the War, culminating in the Federal right wing and part of their centre being swept from the field. The remainder of their army, under General George H Thomas, then held a position on Snodgrass Hill throughout the day against fierce Confederate assaults, enabling the Federal army to retreat in good order to Chattanooga. For this stand, Thomas earned the name 'Rock of Chickamauga'. Besieged in Chattanooga, the Federal army were eventually saved by the arrival of Grant with reinforcements, but in November, the Confederates still occupied Lookout Mountain, Missionary Ridge and the line between them.

On 23 November Grant's men attacked and routed the Confederates from their positions on Orchard's Knob; on the following day, aided by fog, Hooker's forces moved along the slopes of Lookout Mountain to gradually drive the Confederates from their defences around the Craven House. With most of Bragg's force now on Missionary Ridge, Grant attacked with Sherman and Hooker, but they could not break through; Thomas was ordered to assault the rifle-pits along the base of the Ridge, which they carried at a rush. Then, without further orders and with wild enthusiasm, these men scaled the heights in one of the great charges of the war, causing the Confederate line to collapse, and Bragg's troops fled to the rear. This precipitated a general retreat of the Confederate Army across the border into Georgia.

Chickamauga Battlefield is nine miles south of Chattanooga on US27, and the Visitors' Center is at the north entrance of the battlefield on that route. There is a highly detailed system of battle-line tablets, stone regimental markers, memorials and monuments, besides innumerable cannon; the woods and fields in the area have been kept in roughly their wartime condition. There is a seven-mile (11 km) self-guided auto-tour available, with maps from the Visitors' Center; and in the Center is a multimedia presentation of the battle. One feature of this battlefield which should be noted is that, unlike many other Civil War battles fought on open fields, Chickamauga was fought in dense woods and thick underbrush – battlefield markers, etc. make it possible to understand the conflict on the field, as it is now.

In Chattanooga town is the Confederama Hall of History – a three-dimensional, 480 square foot reproduction of the battlefield, with more than 5,000 model soldiers showing where armies moved; guns flash and puff out smoke in an intricate, electronic automation system activating more than three miles of electric wiring and 650 flashing lights. Anyway, that is how the adverts describe it! However, it is interesting and unusual and worth a visit.

Cryptic battlefield notes taken by our party reveal the following salient points of interest at Chickamauga: Visitors' Center; Battleline Rd; 15th US Infantry Memorial; Viniard Field; and the Artillery Demonstration.

Chattanooga boasts an Incline Railway climbing for a mile up Lookout Mountain, with grades as steep as 72.7 per cent near the summit, from which views and panoramas of the area can be obtained; three blocks from its Upper Station is Point Park, where one can stand on that same bluff from which General Ulysses S Grant watched the 'Battle Above the Clouds' unfold. There are many battlefield walker's bonuses down south! Yet another is Fort Oglethorpe in Georgia, lying between the two battle-fields south of Chattanooga and immediately north of Chickamauga on Route 27. The museum of the 6th US Cavalry is proudly manned by veterans of that regiment, which played a distinguished part in the Civil War at Gettysburg and also in the Boxer Rebellion in China at the turn of the century and in wars since.

The experienced battlefield walker will long ago have claimed kinship with the words of the chorus in William Shakespeare's immortal *Henry V*, who says, among much else: 'For 'tis your thoughts which now must deck our kings, Carry them here and there; jumping o'er times. Turning the accomplishments of many years into an hourglass' and so on. And again we are doing just that, by jumping from autumn 1863 forward a year, to November 1864, when Confederate General Hood invaded Tennessee, where he eventually confronted Union General Schofield, snug in previously prepared defences at Franklin, fifteen miles south of Nashville. Impetuously, Hood attacked piecemeal with only two-thirds of his army, to be thrown back with huge losses.

A smallish field, with no Visitors' Center as such, but with descriptive battlefield markers and maps, it is possible to stand on the site of Hood's Command Post on Spring Hill. Gazing over the land ahead where the battle was fought, the diagrammatic orientation-table placed on the mound enabling an understanding to be reached of the course of events: the Confederates attacked from the front of the mound, towards the town of Franklin which is visible ahead. Within the area, at Carnton, is a Confederate Cemetery, claimed to be one of the few existing, as Confederate soldiers were usually buried where they fell.

Digressing, it is interesting to mention that among the American battle-field walkers with whom we were travelling was a very attractive young lady, Margaret Grant, a direct descendant of Ulysses S Grant.

Union General Schofield retired his force that night to Nashville and, emulating him, so did we; without knowing where he rested his head, we stayed the night at Comfort Inn, alongside the Elvis Presley Museum. In December 1864, Hood invested Thomas's force in Nashville, but the indomitable Thomas was not prepared to stay besieged and sallied forth to completely destroy the Confederate army on 15 December 1864, in what has been described as being among the most decisive tactical victories gained by either side in a major action of the war. In the intervening years, Nashville has changed to the extent that the battlefields have long-since gone, and the town's most famous citizen and focal point is the late Elvis Presley – so our party felt it not unfitting that we should extract a bonus from all this by going to that most American of all Entertainments, the Grand Ole Opry, where we indulged in an evening of tuneful country and western music in an atmosphere as alien to us as if we had jumped onto another planet! However, the party did manage to raise the energy next morning to visit the Tennessee Military Museum in Nashville, where little is mentioned of the fact that Nashville, without a shot being fired, was captured by Union troops in late February 1862 – the first Confederate State Capital to fall. A reconstructed log fort on Nashville Waterside is worth visiting.

With that date in mind, our party again jumped the bounds of time, going back to the very end of 1862, when Union General Rosecrans marched his 43,000 men out of Nashville, with the intention of driving on to Chattanooga, after sweeping from his path Confederate General Bragg's army of 38,000 positioned three miles out of the town of Murfreesboro along a meandering stream, Stones River. Here Rosecrans found them and, within sight of each other, the two armies camped for the night of 30 December 1862, with fires flickering and sentries tramping back and forth. Then an army band struck up a patriotic air, answered by an enemy band, blowing vigorously, and the still night air soon echoed with 'Hail Columbia' battling 'Bonnie Blue Flag', and 'Dixie' seeking to drown-out 'Yankee Doodle'. Then a band struck-up 'Home Sweet Home' and the homesick soldiers of both armies singing together on the penultimate night of the eventful old year made the frosty night air melodious.

All this sentiment was forgotten next morning, however; only the roar of guns and the rattle of musketry filled the air, with the Union army being driven back, although contesting every inch of ground until establishing a new line along the Nashville Pike. Both armies rested on New Year's Day, but resumed fighting on 2 January 1863, when the Confederates renewed their assault, but the Federals held and the battle petered out, with 13,000 Union and 10,000 Confederate casualties. Bragg withdrew next day to Tullahoma, forty miles south-east of Murfreesboro, occupied by the Federals on the next day, 4 January.

There is plenty to see at the Stones River National Military Park, a 344-acre site containing important areas of the battlefield, and the National Cemetery containing 6,400 graves, almost 6,000 being Union soldiers, 2,562 of them unknown. How many of them sang 'Home Sweet Home' on the penultimate day of December, without knowing they would never again see it? Just south of the Cemetery is the Hazen Brigade Monument, erected early in 1863 by members of the Brigade and possibly the oldest memorial of the Civil War. A small plot of ground, detached from the principal part of the Park, memorialises the site of Mendenhall's 58-gun concentration that decided the outcome of the battle on 2 January 1863. The Park Visitors' Center is worth seeing and details can be obtained there, with maps, for both walking and auto self-guided tours.

Notes taken to accompany photographs taken on the field reveal that there is much to see: 'Abandoned artillery in wooded area at centre of Confederate left-hook, near the rocky outcrop Slaughter Pen; the Cotton Field, the "no-man's-land" over which Confederate infantry made numerous charges from noon until dusk on the last day of the battle'. A picture taken at a marker telling of:

> Parson's Battery, the most powerful Federal battery on the field, armed with 4 three-inch Ordnance Rifles and 4 12pdr howitzers. Manned by battle-hardened Regulars, the battery poured charge after charge of canister at less that 600 yards range, to help stifle the Confederate massed infantry attacks on the area around the Nashville Pike. At times the Confederate infantry were on three sides of the battery but it gave no ground; during the action it fired more rounds than any other battery (2,299 rounds) and suffered very few casualties because of the havoc caused by its very accurate fire.

There is a touching photograph of the Hazen Monument, with the inscription: 'Hazen's Brigade. To the memory of its soldiers who fell at Stones River on December 31 1862, their faces towards Heaven, their feet towards the foe'. Notes taken at the time on the field also mention the monuments to the artillery and to the regulars as being of interest.

It has long been a matter of habit for eyes to be kept open, so we fell fortuitously upon a real prize bonus, situated in the Moss-Wright Park in Goodlettsville, just north of Nashville, reached by taking Long Hollow Pike Exit 97 off 1–65. Historic Manskers Station is an authentic reconstruction, based on research, of a frontier fort-station, consisting of two blockhouses and four cabins built by Kaspar Mansker and other settlers during the winter of 1779. It sheltered the families living there, along with others forced to flee through Indian attacks on their stations and homes. The fort lasted but one year before Indian pressure forced its abandonment, but later Mansker returned and built a second fort, where he lived until his death in 1821. Today, it is a 'Living-History' Museum and Re-enactment Center, where families, appropriately dressed, live within it in the same manner as did their ancestors 200 years ago. Our party was made warmly welcome by them and an enjoyable morning was spent there.

Anomalously, the earliest fought battle among those we sought was the final one visited during the party's Southern tour, which was Shiloh (Pittsburg Landing) in Tennessee, the first great battle in the West of the War Between the States, fought over 6 and 7 April 1862. Situated on the west bank of the Tennessee River at the intersection of State Highways Nos 22 and 142, the Shiloh National Military Park is about seventeen miles north of Corinth, Mississippi and five miles south of US54, the main route between Chattanooga and Memphis.

The Confederate General Albert Sydney Johnston had concentrated 44,000 men at Corinth, Mississippi; Grant's Federal army of 40,000 troops steamed up the Tennessee River to Pittsburgh Landing, twenty-two miles east of Corinth, where the Union General awaited the arrival from Nashville of Buell's army, with whom he would combine and attack the enemy at Corinth. Johnston was determined to strike before the two armies combined and, after a strenuous march, formed his battle-lines near Shiloh late in the afternoon of Saturday 5 April 1862 and next morning made a surprise attack on Grant's inadequately posted bivouacs in the area of Pittsburgh Landing–Shiloh Church, driving them back. The Union centre managed to withdraw to positions in the Peach Orchard and the Hornet's Nest, a natural fortress of dense woods and thickets; the Confederate commander General Johnston was mortally wounded near the Peach Orchard and was replaced by General Beauregard. Confederate General Ruggles massed sixty-two guns and concentrated a

The Bloody Pond at Shiloh National Military Park.

deadly fire on the Hornet's Nest; the Confederate infantry made charge after charge on that position and on the Sunken Road, defended by the Federal troops for eight hours, and the twelfth charge forced surrender. Despite Grant's vigorous personal efforts, the Federals were steadily forced back until, when darkness fell, they were lining the bluffs above the Landing with their backs to the river.

During the rainy night, Buell arrived with 25,000 troops, and when they resumed attack at daybreak, the Confederate 34,000 found themselves faced by 54,000 Union troops, forcing the Southerners to reluctantly give ground until at 2 pm Beauregard ordered his outnumbered forces to withdraw from the field. The North had 13,047 and the South 10,699 casualties.

Shiloh is a wonderful battlefield to walk, beginning at the Visitors' Center for maps of individual tours, and a 25-minute film provides a fitting introduction to the suggested battlefield tours, which encompass all the main points, as follows:

1.   Iowa Monument.
2.   Grant's last line.
3.   Michigan Monument.
4.   UDC Confederate Monument.
5.   The Hornet's Nest.
6.   Sunken Road.
7.   Ruggles' Batteries.
8.   Confederate Burial Trench.
9.   Water Oaks Pond.
10.   llinois Monument.
11.   Shiloh Church Site.
12.   Fraley Field.
13.   Union Defence Line.
14.   Site of Tent Hospital.
15.   Johnston's Death Site and Monument.
16.   Peach Orchard.
17.   Bloody Pond.
18.   Tennessee River Overlook.
19.   Pittsburg Landing.

Numbered markers are placed at all these points of interest, and correspond to those set out in the guidebook and on the available map. Ulysses S Grant, writing later about the battle, said: 'Shiloh . . . a case of Southern dash against Northern pluck and endurance . . . the troops on both sides were American . . . united they need not fear any foreign foe.'

Moving on from the battlefield, our party was taken to Savannah in Tennessee, where a reception was laid on with costumed members of such

American groups as Daughters of the Confederacy and Confederate Veterans all adding to the attractions of the plentiful food and wine. That night we were guests in a wonderful period house, like Tara in *Gone With the Wind*, where we sipped Bourbon on the columned verandah into the small hours and slept on four-poster beds. Truly, American hospitality is a wonderful thing!

Next day, the party split up, half going on to Vicksburg, New Orleans and Charleston, while the others went north to attend a convention held in Harrisburg, Pennsylvania.

Since then, through the good offices of a Kansas City club HATSOFF (Heart of America Tactical and Strategical Order of the Followers of Featherstone) the opportunity has arisen to complete our education of the battlefields of the American War Between the States by visits to the battlefields of Wilson's Creek in Missouri, fought on 10 August 1861, and Pea Ridge in Arkansas, which took place on 7/8 March 1862. Both fought for the control of Missouri during the first year of the war. The first was won by the Confederates who were not able to take advantage of their victory; the second by the Federals, enabling Missouri to remain in Union hands. However, that was not the end of things as, for the next three and a half years, the state saw savage and repeated fighting by guerrilla bands, so that Missouri can claim to have witnessed so many battles and skirmishes that it has the dubious claim of being the third most fought-over state in the Union.

Wilson's Creek National Battlefield Park is situated ten miles southwest of Springfield, Missouri; it has a Visitors' Center providing a film, a map of the field, and a museum, and living history demonstrations take place there in the summer. Details can be obtained of the auto-tour route on a 4.9-mile, one-way loop road taking in all the major points on the field. There are also walking trails, including a well-mapped three-quarter-mile route in the Bloody Hill area; each route has marked information markers at numbered stops. Acknowledging that time has changed the appearance of the field, steps are in hand to restore a semblance of the battlefield's historic 1861 appearance.

Lyon, the Federal commander, was encamped at Springfield with about 6,000 men and, hearing that a Confederate force of about 12,000 was approaching, decided to attack it despite his lack of numbers. A five-hour-long fierce battle took place on Bloody Hill, with heavy losses to both sides. Federal General Lyon was killed, and with ammunition nearly gone, the Federals withdrew to Springfield; the Southerners did not pursue.

The Battle of Pea Ridge – claimed to be the 'Battle that Saved Missouri for the Union' – marked the end of a campaign that began on Christmas Day 1861 when General Samuel Curtis was appointed commander of the Union forces in the south-west district of Missouri; by mid-February he had chased most of his Confederate opponents into Arkansas. In early March, Confederate leader General Earl Van Dorn marched his 16,000-strong force northward, intending to capture St. Louis, but across his path on bluffs overlooking Little Sugar Creek, not far from Elkhorn Tavern and Pea Ridge, were about 10,500 Federals. Van Dorn tried to encircle Curtis's right flank; Curtis discovered the movement and his counter-attacks of combined infantry and cavalry began to push back the Confederate forces. By mid-morning Van Dorn realised ammunition was running short, and withdrew.

The Pea Ridge National Military Park lies ten miles north-east of Rogers, Arkansas, and its park entrance is on US62; it has a Visitors' Center with all the usual amenities such as coloured illustrated guides and maps, museum exhibits, etc; there are available detailed auto-route and walking self-guided tours, with marked stopping places. Pea Ridge bears a singular distinction in that it was the only major Civil War battle in which Indian troops were employed; a thousand Cherokees from Indian Territory (now Oklahoma) cast in their lot with the Confederates, participating in a successful charge against a three-gun Union battery, but took demoralised cover in woods when taking other artillery fire. Their further participation was limited to scouting and patrolling.

On two occasions these mid-West trips included notable battlefield bonuses in escorted tours around Fort Leavenworth in Kansas, viewing the new Dwight Eisenhower Library and buildings, and the Corridor of Fame, with its superb stained-glass windows, stands of Colours, and huge pictures of leading American Generals; and the impressive Buffalo Soldiers Monument to the Negro cavalry units who fought the Indians later in the nineteenth century. As this is both the American Staff and Command School (approximating to the British Staff College at Camberley) and the American Military Penal Settlement (with more than a thousand prisoners) it is not generally open to the public, so a bit of 'pull' is required! However, it is possible to visit the Frontier Army Museum at the Fort which blends the history of Fort Leavenworth with that of the Frontier Army, from 1817 to 1917, with exhibits providing insight into Indian relations, American western expansion, and army life on the frontier. It also boasts the largest collection of horse-drawn vehicles in the world. Leavenworth is about thirty miles north of Kansas City on Route 73.

39 *The American Civil War Remembered*

Mᵒʳᵉ than any other country in the world, America cherishes its historic battlefields, honouring their ancestors who fought thereon by offering vivid reconstructions of the events which took place upon them, aided by every artefact and device, such as audio-visual and film performances, plus Living-History demonstrations. Most of the battlefields are part of the national Park system, and have first-class Visitors' Centers, providing guides, self-guided tours, maps and literature, mostly free of charge.

Here is a list, by state, of the parks and museums open to the battlefield walker.

Arkansas	Pea Ridge National Military Park
District of Columbia	Ford's Theatre National Historic Site Lincoln Memorial
Georgia	Andersonville National Historic Site Chickamauga and Chattanooga National Military Park Fort Pulaski National Monument Kennesaw Mountain National Battlefield Park
Maryland	Antietam National Battlefield
Mississippi	Brices Cross Roads National Battlefield Site Tupelo National Battlefield Vicksburg National Military Park
Missouri	Wilson's Creek National Battlefield
Pennsylvania	Gettysburg National Military Park
South Carolina	Fort Sumter National Monument
Tennessee	Fort Donelson National Battlefield Park Shiloh National Military Park Stones River National Battlefield and Cemetery

Virginia

Appomattox Court House National Historical
 Park
Arlington House, The Robert E Lee Memorial
City Point National Historic Site
Fredericksburg and Spotsylvania County
 Battlefield Memorial
National Military Park
Manassas National Battlefield Park
Museum of the Confederacy, Richmond
New Market Battlefield Military Museum
Petersburg National Battlefield
Richmond National Battlefield Park
Sailor's Creek Battlefield Historical State Park
White House of the Confederacy, Richmond.

Recommended Reading

Part Two: The Hundred Years War 1337–1453
Burne, Alfred H, *The Agincourt War* (Eyre & Spottiswoode, 1956)
Burne, Alfred H, *The Crécy War* (Eyre & Spottiswoode, 1955)
Featherstone, Donald, *The Bowmen of England* (Jarrolds, 1967)
Hardy, Robert, *The Longbow* (The Mary Rose Trust, 1986)
Holmes, Richard, *Fatal Avenues: Traveller's History of the Battlefields of Northern France* (Pimlico, London, 1992)
Holmes, Richard, *War Walks from Agincourt to Normandy* (BBC, 1996)

Part Three: Waterloo 1815
Holmes, Richard, *The Army Battlefield Guide – Belgium and Northern France* (HMSO, 1995)
Weller, Jac, *Wellington at Waterloo* (Longmans, 1967)

Part Four: The Peninsular War 1808–14
Featherstone, Donald, *Campaigning with the Duke of Wellington and Featherstone* (Emperor's Press 1993; Greenhill Books, 1994)
Weller, Jac, *Wellington in the Peninsula 1808–1814* (Nicolas Vane, 1963)

Part Five: The Zulu War 1879
Claband, J P and Thompson, P S, *A Field Guide to the War in Zululand 1879* (University of Natal Press, 1979)
Emery, Frank, *The Red Soldiers* (Hodder & Stoughton, 1977)
Morris, Donald R, *The Washing of the Spears* (Jonathan Cape, 1966)
Smail, J T, *Historic Monuments and Battlefields in Natal and Zululand* (Howard Timmins, 1965)

Part Six: The First Boer (Transvaal) War 1881
Ransford Oliver, *The Battle of Majuba Hill: The First Boer War* (John Murrray, 1967)

Part Seven: The South African (Boer) War 1899–1902
Packenham, Thomas, *The Boer War* (Abacus, 1979)
Ransford, Oliver, *The Battle of Spion Kop* (John Murrray, 1969)
Selby, John, *The Boer War: A Study in Cowardice and Courage* (Arthur Barker, 1969)

Part Eight: The American War of Independence 1775–83
Boatner, Mark Mayo, *Cassell's Biographic Dictionary of the American War of Independence 1763–1783* (Cassell, 1973)
Symonds, Craig L, *A Battlefield Atlas of the American Revolution* (The Nautical & Aviation Publishing Company of America, 1986)

Part Nine: USA – The War of 1812
Mackay Hitsman, J, *The Incredible War of 1812: A Military History* (University of Toronto Press, 1965)

Part Ten: USA – The War Between the States
Boatner, Mark Mayo, *Cassell's Biographic Dictionary of the American Civil War 1861–1865* (Cassell, 1973)
Griess, Thomas E (ed.), *The American Civil War* (The West Point Military History Series, Avery Publishing Group Inc., 1987)
Keegan, John, *War Paths: Travels of a Military Historian in North America* (Pimlico, London, 1995)
Kennedy, Frances H (ed.), *The Civil War Battlefield Guide* (Houghton Mifflin Company, 1990)

Index